DATE DUE

DEC - 3 1998	
NOV 24 1999	
FEB 1 8 2002	
MAR 2 4 2003	

BRODART   Cat. No. 23-221

WHEN
PASSION
REIGNED

WHEN PASSION REIGNED

Sex and the Victorians

by

PATRICIA ANDERSON

BasicBooks
A Division of HarperCollinsPublishers

Designed by Joseph Eagle

Library of Congress Cataloging-in-Publication Data
Anderson, Patricia (Patricia J.)
    When passion reigned : sex and the Victorians / Patricia Anderson.
      p.   cm.
    Includes bibliographical references and index.
    ISBN 0–465–08991–7
    1. Sex customs—Great Britain—History—19th century.   2. Great Britain—Social life and customs—19th century.   I. Title.
    HQ18.G7A7   1995
    306.7'0941—dc20   95-4108
                                                  CIP

95 96 97 98 ❖/HC 9 8 7 6 5 4 3 2 1

To Bill

Contents

Preface

When Passion Reigned began with a steamy encounter in the British Library.

It was late afternoon on the final day of a research trip to London, and I would be flying home to Vancouver the following day. I still had one more source to look at, an obscure, apparently dry pamphlet published in 1850. Suspecting it would be of limited use for my work at the time, I was tempted not to bother with it. Besides, it was available only on microfilm, and my past experience with microfilm readers had generally been dispiriting.

In the end conscience won out, and I dutifully threaded the reel into the machine. Twenty minutes later I was immersed in an erotic world I'd had no idea ever existed. The "dry" pamphlet turned out to be a collection of quotations about voluptuous visions, oversexed vicars, palpitating bosoms, and the inflamed toyings of masculine hands as they moved ever downward.

At first I thought I'd come across a sampling of Victorian pornography. But reading on, I realized this was not underground erotica but popular entertainment, once sold openly at any corner newsagent's. As a historian of the period, I already knew that the Victorians were by no means as Victorian as we used to think. Yet the kind of public, exuberant sexuality that I encountered that day in the library was news to me. I didn't jump up and shout "Eureka!"—this was the British Library, after all, and I wanted to be allowed back in. But in my accidental discovery I was excited to see the beginnings of a book.

During the research that followed I unearthed some attitudes and images that profoundly disturbed me; these came mostly from occasional brushes with pornography. Elsewhere, and more often, I uncovered the sexual variety, humor, expressiveness, and compassion of our Victorian ancestors. All of it, the bad and the good, became a mirror through which I reassessed the sexuality of our own time.

This book, then, is not just about the Victorians. It is also about ourselves—and what we can learn from our sexual past.

Financial support from the Social Sciences and Humanities Research Council of Canada enabled the writing of this book, and I am indeed grateful. The expertise of Julie Anne Wilson and her staff at the Bodleian Library's John Johnson Collection, and the unfailing good nature with which they responded to my questions and requests, were a great boon to my research. I am also indebted to the staff of the British Library and the Library's Photographic and Photocopying Service for years of assistance in ways too diverse to enumerate.

A number of people have encouraged me during the planning and writing of this book: Kim Adams, Peter Bailey, Geraldine Beare, Roddy Bloomfield, Michael Harris, Paul Heyer, John Springhall, and Eileen Truscott. Special thanks to my husband, Bill Anderson; my agent, Lettie Lee; my father, Dave Runnels; and my friend and mentor, Jim Winter.

Introduction

Sex scandals in the tabloids. Steamy soap operas. Bookstands of paperback sex guides. Titillating talk shows. Sexy movies. Adult videos. Erotica in advertising. These are signs that ours is a highly sexualized world. Yet in writing this book and looking back to the nineteenth century, I became ever more aware that there is a sense in which sex today is a shadow of its Victorian self.

As most people of the day understood it, sex was robust and passionate. It expressed itself through the entire being—through intense physical sensations, fervid emotion, overwhelming pleasure, and release. But as the nineteenth century progressed and turned into the twentieth, sex increasingly attracted the professional attention of legislators, doctors, educators, Freudians, and the like. They sorted and separated it into categories and behaviors. They analyzed, labeled, and discussed it. In the process it acquired a new dimension of abstract meaning—and began to lose substance as a powerful and complete human experience.

Meanwhile, in the more widely familiar reaches of popular entertainment, fashion, and everyday pastimes, sex also underwent a change. It became more standardized in its expression, less exuberant in its presence. Initially, this was not a dramatic turn for the worse. The "ologies" and "isms" that had attached themselves to sex in professional spheres were slower to take hold in ordinary life. And they had yet to join forces with a highly commercialized twentieth-century mass media. As late as 1900, sex for the most part held its own as vigorously felt emotion and tangible desire.

But this vitality would eventually dwindle. With the increasing commercialization of entertainment, the growth of the mass media, and the popularization of medicine and the social sciences, sex progressively lost its healthy autonomy and, with that, much of the special poignancy that had characterized its Victorian phase. Now, routinely, it is the staple of the paperback trade in popular psychology and sociology, the apparently inexhaustible subject of daily television talk shows, the principal commodity of the fashion, beauty, and film industries, and the central ploy in the advertisement of almost everything.

In other words, sex in some form is all around us, but the wholeness of passion is not so evident. This prompts me to raise a series of questions about sex as it is—and was. Before its dissipation into psychology and sociology, advertising, and cultural obsession, did it once have a physical and emotional vigor now virtually unknown? In an age unlike ours, when people did not talk endlessly about it, was intimacy more intimate? And desire more desirable? A century or so ago, was sex sexier than it is today? The Victorian experience suggests that the answer may well be yes.

Twenty years ago it would have been highly unlikely that anyone would have raised questions of the kind I ask here—let alone have answered them in the affirmative. Historians of the 1970s commonly assumed that on the one hand most Victorians were prudish and repressed, while on the other they hypocritically allowed pornography and prostitution to flourish for the pleasure of an uninhibited few.

In 1976 the influential *History of Sexuality,* by the historical philosopher Michel Foucault, cast the first serious doubt on the supposed fact of Victorian repression. Another landmark, the historian Peter Gay's 1984 and 1986 volumes on the private lives of middle-class Victorians, showed that passion and respectability were by no means mutually exclusive. Subsequent research has continued to expose the sex lives of our Victorian ancestors—an ironic postscript to an era that valued its privacy. The result, a virtual explosion of new knowledge, has shattered the former stereotype. With only an occasional exception, historians now refute the earlier twentieth-century view of the Victorians as dreary sexual prudes and hypocrites.

But outside of specialist circles the old orthodoxy still widely prevails. One professor of history often begins his introductory lectures on the nineteenth century with a word-association exercise. He says "Victorian" and the general response is "prudish." Not uncommonly, when I tell people that I am writing about Victorian sex, they are surprised that anyone could be so misguided as to tackle such an unpromising subject. "It'll be a short book," several wits of my acquaintance have predicted.

Many others have offered specific observations about the Victorians themselves. They never took their clothes off to have sex. At the dinner table they asked to be passed the chicken bosoms because they were embarrassed to say breasts. For the same reason, they always referred to limbs, not legs. They even made trousers for their pianos so they would not have to look at naked furniture legs—that is, limbs. Except for prostitutes, the women were all frigid. Sex was always a duty, never a pleasure.

In today's popular perception the subject of Victorian sex is a source of both continuing fascination and misinformation. The myth of Victorian prudery is thriving, while almost two decades' worth of new information has yet to gain currency. Conspicuously missing from bookshelves allotted to works on Victorian sex is an up-to-date synthesis for the general reader, one that blasts the myth of prudery without the heavy artillery of theoretical terms and specialist arguments. Within the limitations described below, this book helps to fill that gap on the shelves.

Beyond synthesizing the work of others, I have drawn upon many previously untapped Victorian sources—advertisements, valentines, and songs, as well as poetry and romances once widely read but now mostly forgotten. A part of common experience a century ago, these sources today illuminate a seldom-explored side of Victorian sexuality. Historians for the most part have overlooked that the erotic permeated respectable heterosexual life at all levels—public as well as private. I have made an effort to evoke this unrecorded reality, to re-create that pleasurable interplay of openness and intimacy that the Victorians so well appreciated.

Without deviating from this, my main purpose, I have also revived examples of pornography. Although undoubtedly the secretive taste of a minority, it was neither an entirely distinct subculture nor the ultimate expression of hypocrisy. Rather, it was one extreme of the sexual spectrum. Not only do the forbidden indulgences of a few help to complete the picture of Victorian sexuality, but they sometimes enhance our understanding of widely acceptable attitudes and practices. Distant though they were, the proscribed and the prescribed occupied the same sexual world.

In exploring the terrain of that world, I have concentrated on England and only occasionally looked to the rest of the United Kingdom, the Continent, and North America. Except for a few glances ahead, I have ranged in time from 1840 to 1905, a period largely coincident with Victoria's reign from 1837 to 1901. Although

"Victorian" is a useful catchall description, it does not mean that the era was uniform and static. Certainly there were many continuities, and these I have chosen to emphasize. But at the end of appropriate chapters I have also indicated the ways in which sex at the close of the nineteenth century was not what it had been some fifty years earlier.

The queen who gave her name to the age receives only passing mention in these pages. I have preferred to devote my attention to the sexual ideals and realities of ordinary people—the middle class mostly, but when I could glean the information, the working class as well. The works of the great literary personalities of the day—Dickens, Eliot, Tennyson, Thackeray, and so on—figure in the background, if at all. Instead, I have given prominence to more obscure writers who often treated sexual themes with less artistry and greater transparency. Sold in weekly parts or serialized in magazines, the potboiling fiction they churned out was the daily fare of an enormous readership. To dip into its pages is to experience, however imperfectly, the fantasies and romantic expectations of a now nameless majority.

In this book I have focused on that majority, who were adult and heterosexual. Then, as now, there were other sexualities, but it was heterosexuality that most Victorians experienced and believed to be "natural" and "normal." It was equally the accepted order of things that men enjoyed most of the political and economic power. But in social and sexual spheres—the drawing room, the bedroom, even the brothel—the balance often shifted, putting women in charge. On such occasions, figuratively and sometimes literally, the hand that held the whip was female. Since men's power was extensive but not absolute, I have not insisted on the idea of women's "otherness." The Victorian woman was not merely the oppressed "other"—nor was the contemporary man simply her oppressor.

Without denying differences and unfair inequalities, I have tried to flesh out, as it were, the relationship of the sexes with a measure of empathy, tolerance, and good humor. Whether the subject is genteel sex or unbridled lust, I have also considered it no less than proper to limit my use of both clinical jargon and the kind of informal language that many would consider vulgar. Although this has not been entirely workable, particularly when dealing with pornography, I have tried to be as inoffensive as possible. Generally speaking, I have taken my cue from the Victorians—those mistresses (and masters) of suggestive euphemism.

For the moment, though, I need to say plainly what I mean by "sex." Not only does it signify the act itself but also what comes before—initial attraction, flirtation, falling in love, and courtship. It takes in male and female sexuality and the body images associated with sexual appeal. It is inseparable as well from the idea of gender, the social and cultural overlay on biological sex.

Because it was not the Victorian way to talk constantly and graphically about sex, I have had to gather much of my information visually, by studying book, magazine, and songsheet illustrations, theatrical costumes, and everyday clothing. Ladies' underwear, especially, has turned out to be eye-catching. (Men cagily guarded against the emasculating effect of exposing their underthings to the public gaze, but on occasion I have also managed to catch a glimpse of masculine unmentionables.)

From these and other commonplaces of a time past, from between the lines of sentimental verse, penny romance, diaries, and love letters, there emerges what we today must stretch our historical imaginations to grasp. In its all-encompassing sense, Victorian sex was a profoundly moving event of the mind and body, an intensely human experience that did not merely take place in the bedroom. It was not yet a celluloid image, nor had it become the abstract subject of popular psychology, medicine, and social theory. In a time before sex turned into talk, "quivering with passion" was no mere figure of speech but a poignant reality. The Victorians felt arousal profusely and perceptibly—in blushes, glances, gestures, and trembling. Theirs was an age when corsets, bustles, and stovepipe trousers were palpably sexual, when women's bosoms heaved with the fervency of their emotional and physical feelings, and when strong men became weak with desire. Theirs was an age when passion reigned.

CHAPTER 1

The Victorian Sexual Mystique

My hands are perfumed with her delicious limbs, and I cannot wash off the scent, and every moment the thought comes across me of those mysterious recesses of beauty where my hands have been wandering, and my heart sinks with a sweet faintness and my blood tingles through every limb.

—Charles Kingsley, letter to Fanny Grenfell,
October 24, 1843

Such was the erotic intensity with which the clergyman and novelist Charles Kingsley remembered an amorous interlude with his wife-to-be Fanny Grenfell. Lean and athletic, with strongly defined facial features, he was endlessly captivated by her feminine plumpness and gentle, pretty face.

In appearance a study in contrasts, the couple was well matched in ardor. A few months before Charles's passionate reminiscence, Fanny reflected on a long kiss the two had shared: "My blood boils and bounds as I recall it," she feverishly confessed. They exchanged many such fervid confidences during their engagement in 1843 and after their marriage the following year. At once passionate and articulate, the Kingsleys were among those whose erotic outpourings belie the conventional wisdom that the Victorians were prudish and repressed, unwilling if not unable to express sexual feeling.

What does in fact distinguish their sexuality from that of later eras is talk—a particular way of talking about sex. Most Victorians lacked the notion of sexuality as a subject for clinical, professional, or otherwise explicit discussion. They allowed sex a life of its own by preserving a measure of silence about it. With almost reverential circumspection, they protected and sustained its mystique of acutely pleasurable naughtiness. They favored engaging euphemism over the language of the clinic, suggestive reticence over verbal exhibitionism. Misunderstood by later generations, their preference for the combined joys of sex and silence gave rise to the myth of Victorian prudery and repression. From this grew further myths and errors, one building upon the other, until the erotic dimension of Victorian life was all but forgotten. To remember is to chip away at the long-standing wall of misconception.

Pearls and Piano Legs

A great error of post-Victorian times has been in thinking that euphemism and suggestion reflected inhibition. Rather, they enabled the free play of sexual feelings and meanings. Take the simple and in many senses innocuous image of the pearl. Traditionally, it had been a symbol of the ideal spiritual union of men and women. In the Victorian era, it carried more concrete associations with feminine sexual attractiveness. Pearl-like teeth were a mark of beauty in the fortunate few who had them. Some women even enhanced their complexions with pearlized powder. Many more adorned themselves with strings of pearls, which not only flattered the face and neck but drew attention to a deep cleavage.

The pearl was also a euphemism for the clitoris. In 1879, when the underground pornographic magazine *The Pearl* first appeared, the sexual implication of its name would not have escaped most potential subscribers. There would have been few who needed to sample the "very vast amount of voluptuous reading" in order to have understood that this was not a trade paper of the jewelry profession. Small wonder, then, that at the beginning of her career as celebrated courtesan and toast of the Paris gossip columnists, Emma Crouch of Plymouth, Devonshire, changed her name. By the time she had bathed publicly in champagne, and long before an all-male dinner party at the Cafe Riche in Paris had enjoyed her served up on an enormous silver platter—entirely naked, so the story goes, except for a sprinkling of parsley—she was already notorious on both sides of the Channel as Cora Pearl.

Ironically, what has become the best known of Victorian euphemisms hardly qualified as such a thing in its own day. Use of the refined word *limbs* to avoid the supposedly vulgar mention of legs was by no means a universal Victorian habit.

Certain overly genteel circles no doubt preferred *limbs,* and possibly this preference was more widespread in America than in England. The majority of English Victorians appear to have referred to *limbs* and *legs* interchangeably, without regarding the former as a euphemism. From gentlemen admirers of the female form to fashion reporters writing elegant prose for respectable magazines, people of all kinds seem never to have so much as blushed, let alone recoiled in priggish horror, at the thought and mention of legs.

Neither, generally, did the sight of them provoke any flustered or excessively prurient reaction. After all, half the population's legs were never much a matter of concern in any case. Men, it had long been accepted, were free to display theirs in knee breeches, tight trousers, and various athletic costumes. Although women's clothing by no means offered its wearers an equal advantage, fashion and some recreational attire at least put the female leg in view, while keeping it more or less properly covered. By the end of the century, swimming costumes consisted of either a short skirt and bloomers or the more up-to-date combination of skirt and stockings. Throughout the Victorian era, if a respectable lady dressed up as a fairy or milkmaid for a masquerade party, she might appropriately show off her legs in tights. Some fashions in ordinary daytime wear could also be revealing. There was, for one, the stylishly form-fitting dress of the 1870s and 1880s. This not only hinted at the outline of a woman's legs when she walked but often, with or without movement, hugged the contours of her thighs so tightly that there was little left to the imagination.

No one, it seems, found such leg-defining dresses and skirts objectionable. Even legs entirely bared were not necessarily a source of consternation. This was particularly true in England, even among the highly respectable. One man of the cloth, Reverend Francis Kilvert, was an observant and appreciative frequenter of bathing beaches. His diary shows that sometime in the 1870s he happened upon a young woman bather who had not bothered with bloomers or stockings. With frank enjoyment and no apparent embarrassment, the reverend studied what he referred to initially as her "legs" and later, his recollected enthusiasm mounting, as "the graceful roundness of the delicately beautiful limbs."

American propriety, on the other hand, was not so relaxed when it came to the recreational exposure of women's legs. According to the London fashion columnist Iris, who disapprovingly relayed this tidbit to the mostly female readers of *Bow Bells* magazine, there was in the 1890s an American law passed to regulate the amount of leg that lady cyclists could show. Such a law did not, however, reflect the entirety of American morality. As Iris explained, it was very unpopular with the women of "that great and free country where the female does nothing by halves." She hastened reassuringly to add that in England "we have no censor of legs."

Before leaving the largely apocryphal subject of Victorian limbs, it is more than time to address some common sense to one of the most prevalent and enduring clichés about sex and the Victorians. This is the much-repeated idea that they prudishly covered the legs of pianos and other furniture with lace and frills so that they would not be reminded of the lower parts of their own anatomies. In fact, such a practice does not appear to have been widely popular. There are at most a handful of American instances that English travelers recounted to their country-men. The English, it seems, generally considered these to be a source of amuse-ment rather than a fashion to be emulated.

Whether or not the Victorians commonly concealed the legs of their pianos, there is no question that they ruffled, fringed, and covered practically everything else. On any available flat surface embroidered table runners, wax flowers, china, brass, and other bric-a-brac told of their owner's taste and personal history. Walls groaned with pictures, patterned paper, and hangings. Chairs and sofas, already brocaded and tasseled, additionally boasted feather cushions and crocheted doilies. In such a setting, frilled piano legs could hardly have been anything other than one feature of a decorating fashion based on the principle of abundance.

But if the adornment of furniture legs had some other significance, more likely than not it was sexual. When it came to the clothing of people, covering and con-cealing had as much to do with sex as they did with modesty. An 1897 article, "Dress in its Relationship to Sex," proclaimed this point to readers of *Adult: The Journal of Sex*, a self-styled "organ" for exploring "important phases of sex questions." Orford Northcote, the article's improbably named (presumably pseudonymous) author, took strenuous exception to women's "bifurcated garments"—bloomers, that is. His objection was not that such clothing was indecent in its exposure of women's legs, but that it could not match the voluminous skirt for pure sexual at-tractiveness.

"The externals of the female generative organs," he explained, "are by nature hidden from sight, and when to this is added the entire encasement of the lower part of the body in one garment, the area of sexual mystery, due to this conceal-ment, is enormously enlarged. The whole space so enclosed becomes sexualised." If what was true of women's skirts can be extended to furniture, then covered piano legs might well have focused attention on those very parts—and triggered the contemplation of more tantalizing human appendages. And perhaps other furniture also piqued the erotic fancy of the Victorians. As magazine illustrations of the day show, the well-padded backs of many a chair bore a distinct similarity to the stylishly ample female posterior.

Dress and Undress

Although certain individuals might have failed to appreciate the sensual overtones of their interior furnishings, collectively the Victorians possessed a sexual imagination of some breadth and flexibility. Besides grasping the erotic potential of covering up, they fastened readily on the titillation to be found in the interplay of concealment and exposure. The appeal of wearing an evening gown, for instance, arose from the opportunity such attire gave for the simultaneous expression of a woman's sexuality and the relative preservation of her modesty. She might combine to alluring effect a heavily boned bodice and long full skirt with bare arms or shoulders and a plunging neckline—accentuated, not infrequently, by a strand of pearls.

Stylish interior and posterior, London Journal, *1874*

Beyond the sight of the respectable world of dinner parties and elegant décolletage, pornography lurked with its own more extreme version of erotic dress and undress. Postcards and other kinds of pictorial erotica regularly featured nubile women in semiclad poses. With apparently absentminded modesty, the models clutched their garments to their bodies while negligently leaving their upper torsos fully exposed. Or, entirely clothed on top, no touch of lace and pearl omitted, they assumed coy facial expressions, lifted their heavy skirts high, and showed off the stylish boots or shoes that complemented their otherwise naked lower bodies.

Also showing nudity offset by strategic clothing is a series of six turn-of-the-century photographs apparently taken in a conventional middle-class parlor. Intently observed by her male companion, a partially clad woman plays the piano or poses suggestively on various pieces of furniture. In one scene she bends over a chair and shows off knee-length drawers, her only garment. In the others she is unclothed except for the boots or shoes on her feet and the stockings covering her legs to midthigh. The piano legs are hidden from view by an object in the foreground, but it is probably safe to assume that they are shamelessly stark naked.

While the erotic appeal of the footwear and stockings in these photographs is enhanced by the near-nudity of their wearer, such items of feminine apparel were in themselves a source of sexual stimulation for many Victorian men. According to experienced contemporary observers, masculine attention would fix first on the stocking itself. Fantasy would then take over, seeing through to the leg beneath. From there it would explore freely upward. The resultant sexual charge appears to have ranged from mild arousal to the obsessive interest of the foot and leg fetishist.

Outside the partial undress common in pornography, there was one proper form of attire with comparable ability to provide a stimulating eyeful of buttoned boot and silk stocking. This was the hooped crinoline, an indispensable fashion item from about 1855 to 1870. Easily tipped or swayed, it afforded many generous glimpses of well-shod feet, stockinged legs—and possibly more, for these were the days when respectable ladies often went without any garment whatever under their crinoline and petticoats. Presumably this was for coolness in warm weather and for convenience when dependent on facilities away from home. On other occasions it was most common for women to wear drawers, an ankle- or knee-length garment that was made of two sections, one for each leg, and tied at the waist. It covered the pelvic area loosely and, for practical reasons, was slit at the front and back. With such an open-ended garment—or nothing—beneath it, the crinoline had perhaps the greatest capacity of all ladies' wear to envelop and reveal the female body.

This was frequently an inconvenience for the women who wore it, and perhaps the reason why it did not match the corset or bustle for fashionable longevity. As one gentleman commentator who had grown up during the Victorian period recalled, women in crinolines "were, indoors, in trepidation on staircases and, outdoors, were equally in fear of the wind and of stumbling, and they dared not go up the steps to the tops of buses." But what was annoying for its wearers was riveting to others. In 1863 another masculine observer, the barrister Sir William Hardman, later editor of the *Morning Post,* had been studying the matter carefully for some time and was moved to remark that "women getting into omnibuses, servant girls cleaning door-steps, and virgins at windy seaside watering places all show their — on occasion." Just which bodily feature had so often caught his eye is open to question. Most likely, though, he was not referring to limbs—nor even to legs.

Hardman may also have been the originator of a riddle of the day: "Why may the crinoline be justly regarded as a social invention? Because it enables us to see more of our friends." In at least one instance the crinoline was also the subject of a photographic spoof of midcentury conventions of courtship. The scene shows a young lady whose intimate interlude with an admirer has been unexpectedly interrupted by her stern mother or chaperone. Only just in time has the surprised lover managed to conceal himself—under the young lady's spacious crinoline, from which he peeps out with a leering expression. Modern viewers might need to be reminded of the source of both the leer and the picture's humor. But no Victorian of wholesomely naughty mind would have forgotten for a moment that underneath her hooped crinoline, this properly well-dressed lady would have been wearing very little—or nothing at all.

Problems with Panties

Such occasions of amiably prurient humor were commonplace among those supposedly grim and sexually unbending Victorians. There were also a few instances when the very flexibility of their collective libido could lead to a certain amount of confusion.

This showed notably in controversies over feminine underpants. These garments were comparatively late entries into the feminine repertoire of intimate wear and only began to be widely accepted after 1870. There were two versions. The first was a shorter, midthigh variant of the old long drawers; the second was "whole-seated," with a back flap that buttoned on each side and could be let down when necessity demanded. By the 1880s in England both types appear to have been known as *knickers,* although the older term *drawers* also continued in use for the first.

In its own way, each of the two kinds was the focus of concern and debate. Some people questioned the decency of the short drawers because they associated these with the dubious sexual morality of courtesans and licentious female aristocrats. Others were upset because such garments were not erotic enough. Gentlemen of the old school, who remembered when many women did not routinely wear drawers, missed the seductive possibility of catching an accidental glimpse of the intimate female parts that were now covered. The same objection applied even more to the closed underpants.

Many men and women also considered that these whole-seated garments lacked feminine allure because they were an adaptation of masculine clothing—the word *knickers* derived from *knickerbockers*, a form of men's knee breeches. A few dissenters, on the other hand, deemed them dangerously erotic because of their stimulatingly close contact with the body. Still others objected to them on hygienic grounds: the loss of free air circulation around the female organs would be detrimental to their healthy functioning. To add to all this confusing controversy, there were also those who took the opposing stance on the health issue and argued that the warmth and protection that both sorts of undergarment afforded would reduce colds and infection.

It was perhaps this ability to insulate against drafts, and the relative convenience of feminine underpants, that led to their almost universal adoption in one form or the other by the turn of the century. With their growing popularity among wearers, reservations about their erotic value subsided and knickers became progressively sexualized. Much of the titillating charge of the cancan (introduced into England in the 1860s) arose from the dancers' blatant display of their underpants. Ever eclectic, pornography, too, was quick to add the garment to its pictorial stock. Rear views of large-bottomed women posing in ruffled knickers became standard. And the always good-natured and accommodating sexual fancy of the average Victorian male now obligingly divided its attention between those white ruffles and the still-inviting zone they enclosed.

By the Sea, Barely

While underpants and other suggestive covering for the body were undoubtedly erotic to many people, the Victorians did not by the same token have an overly modest distaste for out-and-out nakedness. In good weather the English flocked to the seaside resorts that, better even than the crinoline, enabled them to see more of their friends. Until the 1870s, and possibly somewhat later, nude bathing on English beaches was customary among men and not unheard-of among women. Unlike France and North America, where both sexes shared one beach and bathing costumes were obligatory, the practice in England was for men and women to bathe separately. Their respective beaches were usually within sight of one another, however, and the barriers between them nominal. A woman emerging from the bathing machine, then lowering herself into the water, might do so in full view of a long line of men, some with telescopes and opera glasses, watching her from the adjacent beach.

Such seaside voyeurs were not necessarily leering rowdies fresh from the local pub. Reverend Francis Kilvert, for one, was both a pillar of the established Church and seaside habitué, a contemplative diarist and polite yet keenly interested observer of nude female bathers. On one occasion he was captivated by "girls with shoes, stockings, and drawers off, wading in the tide, holding up their clothes nearly to the waist and naked from the waist downward." On another beach he looked with delight upon a "beautiful girl . . . entirely naked on the sand." Not only did this bather's legs draw his admiring gaze, but he was also taken with the "tender swell of the bosom" and "above all with the soft exquisite curves of the rosy dimpled bottom and broad white thighs."

Other seaside sights invited what a certain Dr. Thompson, author of the 1860 *Health Resorts of Great Britain*, uncharitably described in his book as "the unblushing intrusiveness of the fair sex." At about the same time the *Saturday Review* took a somewhat more tolerant view of the "strings of respectable women" who positioned themselves on the shore, only yards away from the men's bathing machines. The *Review*'s commentator remarked:

> There they sit, happy, innocent, undisturbed—placidly and immovably gazing at hundreds of males in the costume of Adam. There does not seem to be a notion that there is anything improper—there are no averted looks, no side-long glances, no blushes or shame. Naked men are treated as one of the products of the place, like lobsters, or soles, or pebbles.

The voyeuristic pleasures of women at the seaside were not confined to any particular age group. It was frequently reported that "young ladies" availed themselves of optical devices that they trained on naked male bathers who might be wading in water no deeper than their knees. George Meredith, a correspondent of that sometime observer of crinolines Sir William Hardman, also recalled seeing "antique virgins with spy-glass in hand," stalking the beach at Eastbourne in 1870.

Their target was purportedly a group of fat men, each one disporting himself in the sun and the waves, with "a glistening on the right cheek and the left." With his characteristic wit, Hardman suggested that the efforts of female spectators were apt to result in disappointment. "The action of cold water" on the naked Englishman, he explained, "produces an unsatisfactory effect, and leaves nothing worthy of a passing glance to the innocent but pruriently curious maiden."

Others lacked Sir William's easygoing sophistication and objected strenuously to nude bathing. One upright family man who wrote to *The Times* in the mid-1850s condemned the practice as "truly disgusting." "But what is more disgusting still," he added, "is the fact that these exhibitions are watched daily by large numbers of ladies who spend their mornings in close proximity to scores of naked men. . . . The whole affair is abominable and ought to be abated." During the last three decades of the century such voices of disapproval progressively became the dominant ones, and by the end of the 1890s bathing costumes had become the rule for both sexes. But not without a good deal of regret on the part of those who had once known "the delicious feeling of freedom in stripping in the open air and running down naked to the sands where the waves were curling white with foam and the red morning sunshine glowing upon the naked limbs of the bathers." This was yet another recollection by Kilvert, who would later write irritably of the new need to don some "wretched rag" for bathing. He would have found a sympathizer in Hardman, for Sir William likewise had no affection for the "damp, unpleasant, clinging garments" that eventually became required wear on every English beach.

What is most telling about nude bathing and the Victorian sexual mystique is not that some people objected to the practice. More striking is that among both those who indulged in it and those who watched, there seems to have been a total absence of shame. There is no record of seriously discomposed bathers, and the majority of lookers-on appear to have been unabashedly entertained, certainly not recoiling in real (or even pretended) outrage. Reverend Kilvert would never likely have joined a line of neck-craning spectators—a clergyman, after all, had his dignity to maintain. He also presumably sought out seclusion to inscribe his memories of seaside visits—for before it is subjected to the prying eyes of the historian, a diary is a private thing. But to have been able to remember and, in solitude, to write down such vivid impressions of naked women bathers, the reverend could not have acted altogether differently from most shoreline voyeurs. He must have looked openly and at some length, each time in full view himself on a public beach.

This instance of one gentleman's unapologetic voyeurism raises the ghost of yet another misconception about sex and the Victorians. As myth would have it, they confined sexuality to some shameful secretive realm—the brothel or the pages of pornography—while in more open arenas a neutered hypocritical respectability held sway. There is a spark of truth in all this. The Victorians had no shortage of pornography; brothels, too, were a part of some people's experience. Where the myth goes wrong, however, is in failing to recognize the larger, public world that not only accommodated the sexual side of life but generally tolerated and often enthusiastically embraced it.

Sexuality played its part in the spectacle that was enacted on public beaches, as well as at costume balls, evening parties, and any place that crinolined ladies might frequent. It also made itself known in greeting and visiting cards, and in the plots of best-selling fiction. It paraded across the music hall stage and showed itself at recreational activities, from parlor amusements to sporting events. What it did not do was withdraw, all but disembodied, into the ether of clinical language and immoderate talk. That would come later.

Sex and Marriage

This is not to say that sexuality had free public rein as long as people spoke of it in elegant euphemisms or ogled it in silence. For all that the Victorians were not the prudes and hypocrites of modern myth, their sexual world was not a place where biology and its urges went unrestricted. Indeed, what helped to make sex a potent force, and an unabashed presence in even the most polite of company, was the Victorians' ability both to express and to contain sexuality. Like good parents, they nurtured it lovingly while imposing the measure of discipline that respectability required. They adhered to a tolerant yet firm policy of pleasure—but within clear limits.

Those limits were set by the prevailing idea of "natural" or "normal" sex: that is, heterosexuality. And, increasingly, as the Victorian period wore on, "normal" heterosexuality appeared in one guise. This was the romantic and sexual attraction between men and women that led "naturally" to marriage and the creation of a family. "Normal" sex was consistent with the values of Victorian industrial society—it was yet another mode of production. As long as it managed to show itself in that light, it could remain in the public arena, acknowledged, accepted, and frankly enjoyed.

The procreative marriage was not, of course, an invention of the Victorians. Nevertheless, as *the* norm, it had never before held sway to the extent that it would by the end of their era. In the eighteenth century, for example, marrying and having children had also been the generally favored way of enacting heterosexuality. But at the same time liaisons before and outside marriage enjoyed a measure of public acceptance that would decline during the nineteenth century. In other words, as there developed the overriding Victorian values of respectability, family, and productivity in all things, the character of publicly countenanced heterosexuality changed. With growing insistence society emphasized, and propriety demanded, the childbearing marital union.

This was not a sudden or dramatic development, nor were the Victorians entirely unbending toward sexual irregularity. Taking popular fiction and humor as a guide, from the 1840s to as late as the 1870s there was a fair level of public tolerance, even sympathy, for divergent heterosexual types—oversexed squires, loving mistresses, and common-law spouses. People were even apt to commiserate with philandering husbands, especially those whose behavior had some good excuse, like an insane wife. Think of Edward Rochester in Charlotte Brontë's *Jane Eyre* (1847). With a raving madwoman and probable nymphomaniac for a wife, how could he help but turn to Jane?

But while the errant husband might find allowances made for him, such generosity was less likely to apply to the fallen woman. Perhaps more than anyone who defied the norm, the adulteress was the recipient of unequivocally harsh moral condemnation. In most fiction she came to one bad end or another—punishment and degradation, illness and physical disfigurement, death, or often all of these unhappy fates. The role of the adulteress as universal scapegoat changed little over the course of the nineteenth century. Meanwhile, other unconventional heterosexuals and their nonproductive gratifications had become more liable for censure at the close of the Victorian period than they had been at its beginning. Sex, as people ever more came to believe, was for faithful husbands and wives, and—providing that they refrained from "going all the way"—for betrothed couples and marriage-minded young lovers.

Potency, His—and Hers

The double standard that permitted the adulterer, but not the adulteress, to indulge with relative impunity reflected the larger condition of Victorian marriage and society. While romantic love and sensual pleasure were ideally the most constant companions of "normal" sex, every couple, however blissful, harbored another, relentless presence. Never absent, it sometimes hovered tactfully in the background; at other times it forcefully asserted itself. This was power or, more precisely, the unequal power that marked the relationship of men and women. Inevitably, men's political and economic dominance shaped their understanding of what it meant to be masculine. Beyond that, it colored their romantic and sexual behavior toward women—the Victorian lover was often what a later age would call "macho."

Because it was mostly created by and for men, pornography was especially apt to cast the masterful male as the potent star of his own play. So it was in the scenario of the cavorting couple in the parlor. The pair may have been sharing a few light erotic moments, but the encounter was by no means equal. He was fully dressed, and the clothing signaled his prosperity and status. She wore only the garments of fetishism, erotic accessories that did not reflect any particular economic or social standing. She was seated, while he loomed over her. Or she assumed submissive kneeling positions or lay face down—available, vulnerable.

This, though, would have been pallid fare for those with truly robust pornographic palates. For such tastes literary pornography dished up dominance more zestfully, never hesitating to thrust right to the crux of male power. In most pornographic fiction, the protagonist was not only a man of authority or privilege—doctor, minister, titled aristocrat—but he was also powerful by virtue of physical prowess. One classic of this kind, *The Lustful Turk*, gripped the Victorian pornographic imagination enough to have merited three editions (two in the 1860s, another in 1893). It features an "Eastern Potentate" who specializes in the forcible deflowering of virgins. Like others of his breed, he is manned with what might sound like a whole toolboxful of "magical" implements, but it is actually just one sublime and (if pornography were to be believed) ever-potent organ with many names: "tremendous instrument," "master-key," "wonderful instrument of nature," "Nature's grand masterpiece."

As most men probably knew, but did not generally care to admit, pornography's infinite penile universe was a cosmos of compensation. For, outside the wishful imagination of the male pornographer, women did not typically submit helplessly to the one-weapon male arsenal. As any well-brought-up Victorian lady was quite aware, properly deployed, *her* sexuality was the greater power. Some men openly confirmed this. Among others, gentlemen authors of popular romance were apt to acknowledge that women's beauty and charm were formidable weapons—their desirable female characters often rendered strong heroes helpless with passion. The late-Victorian poet Alfred Austin was of a more begrudging turn of mind. With a misogyny born of anxiety over rejection and, probably, of plain sour grapes, his poem "The Season" peevishly asked:

What can be Man's, while Woman deems *her* part,
To bare her bosom but to hide her heart?

Heartlessly or otherwise, women commonly exercised their sexuality with a view to attracting a husband. That, anyway, was the opinion of one self-styled "humble bachelor," the anonymous author of *Hints on Husband Catching* (1846), a "manual for marriageable misses." In this slim volume, which he addressed and dedicated to "the spinsters of England," the author, humble though he might have been, was forthright in his version of the feminine pursuit of "the plain gold ring":

> For this you study coquetry; . . . for this you suffer each ball-room booby to clasp your waists and breathe upon your cheeks in the waltz; for this you attempt . . . the polka; for this you leave uncovered the swanlike neck, and the ivory shoulders, and benevolently display to us as much of your beautiful busts as you dare to show.

For all that she might have pursued it with wholehearted energy, marriage was a mixed blessing for a woman. For most of the nineteenth century, she not only gave up her name at the altar but also in effect relinquished her body, her property rights, and her independent legal existence. Still, the ideal of romantic love softened the losses, and marriage could additionally provide more tangible compensations. Sometimes it improved a woman's social position and her material comfort; and, within its domestic confines, it conferred authority and responsibility that an unattached woman living in another's household did not usually achieve. In prosperous and sophisticated circles, it may also have afforded a measure of freedom that the single, well-chaperoned state did not. As the "humble bachelor" advised his feminine readers,

> matrimony, then, is to be to you the signal of emancipation. A married woman may do what she likes, and as long as she keeps within the limits of decorum— that is to say, as long as she is not actually an adulteress—she may flirt, dress, and enjoy herself to an unlimited extent. . . . No wonder then, that you eagerly take your places in the ranks of matrons expectant, and arm yourselves at all points for conquest.

He neglected to mention that dressing up and flirtation were fleeting pleasures. When the party was over, they amounted to nothing but a yellowing dance card, perhaps, or a faded corsage, and a memory or two. Even the more substantial benefits that marriage bestowed on women were small when compared to the social, economic, and political advantages that men enjoyed. By the same token, the overwhelming (and often weakening) effect that one sexually attractive woman could have on an otherwise indomitable man did not redress the inequalities of society at large. But what marriage and the effective use of their sexuality did do was to empower women to carve out space for personal expression and achievement within the constraints on their lives.

Sexuality Throughout Society

For some women the constraints were greater than for others. Many working-class wives faced material hardships that quickly took the gloss off marriage, however joyful it might have been in the beginning. Much the same was true for their men. The exemplary, romantic, fruitful marriage strongly reflected middle-class values. The patterns of femininity and masculinity that most people in some way tried to follow also best suited a prosperous way of life. Those who came closest to realizing the ideals were thus most likely to have come from reasonably advantaged backgrounds.

Yet, apart from class and economic position, an individual's particular family circumstances, temperament, and physical appearance, as well as plain luck, all played their part in each personal experience of heterosexuality. Many who struggled daily with almost unimaginable deprivation were nonetheless fortunate in their choice of mate and able to find sexual fulfillment. This shatters the last lingering myth about sex and the Victorians. No longer tenable is the pervasive belief that unabashed sexuality was the privilege of the upper classes—recreation for the wastrel sons and spoiled daughters of a decadent aristocracy.

Reticent though the Victorians generally were, some left behind memoirs and letters that together are revealing. A few show plainly, while most hint subtly, that behind their drawn curtains and closed doors many respectable middle- and working-class people led sex lives rich in expressiveness and satisfaction. Even where economic distress took its toll on the libido, there was little of that stiff prudery by which the Victorians have so long, so erroneously, been characterized. Neither was there much of that legendary puritanical restraint among those who were prosperous enough to overfurnish their parlors. Except when it came to piano legs—these, as most respectable Victorians well knew, were best appreciated without adornment, in all their naked glory.

Sex Changes

Piano legs would remain gloriously unclothed as the Victorian period began to give way to the Edwardian. Men at the same time would continue to relish the occasional glimpse of female legs—and whatever else they could manage to spot. The rest they would avidly persist in imagining. For those whose cravings were insatiable, pornography and pornographers would thrive through the end of the nineteenth century and for at least a hundred years beyond. Romantic love and marriage would also flourish, and by the turn of the century the procreative norm would be securely established in the minds and lives of most people.

But in the more than half a century that separated the beginning of the Victorian era from its end, many things were bound to change—and did. With the ascendancy of the norm, other sexualities became definitively "abnormal." New words reflected the distinction. Most notably, *heterosexuality* entered into English usage in 1892, followed by *homosexuality* in 1897. What had once been comprehensible only as individual acts of the body could now be labeled and allocated between two broad categories of sexual behavior (there being at the time no developed concept of bisexuality). Behavior of the first sort was to be courted and nurtured; the other, despised or even punished.

The 1890s were marked by a notorious instance of such punishment, the imprisonment of Oscar Wilde for indecency and sodomy involving young men. Apparently, in the minds of the jury who found the famous playwright guilty, "being earnest" paled into insignificance alongside the importance of being "normal." The Wilde case was a tragic outcome of the growing concern to enforce the norm. This had first showed itself conspicuously in the 1880s with the introduction of new legislation against pornography, prostitution, and sex between men (though not between women, for until the 1920s, legislators and the public had little awareness of a distinct lesbian identity). In formulating the language of sexual regulation, legislators helped to initiate a fundamental change in the nature of sex, a shift toward articulating rather than simply feeling it.

At the same time, others played their own small but (in every sense) telling parts. In 1885 a group of radical-liberals, socialists, and feminists came together in London to explore the possibilities of heterosexuality. To these self-conscious intellectuals—the Men and Women's Club, as they called themselves—exploration meant discussion. They debated, disputed, conversed, and expounded upon the sexual issues of the day. Over four years they did their best to turn the carnal into the verbal—spending themselves at last in a torrent of utterance.

It was a mere trickle compared to the wave of verbiage that would engulf sex in the next decade. The 1890s saw the rise of sexology—the professional study of sex—and all the publications, papers, lectures, and discussion that it engendered. In scientific and medical circles the transformation of sex into talk was well under way. A signal beginning had already been made in the last year of the previous decade with the publication of Patrick Geddes and J. Arthur Thomson's biological study, *The Evolution of Sex*. Its use of evolutionary theory as a "scientific" rationale for the status quo of sexual inequality was well received, and new editions appeared in 1890, 1895, 1897, and 1899.

Other experts, meanwhile, were producing their own landmarks in the exploration of sexuality. Richard von Krafft-Ebing's encyclopedia of the "abnormal," *Psychopathia Sexualis*, translated into English in 1892, put yesterday's sins and indulgences on the modern map of sexual pathologies. The norm, too, was charted, most notably by Havelock Ellis in *Man and Woman*, his 1893 examination of "human secondary sexual characteristics." He later widened his compass to take in homosexuality, publishing *Sexual Inversion* in 1897, the first of the seven volumes of his monumental *Studies in the Psychology of Sex*. The sex research that would generate the greatest and most lasting flow of words also became part of the English-speaking world in the 1890s. This was the decade when the Society for Psychical Research and other British learned groups first discussed the ideas of a then little-known Viennese doctor whose name would become a household word in the next century.

But that century had yet to arrive and, outside professional circles, most people had never heard of Sigmund Freud—let alone Ellis and the rest. Nor had they yet acquired the habit of talking incessantly about sex. While an occasional turn-of-the-century observer might complain of offenses against "conversational decorum," the true "abrogation of reticence" was far in the future. As the elderly queen sat out her last few years on the throne, the Victorian sexual mystique was only a little compromised.

For the majority, sex remained primarily an experience of the body, and not an exercise in words. Even if compulsory bathing costumes made visiting the seaside a less purely sensual event than it once had been, there was still, as the century ended, plenty of visible leg—male as well as female—and fantasy to supply what could no longer be seen. And although the crinoline and its revelations had become things of the past, other alluring fashions persisted. Throughout the Victorian period female sexuality was a potent force, and the desirable woman's standard for expressing it always as high as her imposing bosom and stylish bustle.

CHAPTER 2

Bosoms and Bustles

Can anyone suggest a more beautiful sight than what is termed a well-made woman?

—*Revelations of Girlhood*, pamphlet,
"By a Physician," c. 1885

The authority who shared this thought with the public did not hesitate to expand upon what he meant by "well-made." "Note," he exhorted his readers, "the graceful undulations of the body, the rising and falling of parts that are chiefly concerned in giving that prominence to a handsome woman which constitutes one of her principal charms and distinguishes her from man." In other words, the sexually attractive woman was shapely and full-breasted. This was no isolated opinion, but the prevailing point of view. Victorian men and women alike associated beauty, femininity, and sexuality with a rounded figure and well-developed bosom.

In one man's steamy fantasies especially, the generously proportioned, womanly woman was the invariable heroine. Deceptively bland in appearance, with his smooth round face, wire spectacles, and small, prim-looking mouth, George W. M. Reynolds was the best-selling author of dozens of racy romances and the creator of countless bosom-heaving heroines. Sandhurst-educated, married, committed to temperance and social justice, he, like so many Victorians, combined respectability with an apparently tireless sexual imagination. With romance, adventure, and titillation his repeated formula, he captured the imaginations of millions of readers in England and abroad.

Some of these were men, diverted perhaps by all the palpitating sexual tension that distinguished Reynolds's plots. But most of his readers were women, many of them young and single. So great was their demand for romance that Reynolds, popular and prolific though he was, shared the limelight with other writers who also had a large female following. Through romantic fiction Victorian women escaped temporarily from the routines of factories, shops, and domestic service, and from the duties that fell to the daughters and wives of middle-class households. By reading romances, many gained their earliest inkling of the power of female sexuality and took their first lessons in the arts of flirtation and innuendo.

But if romantic fiction contributed to its female readers' sense of their sexual potential, it did so according to the contemporary standard of full-breasted, curvaceous beauty. This popular image was created not just by authors of fiction but also by fashion and beauty experts, advertisers, and glamorous figures such as actresses. There was no concerted effort to impose such an image, nor would women generally have suspected such a thing. Mass entertainment was new, and most people had yet to recognize its capacities and consequences. Reynolds and his kind simply kept on writing. And—breasts uplifted in properly cinched corsets, bustles in place—women kept on reading.

Heaving, Palpitating, Voluptuous Fullness

A reader had only to open at random almost any of Reynolds's works, and there would be his stock character, the beautiful heroine—shapely, bosom-heaving, and often in imminent danger of being seduced, raped, tortured in dungeons, trapped in burning buildings, or threatened by exotic wildlife. In a typical scene from his 1847 novel *Wagner, the Wehr-Wolf,* the intrepid and large-breasted heroine crosses the path of a giant anaconda snake that entwines itself menacingly around her. As she struggles pneumatically in its grip, her disarrayed garment exposes a good deal of breast and a hint of nipple. In another episode a similar-looking female character is abducted into white slavery by an unscrupulous sultan, one of whose minions manhandles her person and disarranges the bodice of her gown to revealing effect.

Reynolds also never missed a chance to place his heroines in happier but no less suggestive situations. His vivid imagination conjured warm tropical shores with "little wavelets kissing snowy bosoms" and gentle breezes strategically lifting

REYNOLDS'S MISCELLANY

Of Romance, General Literature, Science, and Art.

EDITED BY GEORGE W. M. REYNOLDS

AUTHOR OF THE "MYSTERIES OF LONDON," "FAUST," "MASTER TIMOTHY'S BOOK-CASE," &c.

No. 18 . Vol. I. SATURDAY, MARCH 6, 1847. Price 1d.

GRIFFIN & DUVERGIER

WAGNER: THE WEHR-WOLF.

BY THE EDITOR.

CHAPTER XLII.

THE TEMPTATION.—THE ANACONDA.

In the meantime Fernand Wagner was engaged in the attempt to cross the chain of mountains which intersected the island whereon the shipwreck had thrown him.

He had clambered over rugged rocks and leapt across many yawning chasms in that region of desolation,—a region which formed so remarkable a contrast with the delicious scenery which he had left behind him.

And now he reached the basis of a conical hill, the summit of which seemed to have been split into two distinct parts; and the sinuous traces of the lava-streams, now cold, and hard, and black, adown its sides, convinced him that this was the volcano, from whose rent crater had poured the bituminous fluid so fatal to the vegetation of that region.

Following a circuitous and naturally formed pathway round the base, he reached the opposite side; and now from a height of three hundred feet above the level of the sea, his eyes commanded a view of a scene as fair as that behind the range of mountains.

He was now for the first time convinced of what he had all along suspected—namely, that it was indeed an island on which the storm had cast him.

Well-endowed heroine, Wagner, the Wehr-Wolf, *1847*

already scantily disposed garments. Or he conceived intimate encounters between male and female characters, the women bemused and all but breathless with excitement. Octavia was lost "in the dreamlike voluptuousness that enveloped her," he wrote as he worked on an early episode of his 1850 *Mysteries of the Court of London*. "She observed not," he continued, "the encroachment of Harley's hand upon the treasures of her virgin bosom. As he now pressed the glowing,—palpitating,—heaving orb. . . "—and so on. Whatever circumstances he envisioned, the exuberant Reynolds rarely failed to enthuse about "glowing bosoms" and "heaving breasts."

Although his heroines were particularly colorful and noticeably endowed, they were not unique. Beautiful women with elegant décolletage and deep cleavage were virtually everywhere in the popular Victorian romance. Dashing highwaymen, otherwise unregenerate, were softened by their bosomy allure. Prurient vicars and peeping servingmen were inflamed by their "swelling charms." Unprincipled scoundrels seduced them. And heroes rescued them from all manner of predicaments. Often on these occasions, what started out fraught with peril ended up charged with passion.

In an engraved scene in the 1885 *London Journal*, a forerunner of modern ladies' magazines, a "delicate and very fragile" but nonetheless fully developed young woman is plucked from a fiery death by her admirer. Because of the urgency of the situation, he grasps her upper torso more intimately than would normally be acceptable upon short acquaintance. One hand is at her waist, the other presses the underside of her right breast. To readers well-versed in the tricks of the romance trade, this hinted provocatively at the romantic and sexual relationship that would unfold in succeeding pages. Not least of all, it drew their immediate attention to the heroine's bosom—"that voluptuous fullness," as the irrepressible Reynolds would have described it.

Apart from romantic fiction, Victorian women read fashion columns, advice books, and guides to beauty. And there, too, the well-proportioned, full-breasted woman held sway as the model of feminine attractiveness. Although most authorities on fashion and beauty gave due attention to the importance of a delicate hand, white teeth, luxuriant hair, and "speaking eyes," they also generally agreed that a shapely figure was a particularly important female asset. Throughout most of the Victorian period, fashion plates and beauty books promoted a rounded, bosomy silhouette. Meanwhile the minor, often anonymous poets who wrote for popular magazines were apt to extol the "classically" abundant bosom. Justifiably confident, the pamphleteer "Physician" ended his passage on the "well-made" woman with a flourishing rhetorical inquiry—"Who will not admit that a woman with a good, well-rounded bust is to be more generally admired than a flat-breasted girl?" Who indeed?

While women were absorbing the full-breasted body image promoted by everyone from writers to doctors, some men were dipping into their own reading material. Pornography, ever sensitive to the needs of its gentlemen readers, did its best to enhance their natural interest in the "rising and falling parts" that had so taken the "Physician" and countless popular writers. Also enthused was the voyeuristic narrator of *The Disembodied Spirit*, a pornographic romance of the 1860s. In one episode he becomes "more and more excited" as he spies upon a sleeping woman and catches glimpses of "her lovely breasts . . . rounded globes . . . parted between, and crowned each with a delicious pink bud."

Supplementing the written word was the photograph. As early as the 1840s photography's pornographic uses were well appreciated, and there soon grew up a prospering mail-order trade in this new and gratifyingly realistic form of stimulation. To direct particular attention to a model's breasts, the pornographer's camera would capture her fully clothed below the waist and wearing little or nothing above. In one example a woman in skirt, stockings, and garters, her torso exposed, looks provocatively at the viewer. Her right hand toys with the rosary and crucifix at her throat, a blasphemous touch included to enhance both the photograph's forbidden appeal and its subject's large, bare breasts. Thus, in pictures as well as in print, Victorian pornography made its contribution to a widespread and enduring cultural fixation.

Corsets, Controversy, and Orgasmic Excitations

One way or another, there was considerable pressure on women to conform to the ideal of curvaceous beauty. They responded most noticeably through the virtually universal use of the corset. By 1868 Britain was annually producing three million of these popular undergarments and importing an additional two million from France and Germany. Corset advertisements proliferated in magazines and elsewhere, illustrating the shapely form that the wearer aspired to and often attained. As the advertisements indicate, corsets were available in every conceivable style. Apart from standard designs that simply enhanced the curves of women blessed with good, or at least passable, figures, there were more specialized versions: among others, the Self-Regulating Gestation Corset, for ladies in a delicate condition; the Juvenile Elastic Corset, for girls growing too rapidly, presumably due to puberty; the Invisible Scapula Contractor Corset, to develop the chest; and various models, sturdily boned or belted, to reshape bulky torsos.

So central was the corset in popular consciousness—male as well as female—that it was the focus of an ongoing and sometimes heated controversy during the 1860s and 1870s. The corset itself was for the most part uncontroversial; the issue was whether or not it ought to be tightly laced up. Letters and commentary flew back and forth, most notably in an otherwise staid, middle-class ladies' journal, the *Englishwoman's Domestic Magazine.* Some people objected to the tightly laced corset on health grounds, arguing that it caused everything from breathing diffi-culties and constricted internal organs to bad complexions. Others, often men with

Corset advertisements

waist and breast fetishes, ardently championed the cause of tight lacing. Meanwhile, the vast majority of women and men simply accepted a moderately laced corset as an indispensable enhancement to feminine beauty. Writing in 1867 to the *Englishwoman's Domestic Magazine,* one devoted wearer affirmed, "I . . . never feel prouder or happier, so far as matters of the toilette are concerned, than when I survey in myself the fascinating undulations of outline that art in this respect affords to nature."

Whether the result of nature's work or the corsetiere's art, an appealing figure was an undoubted requisite for the desirable woman. But so, too, was what many thought to be her "true beauty"—her goodness. The ideal Victorian woman was loving and nurturing, patient and agreeable, gentle and cheerful, obedient and dutiful. Not least of all, she was as innocent of mind as she was pure in body. In other words, as popular opinion, fashion, and literature would have it, femininity had two sides. On the one hand, the truly womanly woman was sexually virtuous—on the other, sexually attractive.

The corset represented this contradictory demand by fulfilling a dual purpose. It lifted and emphasized the breasts while confining and restraining the waist. In this way it served both the imperative of feminine attractiveness and the virtue of self-discipline. It was not only a conventional fashion essential but a sign of moral rectitude, and no respectable woman of means was likely to appear uncorseted in public. Decency of dress signaled decency of behavior to middle-class Victorians.

But for all that it was an accoutrement of respectability, the corset was also widely sexualized. To most heterosexual men the corseted woman, with her small waist and uplifted breasts, was visually and erotically attractive. The corset was also a source of stimulation for a minority whose sexual tastes tended toward sadomasochism. One representative of this group, "Alfred," wrote to the *Englishwoman's Domestic Magazine* in January 1871:

> There is something to me extraordinarily fascinating in the thought that a young girl has for many years been subjected to the strictest discipline of the corset. If she has suffered, as I have no doubt she has, great pain . . . for many years from its extreme pressure, it must be quite made up to her by the admiration her figure excites.

The majority of women who wore corsets laced themselves moderately and thus did not suffer the level of discomfort that preferences of Alfred's sort demanded. They were generally long accustomed to the feel of waist constriction and were not troubled by it. Many experienced mildly "pleasurable sensations" when laced up, while a few even confessed to orgasmic "excitations." In fact, it is possible that corsets contributed to many women's consciousness of their sexuality. Tight clothing of any sort can enhance bodily awareness.

Whatever were the sensations of individual wearers, there is certainly no doubt that the corset—specifically, its removal—had a widely recognized association with sexual encounter. Laces and stays must surely have figured prominently in many private erotic fantasies. The unlacing of a woman's corset before lovemaking was also a theme in pornography and might be hinted at discreetly in respectable love stories and poetry. As any contemporary would have known, when a still fully dressed Victorian lady dismissed her maid for the night, it was an erotically charged act. A lady's evening gown and much of what went under it, the corset especially, could not be removed by the wearer unaided. And if there was no maid to lend a hand, then who but a lover? . . .

Well-Rounded Women

Along with the corset, the heroines of Victorian fiction in their own way symbolized both propriety and sexuality. With few exceptions, the female characters who palpitated through the pages of best-selling romance were highly principled, sexually virtuous, and—invariably—attractive. The fiction of the day was well populated by worthy and alluring seamstresses, innocent and pretty factory girls, and gentlewomen whose moral sensibilities were equaled only by their sensuous curves.

Among the most eye-catching was Louisa, yet another creation of Reynolds's florid pen. She figured in the same work as the bosom-heaving Octavia, and her image advertised the latest edition in the author's own magazine, *Reynolds's Miscellany*. As the accompanying description expressed it, Louisa was "the personification of virtue, innocence and every good quality." Contemporary viewers might indeed have noted her demure glance and seen virtue reflected there. But they must also have taken in the revealing gown, the curls contrived to fall artlessly on bare skin, and, most striking of all, a corseted shape of pneumatic proportions.

The influence of Louisa and her kind extended well beyond the pages of fiction. Such heroines were the ultimate representatives of the goodness and attractiveness toward which real-life women were expected to strive. It is not difficult to account either for this ideal or for the main reason that most women pursued it. Virtue and sexual appeal—the two sides of Victorian femininity—were important qualifica-

Louisa, Reynolds's Miscellany, *1850*

tions for marriage, the destiny that all women were expected to desire and, if possible, attain. The altar was the goal and reward of most of the virtuous and beautiful heroines of fiction. Meanwhile, advice books and magazine articles also identified womanly with wifely: the ideal woman was, or soon would be, an ideal wife.

In short, to achieve what the world defined as her highest and most appropriate role in life, a woman had to be good *and* good-looking. In responding to this dictate, Victorian women not only enhanced their marriageability but at the same time maintained the contemporary standard of well-managed sexuality. For the Victorians, feminine propriety and female sexual attractiveness existed in perpetual tension. And of this there was no more visible and compelling symbol than the female breast and its popular imagery—the "chaste bosom," "virgin breast," "lily-white orb."

Professional Beauties

Fictional heroines were by no means the only models of full-breasted femininity. Attractive socialites and aristocrats, voluptuous biblical and mythological characters, and monumentally proportioned allegorical figures, such as Liberty or Romance, all from time to time featured in popular magazines and advertising. Even motherhood could be glamorized and sometimes overtly, if judiciously, sexualized. In a Pears' Soap advertisement, for instance, an attractive young mother is about to bathe her infant. At the child's playful tug, her bodice slips low enough to reveal, as if by accident, a good deal of attractive maternal bosom.

One group of women above all vied successfully with fictional heroines for the popular spotlight. Sharing center stage with the Octavias and Louisas of best-selling romance were the real-life women of the theater—actresses, dancers, and music hall entertainers. Their collective credits ranged from Shakespearean tragedy to contemporary melodrama. They gracefully performed the ballet or daringly high-kicked the cancan. Or, like the singer Nellie Power and others of her kind, they rollicked on the music hall stage, bringing to life the popular tunes of the day.

Such women enjoyed great prominence in the public mind. Their careers and personal lives figured regularly in popular print, and their always shapely images adorned theatrical posters, music sheets, and the pages of magazines. Because most of these magazines catered to a family market, their representation of theatrical women was well within the limits of respectable sexuality. Those who wrote articles about actresses tended to emphasize their subjects' gentility, whether or not this was verifiably the case. Meanwhile, illustrators portrayed women who were attractive but not blatantly seductive in either dress or demeanor. The *London Journal*'s artist, for one, showed the actress Fanny Kemble in a demure pose, breasts and shoulders modestly draped.

For all that family magazines played down the sexuality of actresses and other female performers, such women nonetheless eclipsed fictional heroines as the sex and beauty symbols of their day. They led the way in fashion and had an authoritative voice in all matters of grooming and good looks. Their beauty hints and advice graced the pages of the same family magazines that promoted female virtue, and their images and endorsements helped to sell personal hygiene and cosmetic products. Most notably, advertisements for Pears' Soap featured these "profes-

Song sheet featuring music hall star Nellie Power

sional beauties." Among them was "Jersey Lillie" Langtry, the actress and well-known mistress of the Prince of Wales, the future Edward VII.

Such advertisements—especially those depicting partial nudity—not only used the lure of beauty to market their products, but also demonstrated a clear notion of the principle "sex sells." Beyond having pleasing complexions, the actresses and others who endorsed soap and cosmetics were shapely and openly sexual. They allowed themselves to be represented in revealing garments, and they struck poses that drew attention to their bosoms, hips, and pelvic areas. Figuratively speaking, at least one even admitted the public into the intimacy of her bathroom—the operatic singer Adelina Patti was portrayed in her tub, coyly reaching for a bar of Pears'.

Forthright though they could be, theatrical women still maintained a level of decorum in advertising. Elsewhere, they revealed their sexuality more flagrantly.

Lillie Langtry, Pears' Soap advertisement, 1884

Photographs for private circulation and postcards that had to be ordered by mail catered to specialized interests and comparatively small numbers. In these intimate circles, where the sensibilities of the general public were not a factor, female performers and those who depicted them could abandon conventional propriety. Actresses, singers, and dancers were among the favored subjects of those who produced and sold postcards and other photographic erotica.

In pictures taken for more aboveboard purposes, theatrical women might still present themselves as unreservedly sexual beings. In the 1860s the dancer Finette posed for her visiting card clad only in high-buttoned shoes, a short top, and thigh-length underpants trimmed with lace and ribbon. Enhancing the erotic overtones of the photograph was her chosen posture. Unabashedly, she turned her back to the camera and displayed the rear-view charms that had no doubt helped to win her fame as a cancan artiste.

Testimonial from **MADAME ADELINA PATTI.**

I have found it matchless for the hands and complexion.

Bathing beauty Adelina Patti, Pears' Soap advertisement, 1887

Theatrical news reporting might equally emphasize the sexuality of women in entertainment. In a striking illustration from an 1870 issue of the London paper *Days' Doings*, several dressers are busily costuming a chorister for her part as a pantomime pony. Her admirer of the moment watches the scene from a privileged and suggestive vantage point, his monocle in place to afford him the clearest possible view. His gaze is strategically directed at her pelvic area. He has only to glance slightly downward to take in her thighs and their joining, or upward to linger on her corseted waist and breasts.

Pantomime chorister, Days' Doings, *1870*

The erotic charge is further enhanced by the straps and stirrups hanging at her thighs. The vaguely sadomasochistic associations of the leather straps would not have been lost on the urbane viewer as he contemplated this image. The stirrups were more evocative still. As any educated and libidinous Victorian man well knew, mounting and riding were not just equestrian activities.

Sex on Stage

The sexualization of female performers was a commonplace. By the nature of their profession, such women were inevitably linked with carnality, for the work, its demands, and its locale were sexually saturated. The stage was the place where romantic dramas were enacted, where both serious and comic songs celebrated or bemoaned the relationship of the sexes, and where racy dances like the cancan were performed. The stage was also the site where movement and gesture could be more uninhibited than what was allowable in everyday settings. High kicks, lewd winks, provocative body language—all were permissible, indeed expected, behind the footlights.

Most of all, the stage was where the requirements of costuming might defy all the ordinary rules of propriety of dress. Extreme décolletage, translucent fabrics such as those used for ballet skirts, extra-tight lacing, and the visible knickers of the cancan dancer revealed or emphasized the female body more daringly than conventional clothing. Female performers also on occasion adopted masculine attire—there were many melodramas in which the heroine had to disguise herself temporarily as a man. Although such scenarios ostensibly called for the concealment of femininity, their underlying purpose was titillation. Cross-dressing not only showed off an actress's legs in tight trousers, but other accoutrements of masculine costuming—narrow-waisted jackets, cravats, and starched shirt fronts—also called attention to the female curves they purported to hide.

Nudity, even of a partial and not specifically erotic sort, was virtually unknown in the Victorian theater. It was not until the early 1900s that dancers began to perform barefoot and bare-legged. Earlier disrobing acts normally involved the removal of ordinary street wear, under which the performer was still clothed, but in more figure-revealing attire, such as an acrobatic costume. As the turn of the century approached and photographic technology developed, some performances could be more daring because they did not take place live on stage. For instance, an 1897 show at London's Holborn Music Hall included a brief film projection of a woman stripping naked. The performance elicited a complaint to the London County Council but did not otherwise cause any apparent moral outrage.

If actual nudity was not a part of live theater's repertoire, simulated nudity was another matter. Flesh-colored tights to give the appearance of naked legs were a stock item in the wardrobe of dance, from ballet to the cancan. Tights and what were known as "fleshings" or "flesh elastics" (body stockings) were also essential to another popular form of theatrical entertainment, the *tableau vivant*. This was literally what the name suggests: a living picture made up of actresses and actors costumed and posed to reproduce on stage some famous work of art, often a painting of a subject from classical mythology. Undoubtedly the intent of such spectacles was less to promote art than it was to excite the audience—mostly male—with a generous amount of fleshings-clad flesh—mostly female.

In addition to tights, costumes for both dance and the *tableaux vivants* incorporated strategically placed bits of lace, gauze, or other skimpy drapery. The result was an enhanced illusion of nudity. This riveted the attention of at least one observer who described an 1889 ballet performance in which "a number of young girls appear in fleshing tights only to represent the nude figure." He could not help but notice that "a small gauze hung round the waist which could be plainly seen through, thus making things more suggestive than if there were no extra covering around the loins, abdomen, or posterior."

With or without added scraps of fabric, tights approximated the color of skin while hugging the body closely enough to reveal the curves they thinly covered. They thus afforded a powerful stimulus to the erotic imaginations of male viewers—some of whom could almost manage to forget that they were looking at an illusion of nudity and not the reality. One such viewer in the 1890s was disapproving but nonetheless pruriently explicit in his observation of "fully exposed stomach, thighs & legs," which "a very thin piece of gauze, mark you," was "not sufficient to hide." "Of course," he added, as if in afterthought, "I believe there were tights."

Those who more frankly relished the spectacle of women in tights must sometimes have enhanced their pleasure by conjuring visions of what was always a possibility: the accidental ripping of a performer's tights in full public view. This fantasy found humorous and fairly discreet expression in music hall song—"and what I saw I mustn't tell you now." Meanwhile, the authors of pornographic literature indulged themselves freely in descriptions of torn tights. These, not surprisingly, they soon forgot as they focused intently on the "beautiful, . . . silkily smooth, and satinlike" nakedness now exposed to the amorous eye of the theatergoing gentleman.

When it came to ladies in tights, pornography illuminated another aspect of Victorian male fantasy life. Not just visually oriented, it was tactile as well. Illustrating this is the 1882 *Mysteries of Verbena House,* which takes place at a fashionable seminary for young ladies. The plot turns upon the eroticized punishment of "the fair inmates," whose bare bottoms are variously treated to birch rods, riding whips, and hairbrushes. In an aside on the undergarments of "the fair sex," the author conveyed his impression of the intimate contact between tights and female anatomy—and appealed directly to masculine readers' sense of touch:

> The warm close substance that passes close to her flesh, that clasps her loins, and embraces her bum, and insinuates itself, between her thighs, has, all sense-less leather, cloth, or silk, as the case may be, something of the nature of a man's hand in it.

With such fuel to fire male fantasy, it is small wonder that those who wore tights— actresses, dancers, and other female entertainers—were among the most highly sexualized beings of their day.

Satiny Bottoms

As pornography's attention to tights suggests, the Victorian male libido did not live by breasts alone. It thrived as well upon women's legs, thighs, and, especially, their "smooth and voluptuous" buttocks. Whether the focus was theatrical women or other female types—wives, maidservants, virgins, prostitutes, schoolgirls—the pornographic literature of the day dwelled obsessively on their hindmost anatomical part. To evoke an appropriate image of doubleness, authors often referred to it in the plural, writing lovingly of a woman's posterior*s*, not simply her posterior. They also summoned a range of related imagery, and the world of pornography was replete with "merry arses," "cosy bottoms," "plump warm buttocks," and "fair backsides."

While this and even greater explicitness was the stuff of the pornographic underground, it had no place in the respectable public sphere, where sexuality had to be more judiciously expressed. Satiny buttocks were presentable in polite company only when they were covered with the satins and silks of proper feminine dress. In this way respectability was served. Sexuality, meanwhile, found expression through a single device that compelled attention to what it also hid. Openly yet acceptably enhanced with this crucial item of apparel, the posterior came to be second only to the bosom as the visual symbol of female sexuality. This necessary adjunct to fashion and femininity was, of course, the bustle.

Although it was invented some years prior to the beginning of the Victorian period, the bustle did not become fashionable until after the middle of the nineteenth century, about the same time that the crinoline began to decline in popularity. As virtually universal in its use as the corset, the bustle was the other indispensable element in the dress of the attractive and well-turned-out Victorian woman, whether she was a fictional heroine, real-life actress in street wear, or any other woman who aspired to fashion. To meet the requirements of their diverse users, bustles came in a variety of forms, ranging from a simple straw-filled pad to elaborate wire models necessary to achieve the voluminous roundness of formal evening wear in the 1870s or the high and extended look that some fashions of the 1880s demanded.

Retaining one's correct and appealing shape after prolonged sitting was a common concern among bustle wearers, and manufacturers offered purportedly crushproof designs. One 1877 model was named after that paragon of Victorian shapeliness, Lillie Langtry, and advertised as "light, cool, easy to wear, never out of order." It was "arranged with springs" so as to fold up when its wearer was "sitting or lying down," thus enabling her "to lean back against the chair or sofa, the Bustle resuming its proper position upon her rising." The London-based American Braided Wire Co. similarly offered a torsion-spring bustle and several other variants that were also contrived to "properly sustain the heaviest drapery, so that the wearers are never mortified by their being crushed or bent into ridiculous shapes."

Essential as it was to the prescribed fashionable appearance, the bustle was equally a focus for sexuality. In addition to emphasizing the erogenous zone that it also genteelly covered, it could in itself be an erotically evocative object. American Braided Wire's "Paris" model "for high drapery" (at the lower right of the advertisement's illustrated section) was constructed as a series of vaguely phallic shapes. Another and more blatantly suggestive design was the "Cool and Cleanly" (lower center). The two-sided construction of this bustle unabashedly accommodated the pronounced duality of the well-formed posterior.

Most provocative of all, perhaps, was the Langtry bustle and its advertised uncrushability, even when its wearer was "sitting *or lying down*." There were numerous occasions—afternoon visits, dinner parties, and so forth—that required a woman to be seated while fully attired, bustle and all. But why would she lie down while so encumbered? She would certainly have removed her bustle on retiring for the night, and would likely also have done so in order to rest at some other time of day. But what if she unexpectedly found herself alone in a deserted reception room with an attractive suitor and a beckoning sofa? Or some parental oversight left her unchaperoned in the family parlor, sharing the settee with an amorous fiancé? In

Wire bustles, 1888 advertisement

such tempting circumstances even the most well-bred woman might have momentarily allowed herself to subside into a prone position. In the event, a bustle that maintained its "tasteful shape" would have been a distinct boon—to sexuality no less than propriety.

Uncrushable or otherwise, bustle-clad bottoms, along with corseted breasts, were undoubtedly the most widely acceptable expressions of female sexuality. At once erotic and respectable, they made an attractive yet discreet focus for the public eye.

The well-rounded look for evening, 1875

This was a matter of sexual civility rather than any prudish denial of women's primary erogenous zone. Indeed, fundamental female parts were never far from the minds of many Victorian men. It did not take much—a full skirt, a pair of lady's drawers on a clothesline, a glimpse of stocking—to call forth vivid and pleasurable images of "those regions as intimate as they are delicious."

The Beauty Myth, Victorian-Style

Endlessly compelling men's fantasies, such "regions" stayed at the heart of the male sexual imagination throughout the Victorian period and after. Other entice-

The high extended bustle, 1885

ments also persisted. Well-rounded bosoms and bottoms continued to be the publicly favored signs of female sexuality. Women wore corsets up to and beyond the end of the century. Bustles, too, endured as part of the fashionable woman's basic wardrobe. Meanwhile, however blameless their personal lives might have been, actresses maintained their dubious reputation as visibly sexual beings. And the popular heroines of fiction still thrived, breasts heaving, as they embroiled themselves in their various, often sexually suggestive escapades.

As the century wore on, these continuities inevitably intertwined with conspicuous changes. By the 1890s many women had begun to question their purely domestic role; a few sought admittance to universities; others campaigned for the right to vote. Some women also defied the tyranny of conventional feminine clothing and adopted so-called rational dress—bloomers, most notably. These and other new kinds of garments were designed to forego fashion and permit women greater comfort and freedom of movement. Meanwhile, in scientific and medical circles the functioning of the female body was also a concern and, increasingly, the focus of specialized inquiry and professional discussion.

These developments did not necessarily have a direct impact on most women's everyday lives, but there were parallel changes that did. While medicine and science were reducing the female body to a matter of pathology and dispassionate scrutiny, commerce and advertising were objectifying it in another way. As more and more advertisers saw the advantage of equating beauty with their products, sexual attractiveness itself became a commodity. According to advertising, it was something that women could now purchase along with soap or shampoo or the right corset.

Linked to this was the growing standardization of feminine beauty. Like any product, to be successful in the marketplace attractiveness had to associate itself in some way with a guaranteed standard of quality and uniformity. This may also have served the wider social purpose of maintaining the status quo. Perhaps it was not entirely accidental that just when women had begun to look beyond marriage and domestic life, they found themselves facing a distracting and ongoing alternative challenge. Increasingly, fashion, entertainment, and advertising—all basically conservative—promoted a standard of beauty that was not only less open to variation than ever before, but also more difficult for the majority of women to attain.

Distinguishing this standardizing tendency was a generally lowered tolerance for plumpness. In fashion of the 1890s, the ideal feminine figure had become much slimmer than it had been even a decade earlier. The stylish silhouette now emphasized arms and shoulders, not breasts and buttocks, and the bustle had shrunk to a "mere pad." In the theatrical world, the ladies of the chorus were no longer so "heavily-limbed" as once they had been; and, in an 1896 issue of the magazine *Bow Bells*, the actress Virginia Harned publicly confessed to watching her weight. Even the heroines of romance had become less substantial than the well-fleshed beauties in George Reynolds's mid-century potboilers. Among other such slimmed-down heroines was Eily, the main female character in a turn-of-the-century love story in *Cassell's Magazine*. So slender was she that her smitten admirer was moved to describe her as "a sleek edition of an Eton boy." With such influences on the rise, it is probably more than coincidence that cases of anorexic young women increasingly came to the attention of both the medical profession and the popular press. It is likely also significant that between 1881 and 1900 the average corseted waist was twenty-two inches—smaller by an inch than it had been in the two previous decades.

As ideal beauty diminished in substance, it also decreased in age. Ever more prevalent and adamant was the dictum that youth was a requisite of female beauty and desirability. Expert advice typically offered hints on preserving youthful skin and a girlish figure, while romantic heroines, always young in spirit and tender-hearted, now more than ever had to be tender in years as well. This burgeoning cult of youth became apparent even before the 1890s and is illustrated in an 1885 *London Journal* serial, *A Wild Love*. In the opening chapter an aging wife is cast into the shadows by the "fresher charms" of her younger sister, an eighteen-year-old whose "soft, girlish voice" and "unclouded" face have captivated the older sister's middle-aged husband. And the age of this supposedly faded one-time beauty, now an "old married woman"? All of twenty-eight. Beauty and extreme youth were becoming inseparable.

"A sleek edition of an Eton boy": The slimmed-down heroine of the turn of the century

Even so, as late as 1900 the imposition of a new and more rigorous standard of femininity was still an emerging, not a fully developed trend. Slimness was not yet a universally accepted mark of beauty, and youth and attractiveness were not as intimate as they would later become. Many fictional heroines were "beauties," even though their generous curves defied fashion's new rule of slenderness. Pornography, too, continued to favor "richly swelling" breasts, thighs, and buttocks. It even remained possible, if increasingly uncommon, for a woman to be deemed "exceedingly beautiful" without "the advantage of youth." The oppressive union of beauty, slimness, youth, and sexuality was only just in the making.

And almost entirely unchanged at the turn of the century was the desirable woman's socially prescribed goal and most likely destiny: marriage and domestic life. If her palpitating bosom was no longer so ample as it once had been, and her bustle less protruding, the ideal woman nonetheless had marriage on her mind. To that end she still melted willingly, often flung herself passionately, into the waiting arms of her husband-to-be, her male counterpart—the Victorian manly man.

CHAPTER 3

Muscles and Manhood

The gallant young officer . . . begged to assure his beautiful fiancée that in his present state of mind and body it would be quite impossible for him to give proper attention to any serious business, until his burning love for her received some temporary gratification (the plain English of this being that he had a tremendous cock-stand, and felt that if it was not allayed pretty quickly that he must burst). . . .

—*Rosa Fielding, or, A Victim of Lust,* 1867

When it came to "plain English" talk about manhood's fundamental part, the rule of the nineteenth-century pornographer appears to have been "the more and plainer, the better." Pornography, after all, was a phallic world without end. The sphere of everyday life, meanwhile, had its limits. There, men could not with propriety unbutton their flaps (the Victorian equivalent of flies) in the full-frontal manner of pornography. At the same time, total repression was neither practicable nor much desired by either of the sexes. Male sexuality thus posed a certain dilemma for the Victorians. How could they accommodate it openly *and* respectably?

The difficulty was one of basic anatomy. Men lacked a physical endowment comparable in versatility to the female bosom. Women's breasts were at once visible, erotic, and—so far as public sensibility went—acceptably nongenital. They were also ennobled by unimpeachable associations with motherhood and tender emotions.

Men's sexual apparatus, on the other hand, was distinctly problematic. The one male anatomical feature that was specifically erotic, and comparable in prominence to the female breast, was also the one that had to be concealed in polite circles. The phallus was not by its nature a manageable member of the public domain. To accommodate male sexuality in a way both aboveboard and beyond reproach, the Victorians were forced to find appropriate phallic substitutes. This they variously contrived to do—in popular fiction, sport, and music hall entertainment.

Flexing and Thrusting

Writers of fiction were adept at making the phallic substitution. They concocted compelling plots featuring romance, manly action, and the weapons that went with it. Firearms, clubs, knives, and swords were not only the fixtures of robust adventure but also widely known phallic symbols used in the Victorian music hall, in humorous writing, and in informal speech. Through description, pictures, and strenuous action, fiction showed that wielding manhood's weaponry required physical prowess. Like the bosomy, properly feminine heroine, the truly virile hero had one particularly striking bodily attribute. Hard, bulging muscle was both publicly acceptable and distinctively masculine; sometimes on its own, more often associated with a weapon, it proclaimed manly strength and implied sexual potency.

In the opening illustration of the anonymously written *Amy*, an 1847 novel of love, misunderstanding, and rugged exploits, a strapping figure is poised on a ladder. His right hand evocatively conceals what could not be depicted, while his trousers do little to hide the powerful legs that signal his virility. As the story unfolds, other muscular characters, not least of all the hero, Ernest, perform feats of nerve and strength. They engage in hand-to-hand combat, break down heavy doors, and effect daring rescues. More often than not they use their biceps to brandish a manly arsenal of swords, pistols, and muskets. When Ernest at last takes the heroine Amy into his arms, his physical strength and skill with weaponry are well established. Readers could by extension imagine his corresponding sexual prowess and its fitting consummation.

Ernest was among the many of popular fiction's muscular breed. While bosomy heroines heaved, sighed, and palpitated, their masculine counterparts flexed, flailed, and thrust. To leaf through the pages of Victorian escapist fiction is to relive in flashes the brawny, weapon-wielding escapades that once daily enthralled

AMY;

OR,

LOVE AND MADNESS.

A DOMESTIC STORY OF THE HEART'S TEMPTATION. BY THE AUTHOR OF "THE
WIFE'S TRAGEDY," ETC.

CHAPTER INTRODUCTORY.

1845.—THE PHANTOM.

HAVE you not seen him ? Has he
not arrested your attention ? Are you
certain that he has never sat beside you,
never stood beneath the same roof with
yourself ? In all your walks and wanderings about and around London, have you
not met him—has he not rushed by you—have you not looked round and wondered
who he is, and why he is ever restless, ever moving ?
He is an old man—so old, that one might suppose him to have seen a hundred
summers. His form is gaunt, thin, lank, and shrivelled ; his white hair, of which

Muscular manhood in Amy; or, Love and Madness, *1847*

millions. Open any of the numerous tales of swashbuckling highwaymen to find
the gentlemen of the road forever stopping carriages, bowing gallantly to the
ladies, and flourishing their pistols. Dip into life on the high seas, where "black pirates" and the crews of "death ships" engage in perpetual musketry and swordplay.
Or skim yet another ocean where an equally well-armed but more benign bucca-
neer holds sway. In the 1865 *Boy Pirate*, the hero (a young man in his twenties) and
his cohorts tirelessly shoot and thrust from the hip.

In the magazine fiction that adolescent males avidly pored over, pistols, blades,
fists, and muscles similarly held enemies and death at bay. In the 1880s, *Boy's*

Leisure Hour regularly featured sinewy, weapon-bearing heroes resisting assorted human antagonists and threatening animal life—everything from huge birds of prey to giant reptiles. In one scene a gladiator swims naked and powerful, about to wrestle with a hungry crocodile. The water discreetly covers the central part of the gladiator's body, but firmly clenched in his teeth is a phallic substitute in the form of a dagger. In other stories the magazine's heroes exerted themselves to protect women whose breasts were as well developed as their rescuers' muscles. An 1884 illustration shows a warrior using all his strength to keep a stone lintel from falling and crushing a generously proportioned young woman caught below. In the process he displays his own massively endowed calves, thighs, and buttocks.

While inexhaustible stamina distinguished heroes, easily depleted resources marked their villainous adversaries. An anonymous author of magazine fiction applied this principle in *The Silver Digger*, an adventure set in Old Mexico and serialized in the *London Reader* of 1863. As the plot unfolds, two well-armed and muscled heroes, Mion and Diego, are outnumbered by a group of assailants. The pair springs into action, Diego "roaring like a bull." Together they wield carbine

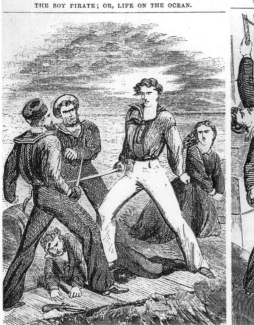

Sword- and gunplay in The Boy Pirate, *1865*

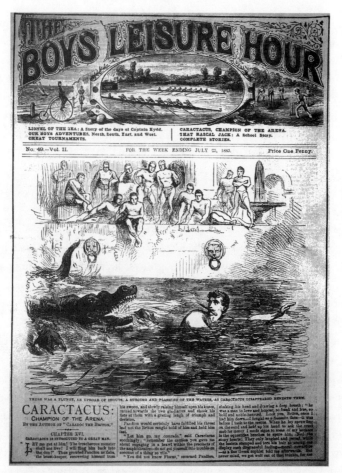

Naked power, Boy's Leisure Hour, *1885*

and club "with a fury equalled only by their dexterity and utter heedlessness of peril." They "leap here and there, . . . clubbing one man in one direction and another in another, . . . soon putting the enemy to rout." In the unmanly fashion of the truly depraved, the would-be attackers fall back, spent and impotent— "bruised and bleeding, with discharged pistols and weary hands." For their part the two heroes, male potency scarcely diminished, clubs still at the ready, withdraw into the loving arms of their women.

A good many of fiction's hefty and heroic characters originated in the minds of male authors. Some women writers, too, were adept at fleshing out their plots with muscular heroes. Among them was Susannah Reynolds, the wife of George

Reynolds, that prolific creator of generously built heroines. A popular author in her own right, she not only invented attractive heroines, but also their powerful, weapon-brandishing men. Perhaps out of feminine propriety, Mrs. Reynolds was comparatively reticent about the bodily attributes of the men in her most famous novel, *Gretna Green* (1848). But considering their impressive stock of knives, sticks, clubs, and swords, it is probably safe to suppose that such characters were as well equipped in their own way as her husband's physically gifted female creations.

Hard Bodies

The well-muscled heroes of fiction had their real-life counterparts in all those who strived after and managed to attain the ideal of Victorian manhood. Such men displayed strength of character, physical toughness, a capacity for action, and endurance in even the harshest of outdoor conditions. At the heart of this model of masculinity was sport, especially open-air team sports such as cricket, rowing, and football (soccer). The public schools, the universities of Oxford and Cambridge, amateur athletic clubs, professional cricket teams (in existence since the eighteenth century), the YMCA (founded in 1844), and boys' papers, many with sporting logos, all promoted the healthy, outdoor, athletic life. The professionalization of football and rugby toward the end of the nineteenth century also gave impetus to the manly cult of muscle, and newspapers and magazines—the mass media of the day—avidly followed the progress of professional sport and its players.

Sportswriters were apt to describe cricket and football heroes in terms that established them as the glowing examples of manhood in its prime—"so steady, so sturdy," "perennially vigorous," "sound and solid. . . ." Words like "steady," "solid," and "sound" not only referred to an athlete's playing ability but also implied his moral worth. Many Victorians made this connection. Among them was Charles Kingsley, who, as a clergyman, allied the morality of the playing field to the honor of the true Christian gentleman. In the late 1850s the idea spread and became widely known as "muscular Christianity."

This and later secular variations served purposes beyond building strong bodies and strong morals. The majority of Britain's dominant middle class maintained that the men who lived by the ethos of sport—"played the game," that is—were the men best qualified to assume positions of leadership in industry, government, and the military. Above all, it was the strong-hearted, firm-muscled disciples of the games ethic who boldly expanded, then staunchly governed the British Empire. According to J. E. C. Welldon, Bishop of Calcutta and headmaster of Harrow from 1885 to 1898, "in the history of the Empire it is written that England has owed her sovereignty to her sports." And, indeed, there was a long period of time when the hand that ruled the world was the hand that swung the cricket bat.

Abroad in the Empire, as well as at home in England, a man's ability to take charge depended greatly upon the productive expenditure of his energies. To that end, most Victorians believed, male sexual energy had to be effectively harnessed. In a society that placed high value on both material and marital productivity, a manly man did not waste his time, his effort—or his seed. Sylvanus Stall, a doctor of divinity and author of the popular information manual *What a Young Man Ought to Know* (1897), associated seminal spendthriftiness with "self-pollution." This could be anything from "evil thoughts" and looking at "nude and nasty" pictures to masturbation and "illicit"—that is, nonmarital—sexual intercourse.

To keep male hormones healthily in their place and to maintain the spermatic economy, espousing sport and fresh air was the Victorian strategy of choice. Stall was convinced that every young man could gain "manly mastery of his sexual nature" if he were only to invest in

> a set of light-weight dumb bells, and if the height of the ceiling and the capacity of his room will admit, also a pair of light Indian clubs. To these may be added various types of exercises. . . . But do not neglect to take plenty of exercise in the open air.

To these wholesome recommendations the Purity Society, a Church of England organization that distributed cautionary tracts to men and boys, added its own suggestions. Work, moderate alcohol use, a hard bed, and plenty of cold baths would all help in winning the "hard fight" to be pure.

Kingsley also lent his voice to the advocacy of masculine purity and the necessary cold baths. But he was careful to align himself with manly, not monastic, Christianity. He was, after all, the same man who had once expressed himself passionately in love letters to his fiancée, Fanny Grenfell. No enemy of sex, he considered monks and their sedentary, celibate life to be unnatural, unsexed, and essentially feminine. In this he was speaking for the majority of Victorians, who shared a general abhorrence of effeminacy.

Not everyone, however, was as convinced as he of the effeminacy of monks. A humorous mid-century photograph depicts the opposite scenario. A burly and enterprising monk returns to his monastery with "provisions" for himself and his brother monks. Slung over his back is a large bundle of strawlike material and, peeping coyly from its center, the most essential "provision" of all—a young and apparently naked woman.

Sex and the Sportsman

The vignette of the unorthodox monastery is an instance of Victorian sexual silliness that helps to illustrate a widely held conviction. For most people of the day, Kingsley squarely among them, male sexual purity was by no means the same as complete repression. The aim of sport was not to deny sexuality but to manage it properly until such time as it could be fully and productively discharged in the marital bed. Sport and the active outdoor life that went with it allowed considerable leeway for the appropriate—sperm-conserving—expression of man's vigorous sexual nature. "Tis the hard grey weather / Breeds hard English men," declared Kingsley in his 1854 *Ode to the North East Wind*. The double entendre in the words "*hard* English men" was no doubt unconscious but, considering its author's preoccupation with sexual matters, this poetic turn of phrase suggests the extent to which the ideal of athletic manhood accommodated male sexuality.

Indeed, Kingsley and those of like mind could become passionately excited about exercise and nature at its most rugged—they even gloried in cold baths. Others, their emotional and physical intensity perhaps greater still, reveled in the sport of hunting. From shooting grouse or following the hounds across the English countryside, to stag hunting in Scotland, to the pursuit of big game in Africa, "the Hunt" was imbued with erotic symbolism. Big-game hunters were apt to exult in the physical demands of hunting and most of all in its reward—the exhilarating release from tension that came with the kill. Later, in the comfort of such male sanctums as the club, the army mess, and the billiard room, horned trophies on the wall helped to foster ardent recollections of the thrill of the chase. Even those who merely drank and listened could enjoy the vicarious excitement to be had from the manly exploits of others.

Hunting was not the only sporting activity with sexual overtones. In 1859 the *Boy's Own Magazine*, one of many wholesome publications for adolescent males, ran an article on fencing, part of a series called "Manly Exercises." The article included two sections on thrusting and seven illustrations of a well-built gentleman brandishing his foil. Many other sports also required the use of distinctly phallic implements—rowing oars, polo sticks, cricket bats, golf clubs. . . . And without balls, a number of the most popular games could not have been played at all.

The analogy between sporting gear and men's physical apparatus is plain to see in an 1890s magazine image of the famous Yorkshire cricketer Lord Hawke. Although seated, he struck an aggressive pose—feet firmly planted, legs wide apart—cricket bat stiff on his lap. Like the upstanding model of athletic manhood that he was, Lord Hawke presented himself as one who was adept in the proper exercise of his sporting, and his sexual, equipment.

In promoting the healthful expression of male sexuality, sport helped, most people believed, to vanquish purity's greatest enemy. Masturbation was a source of widespread anxiety in the nineteenth century, and the subject of countless harangues and dire warnings. This concern has often been remarked upon and attributed to

Well-equipped cricketer Lord Hawke, Windsor Magazine, *1898*

prudery. Undoubtedly there were some Victorians who condemned the "solitary sin" out of sheer narrow-minded priggishness, but others did so on health grounds. Supported by medical opinion of the day, many people were convinced that masturbation promoted a host of mentally and physically debilitating conditions, including insanity, convulsions, and consumption. The more extreme proponents of this view threatened the persistent masturbator with "early decline and death."

The greater number who shared moderate views on the subject, as well as a dawning suspicion that guilt and shame were more damaging than the act, still emphatically discouraged masturbating. It was "an unmanliness" and therefore to be despised—"real men" controlled their sexual urges. Worst of all, as most well-informed Victorians knew beyond doubt, in its profligate wastage of sperm, masturbation was uneconomical and unproductive. Excessive indulgence could lead to impotence or reduced fertility or "an inferior quality of sexual secretion" that would show itself in idiot offspring. The most widely recommended preventives of masturbation and its horrific results were wholesome thoughts, early rising, a hard bed, cold baths, fresh air, and—of course—lots of exercise. Small wonder, then, that men and boys took to the playing fields and a life of brawny activity. The weight of medical and moral conviction left them few other options.

If the regimen of sport and healthy self-control was a strict and unrelenting one, the rewards of "stored-up passion" were abundant. When it finally came time to reproduce himself, the manly man would do so with "splendid energy," eventually generating children as vigorous as himself. And the benefits of this properly self-disciplined manhood extended far beyond a flourishing sex and family life. As James Foster Scott, author of *The Sexual Instinct* (1898), explained it, "the proper subjugation of the sexual impulses, and the conservation of the complex seminal fluid, with its wonderfully invigorating influence, develop all that is best and noblest in men." In other words, the manly man was an empire builder. The masturbator, meanwhile, was not only wasteful but an underachiever. Clearly, the British Empire was better off without him.

Tall, Dark, and Handsome

Apart from his self-control, sporting prowess, and worldly achievements, the mark of the manly man was his handsome physical appearance. The good-looking Victorian man had at least moderate height, even facial features, clear eyes, a healthy complexion, full head of hair, and, when in fashion, luxuriant mustache and whiskers. Most important of all, he had a strong, well-built body. Thomas Hughes, a contemporary of Kingsley and the author of *Tom Brown's School Days* (1857), the classic tale of boys' education and the passage to manhood, was adamant on the subject of masculine physique. In his manly opinion, "round shoulders, narrow chests, and stiff limbs" were "as bad as defective grammar and arithmetic." Others shared this view, Kingsley not least of all. On a walking tour of Germany in 1851, he came as close as a good Christian dared to out-and-out vanity. "My limbs are all knots as hard as iron," he proudly reported.

Although the imperative to be good looking did not exert the same tyranny over men as it did over women, men were not entirely free from such pressure. Images of well-favored men on occasion advertised clothing, soap, tobacco, and other products, thus helping to create a popular standard of masculine appearance. Similarly, the heroes of fiction invariably had admirable builds and attractive faces. One character even managed to achieve position and fortune mainly on the strength of his looks. In the semipornographic *Confessions of a Footman*, the handsomeness of the hero, "a young man of great parts," attracts favorable attention and earns him a speedy promotion from footman to groom. From here his rise is meteoric. He soon marries the daughter of his employer and becomes a gentleman and Member of Parliament. Apart from his good looks, he owes his success to an unspecified but "adept" way of helping his future wife to mount her horse. The unknown author left the matter of sorting out the sexual symbolism of all of this to his readers' ever-keen imaginations.

The serious manly men who won their achievements through greater and more sustained exertions than those of the footman would undoubtedly have disapproved heartily of both the cockiness and the improbability of such a character. Nevertheless, there was some substance in the story's message that good looks brought men luck in love. Or so, at least, many of them believed. Matrimonial advertisements placed by men were a common feature of popular magazines, and if the personals in the *London Journal* for the week of January 24, 1874, are any guide, then the hopefuls in search of a wife rarely failed to point out their manly attractions. Charles P. was "tall, fair, and considered good-looking." Horace was "tall and dark." Cinderford, "a gentleman in good circumstances," described himself as "six feet in height, and good-looking." Pleisiosoris professed to be "an attractive gentleman of thirty-seven." And Charley distinguished himself as the classic "tall, dark, and handsome."

If these men and others like them stretched the truth about their looks, it is hardly surprising. They were simply trying to deliver what women demanded.

The same 1874 issue of the *London Journal* also ran advertisements from women. Millie wished to meet "a respectable good-looking man." A. B. C., who considered herself to be very attractive, wanted "a tall, good-looking, dark gentleman." Alice Maud Mary also required "a tall, nice-looking gentleman." And so on.

Apparently, too, Victorian women could be dauntingly critical of masculine appearance—even to the extent of sending comic Valentine cards picturing skinny, gawky-looking little men. Such cards always included verses that made fun of the caricature. But, of course, the card's recipient was the real target of the often cruel humor:

Oh what a funny stick you are;
All head and little body;
Sure no lady would care
To speak to such a noddy.
With such a figure, such a head,
I really, Sir, decline to wed.

No doubt but that women's expectations had been shaped by the handsome, muscular heroes of romantic fiction.

For men of means who lacked the opportunity or the athletic prowess to remedy their narrow shoulders and spindly legs, the tailor could at least provide padded jackets and the illusion of broad, manly shoulders. After 1876 the new fuller trousers effectively camouflaged skinny legs as well. Good tailoring could also work wonders for the man with too much natural padding. Square-shouldered jackets made the waistline look proportionately smaller, while trousers cut closely at the hips improved their shape. Additionally, underneath his trousers a man might wear drawers with multiple sets of drawstrings for cinching in at the waist. When all else failed, corsets made especially for the rotund figure offered a last resort. Certain men without a weight problem also adopted these multipurpose garments. Some military men wore them to help maintain an erect posture; others used them for back support when horseback riding, or required them for medical reasons.

While the man without serious deficiencies in health or physique had no need of corsets or cinched drawers, he still benefited from the tailor's art. Not only could clothing modify or hide a multitude of bodily defects, but it could also enhance the genuine endowments of the athletic man. Fitted jackets flattered a lean waist, broad shoulders, and upright posture. And, carefully tailored, the tight trousers of the early and mid-Victorian periods tastefully showed off well-formed buttocks, thighs, and perhaps other bulging muscles.

Without a doubt, the man who looked a fine figure in his clothes had appeal for the opposite sex. The problem for the interested woman was to determine whether or not it was the clothes that made the man. Appearances, after all, could be deceiving. The same "humble bachelor" who extolled the benefits of marriage for women in his *Hints on Husband Catching* added some words of warning. Would-be wives, he cautioned, should not put too much stock in a man's outer image. Well-tailored clothing in particular was to be regarded with suspicion. For, as this somehow knowing "bachelor" hastened to remind his feminine readers,

> Ten or twelve hours of *married* life out of the twenty-four are generally consumed by the happy pair side by side in a four-post bedstead; and were your "intended" the "glass of fashion and the mould of form" *in* dress, still, when *un*-dressed, like the jay stripped of the peacock's feathers, or the ass of the lion's skin, he could—to use a slang expression—become "quite t'other thing."

And this "other thing," it is clear, was hardly likely to stir a woman's passions.

If a man were not to be a disappointment in the conjugal bedroom, then he not only had better wear his clothes well, but attend equally to what they covered. There was really only one route to a truly manly physique, and that, of course, was sport. F. Marsh, a London tailor, recognized this in the 1880s. His advertising handbill promoted the comfort and fit of his "Famed Trousers in All Attitudes." He might have said "in All *Athletic* Attitudes," for the handbill pictures four pairs of trousers, disembodied except for the feet showing beneath, all energetically engaged in sporting activities. In one vignette the "famed trousers" kick a soccer ball; in another they leap over a vaulting horse; in a third they go skating. Only the fourth image was perhaps ill-advised—it shows the trousers armlessly and futilely attempting to pick up a cricket bat. Clothes, this suggests, could only do so much—good tailoring or otherwise, it took a real man to "play the game."

Manhood and the Music Hall

As dominant as it was, the sporting ideal of manliness and masculine attractiveness was not universal. One of the most popular of Victorian institutions, the music hall, had a large working-class component among its audience and performers, and

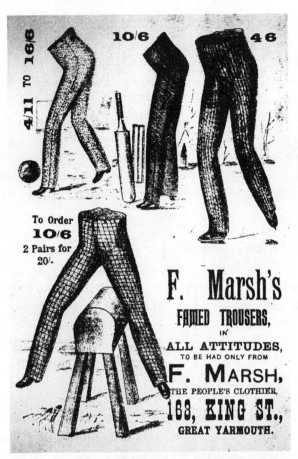

"Famed Trousers in All Attitudes," tailor's handbill, 1880s

was apt to look askance at the predominantly middle-class muscle man. This is not to say that male good looks did not count on the music hall stage. On the contrary, its stars were often good-looking men, and many of their songs and routines concerned love won or lost on the strength of manly physical attractions or their lack. It is just that the music hall tended to regard the handsome man as a product of nature, or perhaps of good costuming and lighting, but not of earnest and perpetual exercise.

The songs and comic acts of the music hall were more likely than not to make light of the sporting man. In one parody, a song called "Slap Bang, Here We Are Again," quintessentially British gentlemen "play cricket, box, and torture cocks." They top off this manly agenda with alcoholic excesses lasting into the small hours.

Another sprig of privilege was the subject of the song "Oxford Joe." The music sheet pictures Joe himself, all decked out in cap and gown, looking self-satisfied and none too intelligent. Surrounding him are scenes of undergraduate activities—fishing, rowing, boxing, and playing cricket. The repetitive words and monotonous rhythm of the song's chorus evoke mindless, intensely physical endeavor:

> Oxford Joe! Oxford Joe!
> I am known as Oxford Joseph.
> Oxford Joe! Oxford Joe!
> Yes, I'm known as Oxford Joe.

The music hall could well afford to disdain muscle as the fundamental symbol of manhood. Its songs and routines bred a rich stock of alternative images to represent masculinity—or, more precisely, phallocentric sexuality. Along with ribald gestures and innuendo, there were suggestive words like "poker," "grinder," "rod," "root," "peg," and the all-inclusive "thing." Endlessly inventive, music hall entertainers repeatedly managed to mention man's unmentionable appendage.

There was no shortage of well-endowed characters in songs like "Captain Pink, of the Plungers." The double meaning of "plunger" would not likely have escaped even the most innocent among the audience. Most would also have connected the name "Pink" to the color of sexual organs and, with a little thought, have remembered that "to pink" was "to prick with a pointed weapon." Combine all of this with the explicit position of the captain's sword in the song-sheet illustration and the weaponry of his brother plungers, as well as Pink's exaggerated hornlike side whiskers, and the result is a phallic universe reminiscent of pornography. The important difference is that the humor and humanity of the music hall raised—that is to say, elevated the status of—the phallus above pornography's constantly grinding, machinelike organ.

Be a Man!

What the music hall's otherwise penetrating wit failed to grasp was the emotional devastation of manhood. But then, how could it? At the time people understood little, if anything, about the price men paid for their masculinity. Despite the general ignorance of its implications, the insistence on manliness was virtually everywhere in the Victorian world. "Be a man!" urged the schools, churches, scouting groups, boys' stories, and wisdom of the street.

"Captain Pink, of the Plungers," song sheet

How men interpreted this command varied according to social class, individual personality, and experience. For middle-class idealists like Kingsley, being a man entailed embracing the ethos of sport and Christian gentlemanliness. For others, it meant taking charge and winning, whether the arena was sport, work, war, or the Empire. For many, many more, it demanded endurance of the hardship and monotony of growing up, getting a little education, and earning a living.

Regardless of class and individual differences, virtually all men associated being a man with controlling the emotions, especially those reflecting vulnerability or empathy. This, after all, was only practical. Fear, sadness, sensitivity, compassion—these were little use on the playing field and battleground, and at the far reaches of the Empire. They were more worthless still for fox hunting and shoot-ing game. They did not win court cases or close business deals. Neither did they have the power to ease a working day in the mills or mines.

As a matter of survival, men learned early to master their tender feelings. At all social levels the realities of passing from boyhood to manhood could be harsh. At age twelve or so, a working-class boy already knew what it was like to toil at a me-nial job for several hours a day and a few pennies. Many, too, had learned early on how to emerge from a street fight with some teeth still in place and no bones bro-ken. But even the most privileged boys were not immune from hardship. When still small, many had to leave the familiarity of home and face the trials of board-ing at public school (so called because it trained the sons of the well-off for high-level public service). At the best of these institutions small heating fires, windows perpetually open, poor food, and too little of it together kept physical comfort at a minimum, while supposedly turning boys into men.

The typical English public school was quite literally "the school of hard knocks." Corporal punishment was the rule, and few, it seems, escaped the mas-ter's cane. Younger or weaker boys also had to contend with the bullying of their heftier schoolmates. In his 1937 autobiography, *Paint and Prejudice*, C. R. Nevin-son recalled his experiences at the Midland school Uppingham around the end of the Victorian era. As a small boy at the bottom of the pecking order, he found "the brutality and bestiality in the dormitories . . . a hell on earth. . . . I was kicked, hounded, caned, flogged, hairbrushed, morning, noon and night."

With violence an integral part of growing up male everywhere from the most exclusive public school to the meanest street, it is not surprising that in self-defense many boys turned into overly aggressive, even bullying men, and that most devel-oped a lifelong habit of shutting off emotion. It therefore fell to women to assume the burden of feeling. The art critic and social philosopher John Ruskin had strong ideas about this feminine responsibility, and these he expressed in his 1865 *Sesame and Lilies*, a collection of essays on the respective duties of the sexes:

> There is not a war in the world, no, nor an injustice, but you women are an-swerable for it; not in that you have provoked, but in that you have not hin-dered. . . . There is no suffering, no injustice, no misery, in the earth, but that the guilt of it lies with you. Men can bear the sight of it, but you should not be able to bear it. Men may tread it down without sympathy in their own struggle; but men are feeble in sympathy, and contracted in hope; it is you only who can feel the depths of pain, and conceive the way of its healing.

Ruskin's willingness to attribute the misdeeds of men to the laxity of women grates on the modern consciousness. Even in his own day he was scarcely typical in his approach to the opposite sex. A man who enjoyed fondling young girls and who, upon marrying, was shocked and disgusted to find that his bride had pubic hair was no advertisement for healthy adult masculinity. Still, his personal quirks aside, Ruskin was an articulate spokesman for a wider point of view. His words help to illuminate the Victorian man's diminished emotional capacity and the extent to which this was unquestioningly accepted. Inevitably, or so it seemed, manhood and the numbing of tender feelings went together.

Popular fiction reflected this clearly. Take Ernest, the typical muscular hero. Whenever the plot dictated that he enfold the heroine, Amy, in his strong arms, he responded on cue. But in any such episode, that action is the extent of his contribution to romance. Once locked in passionate embrace, it falls to Amy to experience the emotions. It is her feelings, her tender heart, her lovingness that are the focus and substance of the encounter—and so it commonly was in the love scenes of fiction. There, as in real life, a man's emotional range was no match for his muscular development.

Happily for the many Victorian women who enjoyed sex, men's ability to suppress emotion did not necessarily translate into sexual repression. The very quest for purity, with its attention to premarital continence and the avoidance of excessive masturbation, must have made many enthusiastic lovers when the time finally came. Ironically, one of the favorite strategies for dampening libido may in fact have stimulated it: unknown to the Victorians, cold baths heighten the level of the male hormone testosterone. But, despite enthusiasm and the benefit of cold water, most men would have been largely incapable of realizing their full sexual potential. Years of conditioning to negate the supposedly weak and feminine emotions, along with the generalized abhorrence of effeminacy, reduced male sexual expression to a limited spectrum.

Additionally, the emphasis that manliness placed on activity, not introspection, ill equipped a man for the subjective experience of his own sexuality. Although Victorian men could behave passionately and romantically, many of them could only lead their love lives in the same way that they conducted their other affairs. Love was a campaign or a game to be won. Like military victory, a secure job, or the winning goal, there was always a sense in which the woman of choice was yet another object of desire.

On the structure of such objects gained, men built themselves—or, that is, a version of themselves that replaced emotional completeness. In the next century this would be popularly known as "the male ego." This is not to say that all men operated by ego alone, or that none were capable of genuine love. Many of them, in fact, were kind and devoted husbands and lovers. Nevertheless, there is no doubt that the masculine ideal could greatly incapacitate an individual in his romantic and sexual life. The male tendency to objectify women was not a matter of design or malice. Victorian men simply did not know any better.

The Birth of Brawn

Men's knowledge of themselves, let alone of women, had not improved by the end of the nineteenth century. If anything, it had deteriorated. The demands of Empire and the second Boer War (1899–1902), increasing industrialization, and, perhaps, a backlash against the female suffrage movement combined to reinforce different sex roles and emotional perspectives. As it long had been, women's domain was the hearth and heartfelt emotion. Men's lot was the world of firm action and cool heads.

Meanwhile, late-nineteenth-century sexology designated homosexuality a pathology and heightened men's fear of their feminine side. Aggressive, active, physical endeavor was the first line of defense against the newly identified "illness" of effeminacy. The moderating ideals of muscular Christianity had become a thing of the past. At the turn of the century, manhood meant muscle, and vice versa. The British Empire was still thriving, but the sun had set on the possibility of sensitive manliness. It would take nearly another hundred years for it to begin to rise again.

Everyday life variously reflected these general developments. As the differences between the sexes became ever more pronounced, women's clothes remained colorful, while men's became increasingly confined to black, navy, brown, and gray. Even the waistcoat, a traditionally bright and patterned garment, became generally drab. The man who still nursed an unhealthy addiction to bright colors was forced to indulge this craving, like a secret vice, in the privacy of his own home, where vivid hues were still permissible for smoking jackets and dressing gowns. At the same time, fictional heroes developed an increasing loathing for dandiness and anything else that smacked of the weak or namby-pamby. The most popular turn-of-the-century fiction writers were those who filled their plots with action, weapons, tobacco smoke, and strong stomachs for violence.

In most of this fiction the muscular hero reigned supreme—as, increasingly, he did in real life. The stars of the playing field attained the status of cult figures, as magazines and papers ever more purveyed their brawny images and recounted their feats. In 1903 a magazine for adolescents, *Boys of Our Empire,* included weekly "presentation plates" (forerunners of collectible sports cards) showing the notable athletes of the day. One of these pictured soccer player William Foulke of Sheffield United. Foulke's nickname, "Baby"—presumably earned by virtue of his bland, round "baby face"—is somewhat ironic. As C. B. Fry wrote in the *Windsor Magazine* in 1898, Victorian football was a man's game, with nothing soft or cute about it. "It precludes sentiment," declared Fry. "It gives no scope for aesthetic appreciation. It is the barbarian in us that loves football." That same barbarian even showed himself in late Victorian advertising. In the early 1890s he began to replace the elegant gentleman of the sort who had advertised Pears' Shaving Soap in the late 1880s. Among others, he was the muscular giant in an animal-skin loincloth who, club and all, helped to sell Titan Patent Soap.

Soccer player William "Baby" Foulke, turn-of-the-century cult figure

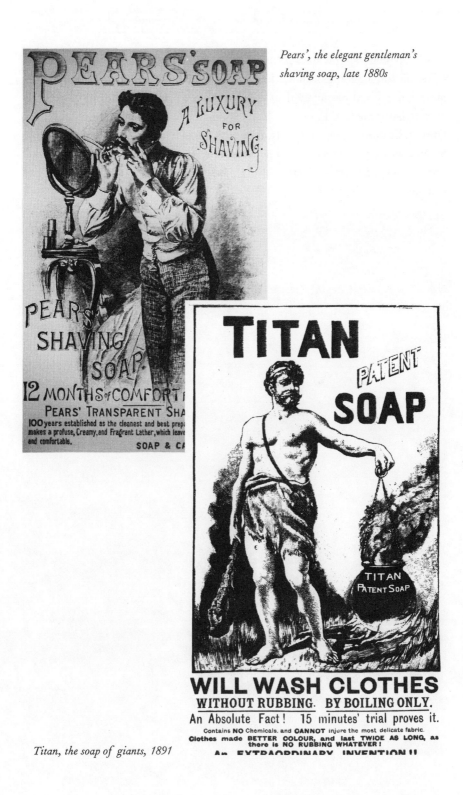

Pears', the elegant gentleman's shaving soap, late 1880s

Titan, the soap of giants, 1891

With brawny figures such as "Baby" and "Titan" increasingly thrusting themselves into public consciousness, the Victorian man had little choice but to go forth,
more actively and resolutely than ever before, to "play the game" in sport, business, politics, war, and Empire. If he did so emotionally and sexually divided from
himself, he barely noticed. Dimly, though, especially as he grew a little older, he
became aware that he had only one hope of retrieving some of the lost self that
growing up had taken away from him. He had to win the love of a good Victorian
woman.

CHAPTER 4

The Making of Lovemaking

Mirror your sweet eyes in mine, love,
See how they glitter and shine!
Quick fly such moments divine, love,
Link your lithe fingers in mine!

Lay your soft cheek against mine, love,
Pillow your head on my breast;
While your brown locks I entwine, love,
Pout your red lips when they're prest!

—Joseph Ashby-Sterry, "A Lover's Lullaby,"
Boudoir Ballads, 1877

In the romantic ardor of his wooing, the lover who composed these lines was much like any Victorian man in pursuit of his chosen woman. Writing verse, though, even if it was far from the standard of Tennyson or Browning, was somewhat unusual. Well-schooled in the aggressive ways of athletic manliness, most men were not poets. For them, being romantic meant taking action.

As they pursued the women of their choice, they individually reflected the romantic and sexual ideals of the day. If Victorian men were not generally poets, some at least dipped into the outpourings of others, as did many of the women they desired. Still more people nourished their romantic longings on best-selling fiction. Meanwhile, songs and other entertainments, greeting cards, love letters, courting customs, and marriage manuals also fostered the relationship of the sexes. Romantic sexual love was a constant, often public presence in Victorian life and popular consciousness. Inevitably this helped to shape people's expectations and behavior in their private relationships. The creation in this way of a widely influential romantic ideal was physical lovemaking's cultural foreplay—the making of lovemaking.

Thrilling Through Every Fiber

The men and women of romantic fiction set the pace. In the typical fashion of his kind, Captain Ainsley Falkland, hero of *Taken by Storm*, an 1885 novel serialized in the *London Journal*, puts his strong arms around the heroine, Beryl, and prepares to "ravish a kiss from her palpitating lips." She in turn responds characteristically to his "sweet kisses"—quick to feel the thrill of physical arousal, the Victorian romantic heroine thrived on passion. "With love's joyous impulse," Beryl nestles her head rapturously on her lover's breast. "'My own Ainsley,' she murmurs, clinging to him in a perfect abandon of love's mystic emotions, that thrills through every fibre of her being."

Other fictional couples were equally devoted and open in showing their feelings. In the early episodes of Charles Reade's *A Terrible Temptation*, an 1871 *Cassell's Magazine* serial, the two principal characters, Sir Charles Bassett and Miss Bella Bruce, are newly engaged and mutually smitten:

> Every day he sat for hours at the feet of Bella Bruce, admiring her soft feminine ways and virgin modesty, even more than her beauty. And her visible blush whenever he appeared suddenly, and the soft commotion and yielding in her lovely frame whenever he drew near, betrayed his magnetic influence, and told all but the blind she adored him.

But even from the blind Bella's passion was no secret. She would also "prattle her maiden love like some warbling fountain" or, seized by emotion, exclaim to Charles, "'I love, and honor, and worship, and adore you to distraction, my own—own—own!'"

Bella and Charles, Beryl and Ainsley, and countless fictional couples like them helped to direct the course of real-life heterosexuality. Each of the stories in which such characters figured might have been enjoyed by a million or more readers. *A*

"Love's joyous impulse," Taken by Storm, *1885*

Terrible Temptation and his other tales of love made Charles Reade at least as popular as Dickens. Whether concocted by Reade or more obscure writers, romance was rife in Victorian fiction. The reading public had only to open a cover and turn a page or two, and there would be the ideal of romantic love created and re-created in compelling plots and illustrations of perfect, happy couples.

Romance All Around

In an age when print was the major source of mass entertainment, fiction played the single greatest role in the making of lovemaking. But other pastimes also made their collective contribution. Those with the leisure and means to attend art exhibitions might feast their eyes and feed their fantasies on paintings of attractive couples in settings of rustic beauty. Improving methods of reproduction made such images available to an ever-wider public. People passing to or from work might pause over portraits of lovers displayed in the windows of print shops, or stop at a newsagent's to browse through the array of illustrated magazines that regularly pictured romantic scenes—a picnic for two, an umbrella shared on a rainy day, or an intimate outing on a secluded river. The new art of photography also assisted the cause of love by capturing the memory of the warm sun and embraces that went with a day off from work, spent courting in a park or at the seaside.

Romance on the river, Windsor Magazine, *1898*

Photography offered yet another possibility for keeping romance on people's minds. One of its offshoots was among the most popular of entertainments in the middle-class home. This was the stereograph, which consisted of two identical photographic images paired together. Viewed through a stereoscope, the forerunner of the twentieth-century Viewmaster, the double image resolved into a single three-dimensional picture. The London Stereoscopic Company (motto: "A stereoscope for every home") and other suppliers offered a wide variety of stereographic images for their customers' viewing—everything from the wonders of ancient Egypt to current events. One of the most popular subjects was the relationship of the sexes. The scenes were generally staged using actors or models posing in studio settings. The tone might be sad ("Broken Vows") or sentimental ("The First Love Letter") or humorous, as in the episode of the suitor who hides under his young lady's crinoline. Whether they inspired tears or titters, the three-dimensional, often color-tinted stereographs showing love between the sexes gave romance a tangible presence in many Victorian parlors.

Romance also made itself felt through another parlor fixture, the piano. During the nineteenth century such instruments became ever cheaper to manufacture, so that by 1880 they were featured in virtually every middle-class household. They were also prestigious additions to the parlors of the most prosperous artisans and tradespeople. In middle-class families at least one female member normally knew how to play—such accomplishment was a common part of a girl's education. In an informal evening's entertainment involving the family or a few guests, one or more of the young ladies might play love songs while others present would listen, perhaps sing along, or quietly let their imaginations stray into pleasurable realms.

The piano also provided an opportunity for young people to enact the rituals of courtship safely in public view, yet with a modicum of delicious privacy. While parents or chaperons occupied themselves with card games or conversation, a young woman and her suitor could enjoy the physical closeness that the piano encouraged. She played, he stood nearby, from time to time bending nearer still to turn a page and breathe in her perfume. New love could thus grow, nurtured by the parlor piano and its romantic strains.

While the piano and stereograph were regular fixtures in the making of lovemaking, there were also special occasions, and on these the greeting card took over. Apart from seasonal motifs, Christmas and New Year's cards often introduced a note of romance. In one, a man takes a woman into his arms under the mistletoe, while a fragment of verse completes the action—"he pressed her, kiss'd her, caress'd her." Another card offered a lighter look at love. It shows a man and

Courting to the strains of the parlor piano, Society, *1885*

woman embracing on a city street; at the same time a servingwoman from an adjacent house empties a bucket whose contents—water, or worse, maybe—are about to hit the amorous pair. The card's message reads, "May there be no damper on your pleasure at this festive season."

The high holiday for the exchange of romantic greeting cards was February 14. The popularity of the valentine grew rapidly in the Victorian period, and the mid-February flow of cards increasingly strained the capacity of the Post Office. In 1841 the English sent a total of 400,000 valentines; by 1871 the figure had risen to one and a half million for London alone. Valentines ranged in quality and price. At sixpence, the most affordable had simple woodcut illustrations enhanced by a half-dozen or so basic colors. Expensive varieties costing several shillings were often exquisitely beautiful, rich in color and decoration—gold or silver leaf, ribbon, lace made of paper or fabric, tiny silk flowers with pearlized leaves, pieces of plush vel-

Inexpensive woodcut valentine, c. 1845   *"Love's Treasure," lavish valentine, c. 1850*

vet, and pink and gold embossed cupids were among the embellishments used on these lavish tokens of love.

Some valentines were whimsically romantic. Particularly popular in the 1860s and 1870s were facsimiles of Post Office telegrams. Bearing the legend "Love Office Telegraphs" and an insignia of two cupids, they were stamped with the postmark "Loveland, Feb. 14." The engraved messages of more conventional valentines were often short and direct: "I love but thee." "Accept my heart." "Affection's token." "Adoration." A few struck a chord of sadness—"I hide my love while it consumes me"—but most were optimistic: "Happy Love." "Ever True." "Yours unalterably." Still others elaborated their sentiments in lines of romantic verse:

How prized the coral and the shell,
And beautiful the pearl,
Who can the hidden treasure tell,

O'er which the soft waves curl.
Yet dearer still art thou to me,
Than all in air, or earth, or sea.

The common practice was to send valentines unsigned or with initials only. The Victorian sexual mystique demanded a little mystery, even if it was only symbolic, and the recipient knew full well who was the sender. Romantic though it was, this secretiveness is a bit unfortunate. It is now often impossible to determine even the sex of the sender, let alone his or her identity. Still, there are occasional revealing exceptions. Among those distinguishable by gender were three men who inscribed their own words of love among the embossed hearts and printed sentiments they sent to the women they loved. The ink of these handwritten feelings is now faint, but their sincerity still resonates clearly across the years. "Accept this token of constancy from your most devoted." "With best wishes and sweet kisses." And, simply, "My dear, from GC, 13/2/1856."

Quivering Lips and Blooming Blushes

Important though they were to the Victorians, there was more to the making of lovemaking than the sentiments and trappings of romance. At the real heart of the matter was sex. In *A Terrible Temptation*, Bella on occasion punctuates her fervent declarations of love for Charles by "flinging herself passionately yet modestly on his shoulder." Her passionate modesty was not a contradiction in terms but one of the many demonstrations of the Victorian gift for the decorous cultivation of sexuality.

Especially gifted in this way were the many writers of fiction who celebrated biology with propriety. Not uncommonly, but discreetly of course, they evoked the imagery of female sexual parts. In describing Bella's beauty, Charles Reade gave loving attention to her mouth. Searching his imagination, he saw "two full and rosy lips. They made a smallish mouth at rest, but parted ever so wide when they smiled, and ravished the beholder." In writing *Taken by Storm*, the author gave his hero Ainsley a constant desire to "sip the nectar" from Beryl's "pretty" and "quivering" lips. Some readers would have taken such passages strictly at the face value they ostensibly presented. Others would have responded to the sexual connotations of ravishing or quivering lips, and let their mind's eye stray downward. "Ravish" and "quiver" both had suggestive meanings, while alluring facial lips were respectable symbols of a more fundamental erogenous zone.

Indeed, the language of such symbolism compared closely to the more literal-minded descriptions in pornography. The difference was that pornographers gave short shrift to faces and devoted themselves directly to other "fair lips" and "pink slits." A reference or two to "dewy moisture" or "sucking the honey of love" completed the picture. True to type, the voyeuristic narrator of *The Disembodied Spirit* was quick to fix his gaze in the direction of what lay between the "quivering thighs" of his current object of desire. Soon his "eyes dwelt on . . . a pair of scarlet pouting lips, whilst the soft mound above thrilled as if longing for some unknown pleasure."

Lacking the literalism of pornography and its relentless taste for the objectification of people, popular fiction exercised greater inventiveness in the treatment of sexual themes. It made much of blushing, for instance. Whenever in the presence of her fiancé, Charles, Bella blushes visibly. Beryl's great love for Ainsley suffuses her complexion with "brilliancy." Similarly, "roseate hues," "vivid blushes," and "love's colors" constantly "steal" into the faces of most other romantic heroines in the throes of passion. It was no accident that feminine blushing was one of the preferred motifs of the Victorian romance. Second only, perhaps, to the palpitating bosom, it identified the true womanly woman.

In 1900 Havelock Ellis's "scientific" analysis of the blush, part of *Studies in the Psychology of Sex,* confirmed what had long been popular consensus on the subject. Blushing was first of all a sign of female modesty, a desirable trait in heroines and real-life women alike. It was also in itself appealing. In February 1858 the author of the advice column in *Cassell's Magazine* assured a concerned young woman that her blushes were a distinct romantic asset: "That face which has lost the power to blush, has also lost the power to charm—true men."

Beyond adding to a woman's general attractiveness, the blush was also specifically sexual. Ellis and others before him argued that physiologically it was virtually the same as the "general rosiness" of the sexual flush and directly comparable to the "erection of sexual organs." It was thus a signal of arousal and, for the unmarried, an appropriate sex substitute. Small wonder that fiction made much of feminine blushes—as beacons of arousal, they undoubtedly titillated readers and stimulated authors' sales.

It almost goes without saying that heroes did not blush. In and out of fiction, real men controlled their sexuality, emotions, and bodily responses—or so they were supposed to do. At times this was difficult, even for heroes. Ainsley found Beryl "perfectly irresistible" and could not stop himself from "ravishing" her lips. Indeed, she was "possessed of such power over him" that he gave up a fortune to marry her, "his only earthly treasure." Charles was also overcome by his passion for Bella. On those occasions when she "flung herself passionately" upon him, he was weakened to the point of feeling "highly gelatinous" and bereft of "all power of resistance." His coloring, though, remained unchanged.

But if even in the heat of passion men were constrained to suppress their own blushing, at least they were always at liberty to take a prurient manly interest in the blushes of women. This the poet Joseph Ashby-Sterry acknowledged, although with less than lyric greatness. In "A Breezy Ballad," part of his anthology for the boudoir, he is delighted with "Old March" wind who "romps with skirts and dresses," revealing "snowy frills" and provoking a "wealth of blooming blushes / Seen through tangled mass of hair!" Here were not only blushes, but suggestively tangled hair, ladies' unmentionables, and romping—a favorite activity of the sexual adventurer. The poet had in fact created an entire erotically charged scenario.

Writers of romantic fiction could be just as thorough. Take the 1870 *Bow Bells* serial *Marion's Fate*, a simmering mix of passion, murder, revenge, separation, and mistaken identity. Marion and Walter, her divorced husband and now her lover once more, are together in Paris and about to marry again. But Marion knows what Walter cannot—that their love is destined always to be thwarted in life. She deter-

Fatal attraction: Walter and Marion, Marion's Fate, *1870*

mines to put an end to this dire fate by poisoning first him, then herself. As the story ends, they die in each other's arms, "passionately entwined as one."

Their final, intense encounter on this earth is imbued with unspoken sexual appetite. After dining intimately in Marion's boudoir, they set to "dallying daintily" with "rich fruits" contained in silver baskets upheld by nude figurines, and spread sensuously over the table. She plays the guitar and sings "a tender love ditty." The accompanying illustration is also infused with the characters' sexual love. Physical union the dominant motif, the figures' eyes are locked; she leans back against his legs. His arm is thrust out, his hand stroking her hair. Apart from its possibly phallic connotation, Marion's guitar is the visual device joining their two bodies. In the making of Victorian lovemaking, passion was no abstraction. With or without actual intercourse, it was a bodily reality, integrally bound up with living—and, in Marion and Walter's case, with dying as well.

Sex Symbols

Outside of the privacy of the bedroom, the passionate fever pitch that romantic fiction could reach was not regularly surpassed. But while Victorian sexuality was not always openly intense, it was still a constant if often coy presence in romantic life.

February 14 provided a formal occasion for some tantalizing glimpses—eroticism was not far from the surface of the frills and sentiment of many valentines. In the verse about hidden treasure, "coral" had a possibly suggestive association with "coral lips," that much-loved image of both romantic and pornographic fiction. "Pearl," meanwhile, was a symbol of female sexuality and figured often in valentine poetry and ornament. Another popular motif was the glove, either in the form of a paper miniature pasted to the card or an entire valentine shaped like a glove. The motif signaled a man's serious romantic interest in the recipient, and often it was an unspoken proposal—"prelude to a Ring." Additionally, as casings into which bodily parts were inserted, gloves were inescapably colored with erotic overtones. Not surprisingly, they were among the most beloved objects of sexual fetishists.

The air of fetishism also lingers about a tiny lady's lace nightcap, complete with real pink silk ribbons, mounted on the paper lace background of yet another valentine. The image was not a common one, but the message—"Good night dear"—captured a recurring theme. Valentine verses were frequently evocative of beds and going to bed. Female breasts were invariably the "pillows" where men longed to lay their heads, while their women lulled them into "balmy rest" and "soothing sleep." Weary from "playing the game" all day, the Victorian man apparently sometimes needed sleep more than sex. Also, perhaps, he occasionally confused being sexual with being mothered.

Finding a mother substitute does not appear to have been foremost in the minds of the young men who gathered around that bare-legged center of courtship the parlor piano. Beyond its connection with innocent romance, it was where male sexuality sometimes aggressively asserted itself. The piano as a scene of seduction showed up in Victorian painting—most notably, William Holman Hunt's *The Awakening Conscience* (1853)—and in popular magazine illustrations of the day. As an *instrument,* the piano was also the object of ribald humor. In the comic song "Tuner's Oppor-tuner-ty," the piano tuner takes a more than professional interest in his client, Miss Crotchety Quaver, a young woman whose versatile "playing" requires regular tuning service:

> And to keep her piano in tune she would have
> A good tuner constantly there,
> And he'd pull up the instrument three times a week,
> Just to keep it in proper repair.

Chorus:

> And first he'd tune it gently, then he'd tune it strong,
> Then he'd touch a short note, then he'd run along,
> Then he'd go with vengeance, enough to break the key,
> At last he tun'd whene'er he got an op-por-tu-ni-ty.

Like many other comic songs, this one was sold as a song sheet and performed, with appropriate gestures no doubt, on the music hall stage. There the nudging, winking style of entertainment enjoyed considerable license. Clothed in humor, the making of lovemaking could "go all the way" in full view, with the general approval of a mass audience. Typically bawdy was an 1890s song called "Starve Her, Joe." It begins with a married man, Joe, whose domestic tranquility is disrupted by the extended visit of his wife's mother. Driven to distraction, he contemplates starving the offending in-law to death. Quickly coming to his senses, he abandons this plan and instead seeks solace with Flo, an attractive lady barber with, as Joe puts it "such a goo-goo eye / I lay back my head and sigh." He then launches into a full-frontal chorus:

Lather! lather! lather me, Flo!
Your little brush, it tickles me so-o-o!
But please don't hurt that pimple below
When you start to lather me, Flo!

As Joe and most of the audience well knew, "pimple" had two meanings—one of which was "a swelling."

Although it did not necessarily go to the lubricious lengths of the music hall, sexual humor still found a place offstage. The repertoire of stereographic entertainment included a lot of light-hearted naughtiness—the suitor under the crinoline, the monk with his naked female "provisions," husbands dallying with pretty

"Tell me where to find the Peg," comic valentine, 1840s

French maids, and so on. Valentines also had their moments of comic suggestiveness. In one vignette a hoydenish young woman (with an impressively large bottom) tries on a type of men's breeches known as peg-tops. The humor rested on the double meaning of "peg"—once clad in the trousers, the young woman is disappointed to find something missing. "Oh dear there's nothing in 'em," she exclaims:

> Call these Peg tops? then I beg
> You'll tell me where to find the Peg.

Cleaving Together

While many Victorians were never averse to a little sexual humor, most did not allow themselves to be long diverted from sexuality's serious purpose—the procreative marriage. As biology proceeded along a decorous course toward matrimony, there were certain rituals and conventions to be observed. Women had their ways of signaling marriage-mindedness—eye contact, blushing, flirting—but men usually made the actual proposal. "Man proposes (or at least should do so) and woman disposes," was the wisdom of the day, and few would have thought to challenge it. The heroes of fiction and their counterparts in everyday life produced gold rings with a flourish, or fell to their knees in romantic entreaty, or otherwise declared their matrimonial intentions. "Name the day . . . that makes thee mine" was the plea of many men who sent valentines, while the poet Ashby-Sterry ended his "Lover's Lullaby" on a similar note:

> Mirror your fate, then, in mine, love;
> Sorrow and sighing resign:
> Life is too short to repine, love,
> Link your fair future in mine!

Although there were always exceptions and variations according to class, the general expectation was that the engagement was the time for a couple to enjoy increasing physical intimacy, but to stop short of premarital sexual intercourse. As the wedding date approached, those who adhered to this regime of going just so far, but not the whole distance, found their sexual tension growing and their restraint weakening. Men and women alike thus looked forward eagerly to the wedding night. Of course, anticipation did not mean that there were no prenuptial anxieties. For all her genuine passion, Charles Kingsley's bride-to-be Fanny confessed to a certain amount of fear mixed with her sexual yearning. Her groom meanwhile was wrestling with his own worry. "The blaze of your naked beauty," he confided anxiously, might dazzle him into impotence.

As it turned out, all went well in the Kingsleys' conjugal bed. Sexual gratification was in fact what a majority of about-to-be-married Victorian couples optimistically looked forward to. Pictures and verses in wedding cards represented this hopeful longing and the imminent joys of consummation. A card from the 1880s depicts a bride and groom in their bedroom, alone at last, kissing tenderly. "What . . . oft they dreamt, and oft they longed for" was about to become, as the card's poet expressed it, "reality at last":

> And the veil, in sweet caresses,
> Yields to love's most ardent touch;
> Gently then they draw the curtain
> To hide love's secret with a blush.

Even pornography, usually unsentimental, was apt to soften a little when it turned to the theme of newly wedded bliss. A turn-of-the-century pornographer's catalogue of "Photographic Novelties" unctuously advertised a series of images of "The First Wedding Night": "The preludes of love, the clever caresses, the endless ecstacies and then the carnal refinements, the search after the new, the unknown and lastly prostrated, the felicity of the total initiation."

After the first joys of consummation had subsided, sex remained at the core of the healthy Victorian marriage. Not everyone experienced sensual fulfillment as intense as that of the Kingsleys—what made for a happy sexual relationship varied from couple to couple. Still, there were broad guidelines for establishing and maintaining appropriate and rewarding marital relations. Those who sought sexual knowledge or the improvement of their conjugal lives could always turn to one of the many manuals whose advice helped to shape marital lovemaking.

Frequency of intercourse was a standard theme. The experts, mostly physicians and doctors of divinity, agreed that sexual moderation was the ideal and that excesses were to be avoided. This view arose not out of prudery but in part out of a belief in the necessity of spermatic economy—the end result of the overexpenditure of seed might be the moral, intellectual, and physical degeneration of the human race. Or so believed a number of commentators, among them Sylvanus

Stall, who wrote several sex manuals published in Canada, England, and the United States. In *What a Young Husband Ought to Know* (part of an 1897–1902 series called Sex and Self), Stall, like other authorities, was concerned for the general health of couples. Too much sex, he cautioned, might be "most ruinous" to the health of the wife and lead to a host of fearful conditions in the husband: "backache, lassitude, giddiness, dimness of sight, noises in the ears, numbness of fingers and paralysis."

But how much was too much? The experts were not entirely dogmatic and, to a point, allowed for individual preferences and circumstances. Most offered some general direction as well. A few recommended relations every twenty to thirty days. A greater number considered once a week to be sounder practice for maintaining a satisfactory bond of "mutual affection" between husband and wife. Pregnancy, however, changed matters. By and large, greater than usual moderation was the rule, although Stall advocated complete abstinence.

It is impossible to know with any certainty the extent to which Victorian couples followed the experts' advice, and how often most actually made love—there were then no national polls or statistical averages. In 1892 Dr. Clelia Mosher of Stanford University conducted a survey of about forty-five middle-class American women. Her sampling was too small to permit sweeping conclusions, but it is not unreasonable to take it as a general indicator of more widespread behavior among the prosperous middle classes. On average the women reported having sex once a week, while a few indulged more often. At the lower ends of the economic scale, it is probably likely that frequency declined. Exhausting labor, poverty, and lack of privacy were not conducive to sexual activity.

Sex and the Married Woman

The writers of marriage manuals tended to overlook the existence of an impoverished working class. In the world of sex experts the ideal of the well-off middle-class family reigned supreme. From such a privileged vantage point, the feeding of extra mouths was not an overriding concern, and the ready consensus was that the primary purpose of sex was procreation. Sexual feeling, wrote Dr. Mary Wood-Allen in her 1899 advice book *What a Young Woman Ought to Know*, "is the indication of the possession of the most sacred powers, that of the perpetuation of life. Passion is the instinct for preservation of one's kind, the voice of the life principle, the sign of creative power."

But the reproductive purpose of sex did not mean a negation of pleasure.

Dr. Wood-Allen was quick to refer approvingly to "throbbing and pulsing in every fibre." In Stall's opinion, pleasure was one of the strongest arguments for moderation. Indulge "every slight inclination" and oversatiation would be the unhappy result, but exercise a degree of moderation and "realize the greatest pleasure and satisfaction." Dr. R. T. Trall, author of *Sexual Physiology*, published in 1870, counseled people to set aside whole days for making love. Whether the object of such activity was a "love embrace merely" or a "generative act," he was convinced that it should be pleasurable to husband and wife alike. "Surely," he insisted, "if sexual intercourse is worth doing at all, it is worth doing well."

It is one of those enduring myths about the Victorians that sexual pleasure was a disproportionately male enjoyment, and that women on the whole were indifferent. The misconception arose principally out of the work of the now notorious Dr. William Acton, an "expert" on the "evil habit" of masturbation and other sexual matters. In his 1857 treatise, *The Functions and Disorders of the Reproductive Organs*, he pronounced with chauvinist certainty that "the majority of women (happily for them) are not very much troubled with sexual feeling of any kind." Of course, he admitted with spurious fair-mindedness, there were exceptional women who experienced "sexual excitement." But this, he hastened to add, invariably progressed to "nymphomania, a form of insanity which those accustomed to visit lunatic asylums must be fully conversant with."

Acton was read widely in his day, and his opinions were undoubtedly given some credence. For instance, they validated the asexuality that was simply some women's nature. Perhaps they also alleviated the guilt of those in whom ill health had diminished sexual interest. But many Victorian authorities on sexuality had grave doubts about Acton's views and even his competence. Others simply ignored him and propounded their own ideas. Stall for one considered that the "largest number" of women took at least moderate pleasure in the sex act. He also acknowledged another, smaller group "in whom sexuality presides as a ruling passion. . . . Such women should never be married except to men of good health, strong physique, large powers of endurance, and with a pronounced sexual inclination."

He also described a third group that on the surface appears to be indistinguishable from Acton's sexually anesthetic women. But a closer look shows that Stall did not regard some women's sexual coldness as either inevitable or healthy. It was a correctable condition whose causes were varied. Indigestible food, late hours, and general debility from too little fresh air and exercise all contributed to sexual malaise. So, too, did excessive novel-reading, tight lacing, and chronic constipation. He did not say so directly, but the implication is also there that some women might have overreacted to Acton and his misogynist kind and come to believe that frigidity was very nearly a virtue.

Not least of all, Stall blamed ignorance. Of this both husband and wife might be guilty, but the greatest onus for knowledge and consideration he placed on the man. Ignorance could lead to clumsy and unintentionally brutal lovemaking on the husband's part—and on the wife's, permanent aversion. An informed and considerate approach, Stall maintained, would make all the difference between a "disgusted" bride and "a union of lifelong happiness." Quoting from Mrs. Eliza B. Duffey, a contemporary authority on "the relations of the sexes," he counseled new husbands to "practice in lawful wedlock the arts of the seducer rather than the violence of the man who commits rape, and you will find the reward of your patience very sweet and lasting."

Getting Satisfaction

No doubt many Victorian husbands never became as well versed as they ought to have been in the fine art of wife seduction. Even so, their wives were not necessarily sexually unsatisfied. Quite the opposite, often. In fiction just-married heroines typically took on "new beauty" or "the blossom of wifehood"—the signals of recently discovered physical satisfaction. In a more forthright vein, greater than a third of the women in Dr. Mosher's survey reported experiencing orgasm "always" or "usually"; another 40 percent said "sometimes" or "not always." Even among the remaining women—about a quarter of the whole group—there were some who at least occasionally felt arousal.

Other middle-class American wives indicated general sexual contentment through their language and tone in letters to their husbands. One woman wrote playfully to her absent husband in the summer of 1873: "How are you this hot day? I am most roasted and my chemise sticks to me and the sweat runs down my legs, . . . don't you wish you could be around just now." Another wife's sexual longing was too great for teasing. "I like you to want me, dear," she wrote to her husband in 1883, "and if I were only with you, I would embrace more than the back of your neck, be sure."

For all their expressiveness, these women, the many others like them, and the men with whom they exchanged loving letters all preserved a characteristically Victorian reticence when it came to what, precisely, gave them erotic pleasure. Even most marriage manuals were unforthcoming about the mechanics of lovemaking. Stall, among others, says nothing on the subject. Such discretion need not be narrowly interpreted as prudery, nor even as fastidiousness with regard to subject matter. Saying nothing about the technical particulars served the sexual mystique of the day. It left room for variation and experimentation, as long as no one violated the general rule of mutual pleasure.

At least one expert, however, was more explicit—and dogmatic. This was a French medical man, Auguste Debay, the author of *Hygiène et physiologie du mariage,* published in 1848 and reprinted throughout the century. Debay insisted that the only "natural" and "normal" way of making love was in the missionary position. His conviction arose from an assumption of general male superiority as much as it did from a notion of appropriate intercourse. In bed or elsewhere, men "naturally" belonged on top. Many of his contemporaries no doubt agreed and, coincidentally or not, enjoyed sex in the missionary position. Nevertheless, it is hard to imagine the populace of a country famed for its lovemaking unanimously and invariably obeying Debay's authoritarian stricture.

And, looking across the Channel, it appears no less inconceivable that upon marriage, versatile English eroticism could universally subside into missionary monotony. Kingsley for one had a lively sexual imagination. How could he have been content with marital relations limited to the missionary position?—even though he undoubtedly had a tendency to mix religion with sex. Take off your clothes and pray, he had once suggested to Fanny. "Then lie down, nestle to me, clasp your arms and every limb around me, and with me repeat the *Te Deum* aloud." Eccentric Anglican clergyman though he might have been, Charles Kingsley was no puritan missionary.

Whatever the ways in which individual couples chose to make love, the joys of marriage, including its physical side, were ideally supposed to last. In his manual for young husbands, Stall hinted at "the later years" of marriage, which could bring with them "the largest possible good and blessing." In 1901 he would follow up the hint with a further volume, *What a Man of 45 Ought to Know.* Romantic fiction offered a similarly optimistic view, and many of its couples continued to enjoy "perfect bliss" and "passionate devotion" long after marrying.

In real life, frequency of intercourse perhaps declined over time—or so the Mosher survey suggests—but in many marriages, romance and sexual pleasure endured throughout the years. Among the love letters preserved from Victorian America, a number attest to the longevity of marital passion. In 1856 Nathaniel Hawthorne, famed author of *The Scarlet Letter* and other novels, expressed the fervid sentiments of many when he declared to his wife of fourteen years:

Oh, dearest, dearest, interminably and infinitely dearest—I don't know how to
end that ejaculation. The use of kisses and caresses is, that they supersede language, and express what there are no words for. I need them at this moment—
need to give them and to receive them.

Not unexpectedly, Hawthorne's enthusiasm was perhaps exceeded only by the
erotic devotion of Kingsley. During a brief separation in the first year of his marriage, he tantalized his wife with the question, "Shall we the first night we meet re-
enact our marriage night?" "Oh!" he exclaimed, "to be once again with you—to
lie once more naked in your arms." A half-dozen years later, in May 1850, separation still made him physically long for her. "These soft, hot damp days fill me with
yearning love," he wrote. "Your image haunts me day and night as it did before we
were married, and the thought of that delicious sanctuary"—but here the fantasy
breaks off. No less passionate but more discreet than her husband, Fanny had carefully inked over his amorous revelation.

To the Bridal Altar Go

While most Victorian husbands might not have been as articulate as Kingsley,
there were many as passionate—and with wives as compatible as Fanny. As the
nineteenth century progressed, more and more people strove toward this conjugal
ideal. The number of marriages grew during the Victorian years, as the marital
norm became increasingly central in the making of lovemaking. Common-law
arrangements progressively decreased until they survived only among the poorest,
who tended to keep quiet about their irregular circumstances. For those of means
marriage had longer been the established norm, but it was more firmly entrenched
than ever by the turn of the century.

Some advertising did not fail to use the norm to its own advantage. An attractive pictorial advertisement for Pears' Soap featured the image of a young woman
sitting in a field and plucking petals from a daisy. Superimposed were a few lines of
appropriately "romantic" verse:

A Maiden's Wishes
—are but three.
O'er all the world, whoe'er she be—
To handsome grow,
And have a beau,

And to the bridal altar go—
All these fruitions of her hope
Come quickly if she'll
USE PEARS' SOAP

With or without the help of Pears' Soap, women not only increasingly got married but, as far as their families could afford, ever more favored elaborate and colorful weddings to mark the day. In the last two decades of the nineteenth century, bridesmaids wore colored gowns, instead of the traditional white. For brides, the shades of preference were cream or ivory, rather than stark white; other popular choices were by later standards startling—claret velvet, purplish-brown satin, gray corded silk. In contrast, the bridegroom and his attendants became less colorful. As the popular notion of masculinity grew more rigid, the male members of the wedding party gave up shades of blue, claret, and mulberry. By the 1890s the only acceptable color for a frock coat was black.

Not everyone was happy with the ideal that middle-class weddings represented. Here and there the voices of dissent spoke out against the marital norm. A number of late-Victorian feminists were critical of marriage and its embedded premise that women were property. These and other women also wanted greater educational and political rights, as well as marital reform. In 1893 still others—men as well as women—founded the Legitimation League to protest against conventional marriage, advocate free love, and demand legal rights for children born out of wedlock. Meanwhile, the majority of men and women took little notice of these voices. As the century ended, they were absorbed in falling in love and planning romantic weddings.

In yet another sphere, still far removed from most common experience, the sexologists were at work distinguishing and describing the "normal" and the "pathological," turning sex into definitions of standard or deviant modes of behavior—talk, that is. Although their efforts escaped the attention of most people, there appeared a few signs in everyday life that sex was already less a total affair of the body than it had been not long before. By 1900 new, matter-of-fact fictional heroines tended not to blush, or at least not so readily as their predecessors. Suitors, accordingly, were not so apt to turn "gelatinous" in their presence. At the same time, the odd sex manual was inclined to equate sexual love with effective technique, rather than with individual passion and bodily response.

But even as the nineteenth century gave way to the next, such signals were still sporadic and faint. The making of lovemaking retained most of its old devotion to passion. At once profoundly romantic and physical, the mystique of carefully nur- tured eroticism had not yet dissolved into analytical talk. Throughout the Victo- rian age, for countless lovers, both courting and married, sex radiated much of the "sweetness and light" that the poet and moralist Matthew Arnold envisioned in a perfect world. Inevitably, though, in a less than perfect reality there were unlit places—shadowy corners where most lovers, content in the felicity of the norm, never cared to venture. In such places passion's aspect darkened.

CHAPTER 5

Dark Desires

They laid her flat on a gorse down pillow,
And scourged her arse with twigs of willow,
Her bottom so white grew pink, then red,
Then bloody, then raw, and her spirit fled.

—"Epitaph on a Young Lady who was Birched
to Death," Victorian flagellant verse

In the dim sexual netherworld known to a few Victorians with esoteric tastes, pain and erotic desires obscenely embraced. Those who harbored such desires did so furtively. As men of means, the readers of pornography and patrons of brothels had reputations and social positions to maintain. Some also had wives and families to protect. Indulging unusual sexual preferences was of necessity a dark, secretive affair.

The writers of pornography, among them the unnamed author of "Epitaph on a Young Lady," similarly preferred anonymity. For their part, the keepers of brothels typically operated under a variety of aliases. Like all purveyors of illegal or questionable goods and services, those who traded in sex did not court publicity.

Much of what went on in brothels involved violence and victimization. These were also the mainstays of pornography, as in the grisly flagellant doggerel. Although in its extreme forms eroticized violence was a minority taste, popular fiction sometimes served up diluted versions. To ensure public acceptability, such fiction usually contained a redeeming moral message. Pornography, meanwhile, rarely allowed moral concerns to interfere with the business of degradation.

Concerned members of the government and the public tried unsuccessfully to eradicate prostitution and pornography. Yet, collectively resourceful, the Victorians achieved a measure of reconciliation between the norm by which the majority lived and the dark desires of a few. For the most part, the patrons of brothels continued to visit their chosen establishments, and the devotees of pornography endlessly and obsessively thumbed its pages.

Buttocks and Birch Rods

In the dark reaches of the pornographic imagination the supreme obsession was flagellation—the beating of the bare buttocks with birch rods, canes, whips, or other punitive instruments. Flagellant episodes did not usually end in death or even bloodshed. But they all enacted the same ritual of punishment, pain, and humiliation—frequently in the presence of one or more voyeuristic witnesses, as suggested by the sinister "they" in the "Epitaph."

One late addition to Victorian flagellation pornography had many precedents and well illustrates standard practice. In this verbosely entitled 1899 "reminiscence," *The Memoirs of Dolly Morton. . . . With Curious Anthropological Observations on the Radical Diversities in the Conformation of the Female Bottom and the Way Different Women Endure Chastisement,* the innocent young heroine Dolly rejects the lecherous advances of a would-be lover. Enraged, he sends his henchmen to punish her. She describes her torment and shame in graphic detail:

> He went on whipping me very slowly, so that I felt the full sting of each stroke before the next one fell; and every stroke felt as if a red-hot iron was being drawn across my bottom. I winced and squirmed every time the horrid switch fell sharply on my quivering flesh. . . . The feeling of shame again came over me as I began to notice the way the men were looking at my naked body, and I tearfully begged them to pull down my clothes. No-one did so however.

Instead her flogger swaggeringly invites the spectators to admire his handiwork: "'There, boys, look at her bottom. You see how regularly the white skin is striped with long red weals; but there is not a drop of blood. That's what I call a prettily whipped bottom.'"

In pornography the recipients of such "discipline" were often women. Far outnumbering them, however, were all the men and boys who suffered at the hands of female flagellators. Incidents of this kind commonly began in a schoolroom setting. In *The Romance of Lust* (1873–76), a four-volume sexual epic with nothing romantic about it, the narrator, Charles, recalls his twenty-two-year-old governess, Miss Evelyn, and the way in which she punished him when he was a student of fifteen:

> "Put down your slate, Charles, and come to me."
>
> I obeyed, and stood before my beautiful governess, with a strange commixture of fear and desire.
>
> "Unfasten your braces, and pull down your trousers."
>
> I commenced doing this, though but very slowly. Angry at my delay her delicate fingers speedily accomplished the work. My trousers fell to my feet.
>
> "Place yourself across my knees."
>
> Tremblingly, with the same commixture of feeling, I obeyed. . . . A rapid succession of cruel cuts lacerated my bottom. . . .
>
> Holding me firmly with her left arm, Miss Evelyn used the rod most unmercifully. . . . The pain was excruciating, and I roared out as loud as I could.

As Charles suggests when he speaks of "commixture of feeling," the flagellant fantasy tempered its "excruciating" pain with acute pleasure. In *The Romance of Chastisement* (1866) Dora, a pupil at a school for young ladies, describes her first flogging at the hand of the school's head governess:

> I was forced upon my knees on the block. . . . I felt that the eyes of all present were riveted on my naked person. . . .
>
> . . . Oh! the unspeakable agony of that first murderous lash! Legions of scorpions fastened on my flesh and dug their fangs into my vitals.

But before long, as Dora tells it,

> a change next to miraculous took place in all my thoughts and feelings. . . .
>
> Fear and shame were both gone: it was as though I was surrendering my person to the embraces of a man whom I so loved I would anticipate his wildest desires. . . . Then, too, there was a thrill in a certain part, . . . which every fresh lash kept on increasing. The added pang unlocked new floods of

bliss, till it was impossible to tell . . . whether the ecstasy was most of pain or pleasure.

Or, as Charles recounts his experience of punishment-induced arousal,

> gradually the pain ceased to be so acute, and was succeeded by the most deli-cious tickling sensation. My struggles at first had been so violent as to greatly disorder Miss Evelyn's petticoats, and to raise them up so as to expose to my delighted eyes her beautifully formed silk clad legs up to the knees, and even an inch or two of naked thighs above.
>
> This, together with the intense tickling irritation communicated to my bot-tom, as well as the friction of my cock against the person of Miss Evelyn in my struggles, rendered me almost delirious, and I tossed and pushed myself about on her knees in a state of perfect frenzy as the blows continued to be showered down on my poor bottom. At last the rod was worn to a stump, and I was pushed off her knees. As I rose before her, with my cheeks streaming with tears, my shirt was jutting out considerably in front in an unmistakable and most prominent manner, and my prick was at the same time throbbing beneath it with convulsive jerks, . . . which I could by no means restrain.

The English Vice

In English pornography countless scenes of flagellation metaphorically whipped devotees to a fever pitch of arousal. Works with obsessively similar titles—like *Mysteries of Flagellation* (1863), *Sublime of Flagellation* (1872), and *Curiosities of Flagellation* (1875)—proliferated. So prevalent was such material that the French and other Europeans, familiar with pornographic imports from across the Chan-nel, regarded flagellation as "the English vice." The English bibliographer of erot-ica Henry Ashbee confirmed the Continental view in his introduction to *Index Librorum Prohibitorum* (1877), the first of his three-volume bibliography of forbid-den books. "The propensity which the English most cherish is undoubtedly flagel-lation," he wrote. "The rod . . . has certainly struck deeper root in England than elsewhere."

Ashbee further noted that even respectable periodicals like the *Family Herald* and the *Englishwoman's Domestic Magazine* (April–December 1870) did not shrink from publishing correspondence on the subject. One of the age's eminent poets,

Algernon Charles Swinburne, was an eager recipient of the "chastisement" of the rod and the author of flagellant verse and a prose piece, "Hints on Flogging," both of which he contributed to the privately published *Whippingham Papers* (c. 1888). Even his obscure contemporary, the inimitably saccharine poet Joseph Ashby-Sterry, discreetly celebrated eroticized discipline in one of his *Boudoir Ballads*, "Pet's Punishment":

> O If my love offended me,
> And we had words together,
> To show her I would master be,
> I'd whip her with a feather!
>
> . . . .
>
> And if she dared her lips to pout—
> Like many pert young misses—
> I'd wind my arm her waist about,
> And punish her—with kisses!

Aficionados of the national vice did not need to resort exclusively to pornography and marginal poetry for their gratification. Specialist brothels catered to those whose taste for pain and pleasure was not just literary. Discreetly worded periodical advertisements offered potential clients "Discipline Treatment—DOMESTIC, THERAPEUTIC, RECIPROCAL, AND PENITENTIAL"; Miss Thornton's "TREATMENT FOR RHEUMATISM, with Pine and Medicated Baths, also Discipline Treatment"; "MANICURE AND DISCIPLINE TREATMENT"; or—simply—"MANICURE, &c." In the establishments of these advertisers, there were some women who would for a price submit to flogging by clients, but this was not the usual routine. More commonly, gentlemen patrons paid generous sums to receive the disciplinary ministrations of "nurses," "governesses," or "schoolmistresses," as flagellant prostitutes euphemistically were known.

There are a number of reasons why men sought out these "services." A frequent side effect, or aftermath, of being beaten on the buttocks is stimulation of the primary sexual organ. Among boys who had been caned at school, there were some for whom this was a formative erotic experience—one they craved to repeat, even in adulthood. The female flagellant was also herself a source of arousal for her client. "Round full breasts" that would readily "heave with exertion" were a general requirement for giving customer satisfaction. Finally, a part of the pleasure of flagellation for the male recipient was the brief abdication of responsibility it afforded, a respite from the usual masculine imperative to be in control. "One of the great charms of birching," wrote Swinburne in "Hints on Flogging," "lies in the sentiment that the floggee is the powerless victim of the furious rage of a beautiful woman." Apparently many men agreed with him—especially, perhaps, those who enjoyed considerable authority in their everyday lives. If Ashbee is to be believed (and there is no reason to doubt him), those who indulged in the "idiosyncrasy" of flagellation included "men of the highest positions in diplomacy, literature, the army, &c." The successful "governess" was well skilled in provoking the release such men sought—in the irresistible combination of pain, arousal, nostalgia, and the temporary relinquishment of power.

According to Ashbee, "the queen of her profession" was London's Theresa Berkley of Charlotte Street, Portland Place. "She was a perfect mistress of her art," he continued, one who well "understood how to satisfy her clients." Although she died in 1836, her establishment became the model for the quintessential Victorian flagellation brothel. Ashbee recorded,

> Her instruments of torture were more numerous than those of any other governess. . . . Thus, at her shop, whoever went with plenty of money, could be birched, whipped, fustigated, scourged, needle-pricked, half-hung, holly-brushed, furze-brushed, butcher-brushed, stinging-nettled, curry-combed, phlebotomized, and tortured till he had a belly full.

Mrs. Berkley enhanced her premises and her legend by commissioning a device that was in effect the prototype of standard equipment used by her Victorian successors. This was the "horse," a form of padded stepladder to which a client could be strapped facedown for efficient flogging. Ashbee referred to "a print in Mrs. Berkley's memoirs, representing a man upon it quite naked. A woman is sitting in a chair exactly under it, with her bosom, belly, and bush exposed: she is *manualizing* his *embolon*, while Mrs. Berkley is birching his posteriors." By the time of her death this enterprising madam and her "horse" had earned £10,000—a small fortune in those days, and evidence that England's favorite vice was no cheap thrill.

Pornography's Phallic Fallacies

Flagellation was only one specialty on offer in the Victorian brothel. For the right price a man might instead purchase anything from group sex to the privilege of deflowering a virgin, who might or might not be the real thing. Pornography's repertoire, meanwhile, was greater still. Ever mindful of the rarefied tastes of their readers, pornographers seldom hesitated to turn their hands to obscure and delicate subjects. Comparatively mild deviations from the norm, like voyeurism and fetishism, were all in their day's work. And neither did they shrink from turning a profit by graphically portraying the extremes of sodomy, bestiality, and incest.

Apart from flagellation, they directed their greatest effort toward purveying rape. Pornography, after all, was the ultimate man's world. Typical of its kind was the 1894 *Raped on the Railway*. To allay any twinges of proper feeling that might have spoiled his readers' enjoyment, the anonymous author hastened reassuringly to elevate rape to a higher plane: "To get a strong bodied wench, in the prime of health, down on her back, and triumph over her virtue, in spite of all her struggles, is to my mind the height of delightful existence, the sum of all human ambition."

The story's male protagonist, Robert Brandon, is a high achiever in this sphere of endeavor. As the plot unfolds, he spots an attractive young woman at London's Euston Station, follows her on board the Glasgow train, and traps her alone in a compartment. He then makes sexual advances, which she unsuccessfully struggles to fend off:

> As she arched up her buttocks that she might better be able to twist sideways and get rid of the intruder, Brandon gave a powerful downward lunge . . . of his big column. . . . She knew then that he had won the game, and woman-like burst into a flood of tears.

The author no doubt thought that his reference to womanlike tears was properly manlike—a convivial aside, just between us men who know how to play the game. But in fact he had merely betrayed his unmanly contempt for another human being.

Except for the somewhat unusual setting, this was a standard rape scenario. But on occasion the pornographer stretched his limited imagination and came up with a variation or two. There were, for instance, different rapist types—dissolute European aristocrats and Eastern potentates were among the stock characters. Additionally, as a side effect of the complete male domination of obstetrics and gynecology by the mid-nineteenth century, there developed yet another pornographic type, the doctor-rapist. In *The Amatory Experiences of a Surgeon* (1881), the main character is invariably overcome by lust when he examines barely pubescent female patients. "I carefully raised up her clothes," he typically recounts. "Everything now lay bare before me, her mossy recess, shaded by only the slightest silky down, presented to my view two full pouting lips of coral hue, while the rich swell of her lovely thighs served still further to inflame me." Thus aroused, he misuses his medical authority, coercing his virginal patients into submitting to defloration as the cure for what ails them.

True to the "more is better" philosophy of their trade, pornographers often intermingled the dark desires they strained to excite. Voyeurism, for instance, was almost always an element of any flagellation episode. Garment fetishism also figured often in flagellant and sadistic fantasies. Usually, as in *The Secret Life of Linda Brent* (1882), the representation of the fetish involved the ritualistic stripping of the victim, followed by an erotic focusing on any remaining clothing:

> They seize her. One by one her garments are taken off, in spite of her struggles, disclosing first her beautiful polished shoulders, her round firm swelling virgin breasts. . . . Her beautiful moulded arms, ripe, well-formed waist, which, as she moved and writhed in their hands, showed suppleness of a most voluptuous character; and, at last, she stands before them panting, naked but for her drawers, which she tenaciously clung round her.

Pornography's most potent combination was undoubtedly rape and flagellation. *Raped on the Railway* in particular exploited the doubly false eroticism of this pair of sadistic desires. Thus the young woman's ordeal in the train compartment does not end with violation by her fellow passenger. She is next forced to endure a brutal beating at the hands of her brother-in-law, who believes she deliberately invited the rape. The lengthy title of the American version told the whole story: *Raped on the Elevated Railway, a True Story of a Lady who was First Ravished and then Flagellated on the Uptown Express, illustrating the Perils of Travel in the New Machine Age.* The title's final glimmer of humor is unusual in Victorian pornography. Apart from occasional unintended silliness and some rare instances of deliberate humor, obscenity was a serious business.

Whatever the topic—flagellation, rape, or other obsession—there was a terrible perverted earnestness about the way in which the pornographer reduced human beings to body parts. This is particularly apparent in *The Romance of Lust,* the same work that featured the schoolboy Charles and his flagellant governess. Its four volumes are little more than compendiums of anatomical objectification. In one scene Charles, now long out of the schoolroom and well versed in sexual acrobatics, enjoys an energetic orgy of "general combinations" with one male and three female companions. The women are identified by their surnames in a way that makes them sound like objects, not people: "the Benson," "the Egerton," "the Frankland." Like the whole of this spurious romance, the episode is recounted with all possible verbal excesses—four-letter words, vulgarisms, and clinical language. The image evoked is a welter of acts and parts all tumbled together, yet mechanical in their operation.

Eventually the group pauses briefly to catch its collective breath, and to add two women and five men to its original number. The twelve devotees to "raging lust" then join together in an unbroken "chain" of organs, apertures, and dildos. And so on—and on and on. With only a few predictable twists and variations, such dreary contortions were what masqueraded as passion in the dark and debauched, infinitely fragmented anatomical world of Victorian pornography.

Dark Fantasies

The dehumanized sex, the eroticized violence—the overall unrelenting dreariness—were unequaled beyond pornography's furtively thumbed pages. But in altered form, their graphicness moderated through euphemism and discreet omission, pornography's grim fancies cast their shadows across the sensational reaches of popular fiction. A penny or two at the corner newsagent's purchased a brief excursion out of the light of the everyday norm and into fiction's lurid regions. Imprinted on paper now yellowed and fragile, the murky scenes still unfold as they did in their own time.

Turn the pages, . . . and a sadistic hangman in the novelist George W. M. Reynolds's *Mysteries of London* (1845–50) takes time off to practice the English vice on his beautiful niece and humpbacked son. . . . In another of the author's classics, *Wagner, the Wehr-Wolf,* a convent houses flagellant nuns. Stripped to the waist, they whip each other across their bare breasts. . . . A female character in *The Boy Pirate* is also half-naked. Her captor ties her to a post and flogs her viciously until her back is torn and bleeding. . . .

Chambers of torture and their twisted proprietors are everywhere—especially in London. The unprotected females in Bracebridge Hemyng's *Women of London* (c. 1856) are perpetually at risk. . . . A bestial lout forces the heroine, Agnes, into a dungeon. . . . Chapters later, a different brute drags her into yet another dank cell. He removes her dress, ties her to an iron bedstead, and subjects her to "the strange and extraordinary torture of the drop of water. . . . Drip, drip. Patter, patter" on her forehead, until she is nearly driven "stark, staring, raving mad."

Leaf through the pages yet again. . . . Kidnappers, seducers, and would-be

Brutal flogging scene from The Boy Pirate, *1865*

rapists abound. A voyeuristic clergyman in *Mysteries of London* peeps furtively at the naked breasts of a woman preparing for her bath. Obscenely aroused by what he sees, he contemplates rape and murder. . . . Harwolf, the gentlemanly looking but villainous antagonist of *The Boy Pirate*, also has rape on his mind. He comes ashore and roughly seizes Lilia, the hero's fiancée. . . . On a different seacoast, the domain of Pierce Egan's *Paul Jones; the Pirate* (c. 1850), another lecherous villain forces his attentions on a hapless young woman. "If you say nay," he threatens, "you go with me now, to a spot where none can find you . . . and there you shall learn to love him you now despise. . . . Either be my wife by your own consent, or my mistress by compulsion."

On other coasts, in different countries, mountain hideaways, and the streets of London, at masked balls, and even in respectable drawing rooms, the women of fiction are abducted, gagged, bound, drugged. Threats of dishonor, defloration, and death dog their footsteps. . . . Others meet with artful seducers—and yield to the honeyed words and false promises. Her "tender sensibilities" skillfully "inflamed," Reynolds's innocent heroine Octavia "gives herself completely up" to her lover and his "infernal artifice."

Riffle the pages of still other volumes . . . and Victorian fiction's consummate seducer looms—ravishing the flesh, the blood, and the life of his victims. In a flash of lightning, the fiendish "vampyre" Varney materializes in a woman's bedchamber. She is "young and beautiful"—"just budding into womanhood." He, gaunt and horrific, divides his grisly attentions between her blood and her "half-disclosed" bosom. Gripping her breast with a clawed hand, he "seizes her neck in his fang-like teeth"—the vampiric version of rape. "Her bosom heaves and . . . her beautifully

Vampire and female victim in Varney, the Vampyre, *1847*

rounded limbs quiver." The vampire "makes hideous sucking noises." His victim shrieks and shrieks. . . .

A half-century later Varney's aristocratic successor journeys to England. The vampire count of Bram Stoker's *Dracula* (1897) soon thirsts after the sweet, high-spirited Lucy. With vampiric lust, he drinks her blood, transforming her from human to vampire—from virgin to "voluptuous" wanton, a "devilish mockery" of her former pure self. . . . His dark desire for the blood of innocent women leads him to the bedroom of Mina, the story's heroine. Eyes flaming red, reflecting his "devilish passion," he takes her—forces her into an obscene rite of union, a bloodily erotic exchange of their body fluids. . . . Mina later recalls her nightmarish violation:

> And oh, my God, my God, pity me! He placed his reeking lips upon my throat! . . . I felt my strength fading away, and I was in a half swoon. How long this horrible thing lasted I know not; but it seemed that a long time must have passed before he took his foul, awful, sneering mouth away. I saw it drip with the fresh blood! . . .
>
> Then he spoke to me mockingly. . . . "You . . . are now to me . . . flesh of my flesh, blood of my blood. . . ." With that he pulled open his shirt, and with his long sharp nails opened a vein in his breast. When the blood began to spurt out, he took my hands in one of his, holding them tight, and with the other seized my neck and pressed my mouth to the wound, so that I must either suffocate or swallow some of the—Oh my God! my God!

Such were the dark fantasies of popular escapism.

Furtive Pleasures and Moral Measures

On the surface of things it is not easy to reconcile the perverse desires of vampires, rapists, and flagellants with the loving sentiments of valentines and popular romance—or with muscular chivalry and idealized womanhood. How did the Victorian mystique of carefully nurtured sexuality manage to accommodate flagellation brothels and violent pornography? Were the Victorians really such hypocrites? Undoubtedly, there were individuals who led a hypocritical double life—ostensibly respectable, even prudish, but secretly obsessed with vice. But this is not sufficient basis for attaching the label of hypocrisy to an entire era. The majority of Victorians neither patronized brothels nor indulged in pornography. Absorbed in the erotic variety and expressiveness of daily life, most had little, if any, precise knowledge of the excesses of a few.

Others, however, were actively concerned. Since its founding in 1802, the Society for the Suppression of Vice had lobbied for criminal proceedings against the publishers of pornography. As a result there were a number of prosecutions and convictions over the course of the nineteenth century. The Society also confiscated pornographic materials, among which were a quarter of a million photographs seized between 1868 and 1880. Its efforts further included a successful campaign of persuasion that led to the passing of the Obscene Publications Act of 1857.

Perhaps the most famous Victorian crusade against vice was launched by the journalist W. T. Stead, editor of London's *Pall Mall Gazette*. In 1885 he ran a four-part exposé of the traffic in young girls. Compellingly entitled "The Maiden Tribute of Modern Babylon," the series was a masterwork of yellow journalism that no doubt titillated as much as it outraged its mass readership. Nevertheless, it impelled the passage of the 1885 Criminal Law Amendment Act, which raised the age of consent from thirteen to sixteen, and increased the power of the police to proceed against brothel-keepers.

Similarly, there had been successful prosecutions under the Obscene Publications Act. These, together with the activities of the Vice Society, had at times managed to curb the English pornographic trade. But the effects were always only temporary, and for the most part pornography continued to thrive. Unable to eradicate it, legislation and lobby groups at least exerted a degree of control. Somewhat ironically, there was also a sense in which the very publications they attempted to eliminate exercised their own measure of self-control. That is, much of pornography and virtually all of popular fiction, however lurid, were heterosexual in their plots and scenarios—and, to this extent, "normal."

Although there was some explicitly homosexual pornography in circulation, as well as homoerotic elements in other works—same-sex flagellation scenes, for instance—pornography generally upheld a corrupted version of the heterosexual norm. So-called gentlemen pursued and deflowered female virgins; or they frequented brothels and enjoyed two or more women at a time; or medical men overexcited themselves while examining female patients—and so forth. Pirates and other villainous males similarly lusted after the virtuous heroines of popular fiction. Some even attempted to legitimate their desires through enforced marriage. Although Stoker's Dracula showed a passing interest in the blood of Jonathan (Mina's fiancé and later husband), it was Lucy, then Mina, whom he actually attacked. The Count, too, was basically heterosexual.

So it was with the majority of reprehensible characters in pornography and sensational fiction. Unproductive, perverted, and violent though their sexuality might have been, fiction's vampires and villains, as well as the rapists and sadists of pornography and real life, were predominantly heterosexuals. They were not, therefore, a serious threat to the norm but, rather, a minority within it—the inhabitants of its dark side. The majority could thus safely ignore the shadowy existence of the few and devote themselves contentedly to their own appropriate and productive relationships. In this way, by a hair's breadth, the Victorians and their sexual mystique evaded the taint of hypocrisy.

The "Natural" Order of Things

Much to their discredit, pornography and lurid fiction lodged themselves within the norm in yet another way. The dark desires—the eroticized brutalities—that such material represented were the cruel extremes of the "normal" disproportionate control that men wielded in most areas of life. Harshly mirroring the overall power imbalance between the sexes, violent behavior—in both fiction and reality—was overridingly perpetrated by men against women. The male vampires of Gothic horror violated the flesh and gorged on the blood of innocent women. The "heroes" of pornography and the patrons of certain brothels deflowered terrified virgins. In everyday domestic settings, some husbands beat and raped their wives. The unscrupulous villains who skulked in the gaslight of melodrama forcibly abducted virtuous heroines. And, night and day, in cities everywhere, men with intentions from mildly caddish to heartlessly sadistic accosted women on public streets.

Most people did not condone male sexual aggression and violence toward women. But it is nonetheless unlikely that anyone would have understood such behaviors as anything other than the loathsome aspect of the "natural" order of things. The assumption was that women were "natural" victims. With this went the insidious notion among men that women were also capable of deriving pleasure or benefit from their victimization. As the ultimate male fantasy, pornography was particularly enamored of this idea. When some male character deflowers a virgin, with or without her consent, the end result is predictable. In inflicting pain, he has done her a great favor—awakened her womanhood, introduced her to the unalloyed joys of the flesh, and so on.

Even when the woman in question is not a virgin, the supposedly beneficial effect of rape is much the same. In *Raped on the Railway,* it is a married woman who is violated. At first she is understandably horrified at what has happened to her. But when her rapist apologizes for his actions, she is suddenly flattered and forgives him. Typically, she also realizes that she had actually enjoyed herself all along. Collectively, she and all the other purportedly satisfied victims of sexual force were pornography's rationalization of rape—and, of all its phallic fallacies, undoubtedly the most pathetic.

Popular fiction, on the other hand, was not so ready to justify coercive sex. Unlike pornography, it catered to a large and diverse market, much of which was female. It was generally careful not to portray women as willing victims, or sadists and seducers as sexual philanthropists. Some scenarios, though, inadvertently incorporated a disturbing ambiguity. Take Varney the vampire's assault upon the young woman in her bedchamber. When he grabs one of her breasts and his long teeth penetrate her flesh, does the eroticism emanate only from him? Are her limbs quivering and her bosom heaving from pain or masochistic pleasure? Are her screams entirely of terror?

Such ambiguity was not the rule in popular fiction, however. For the most part its heroines were neither willing victims in the first place, nor did they in the end come to enjoy their mistreatment. That fantasy was reserved for pornography. The usual scenario in popular fiction depicted the heroine's valiant struggles, her eventual defeat due to the villain's superior physical strength, and her ultimate rescue by the hero—the most brawny character of all.

But there were times when fiction's women turned the tables on men. In *Fortunes and Misfortunes of a Ballet Girl* (c. 1870) the resourceful heroine uses one of the metal stays from her corset to dig her way out of the cellar in which a debauched nobleman has imprisoned her. In the 1868 pirate adventure *Black-Eyed Susan,* by George Emmett, Susan never hesitates to wield pistol and sword to vanquish seagoing ruffians. "'Cowards!'" she exclaims, "her lip curling scornfully" as, weapon still in hand, she rests her "tiny foot" on the nearest recumbent pirate. And, in one of Victorian fiction's ultimate reversals of the standard power relations between the sexes, three rapacious female vampires attack Jonathan when he is alone and vulnerable in the castle of Stoker's *Dracula.*

Beyond fiction, in certain brothels of London, routine business was apparently yet another reversal of the usual power relations between men and women, as "governesses" birched, caned, and scourged their male clients. Such men were undoubtedly deeply dependent on the rod and perhaps truly enthralled with a favorite "governess." To this extent the women involved wielded the power. But in these circumstances appearances were also deceptive—the "punishment" had been ordered and paid for by the men for their own gratification. Although men with a taste for debasement often liked to delude themselves that women "delight in administering the birch," there is in fact nothing to support this belief. The workplace offered women limited opportunities, and those who resorted to the

flagellation brothels were not in search of pleasure. Like many of their female contemporaries, they were simply doing whatever they could to earn a living.

In the larger world, in ways that were real, not illusory, women of all kinds were
beginning to erode the male power bloc. They sought and obtained improved
property and child guardianship rights within marriage. Some began to pursue
higher education and careers outside of the home. In the courts of law a few brave
survivors fought for and occasionally won redress for the violence they had endured at the hands of men. With the exception of works of pornography—dominant manhood's last frontier—fiction increasingly fashioned independent heroines,
"new women" who took assertive action to gain emancipation and realize their
goals.

Although women had always done what they could for themselves within the
restrictions of their lives, these signs of change belong mainly to the late Victorian
period, from the 1870s onward. And there was still a long way to go. For instance,
it would take until 1937 for rape and cruelty to become legal grounds for a woman
to divorce her husband. Nevertheless, in large measure and small, within and beyond the domestic sphere, in fiction and reality—virtually everywhere but in
pornography—their momentum gathering, women were striking back at male su-
premacy and its dark extremes.

Fragmented Bodies

It was possibly no coincidence that as the first wave of Victorian feminism broke
across public consciousness, the women who made their living on the streets of
east London began to fear for their lives. In one sick mind, perhaps, the murder of
prostitutes was a suitable revenge against all women who stepped beyond the
norm. Between August and November of 1888 the killer who would soon become
known as Jack the Ripper stalked London's Whitechapel district. He murdered his
five victims within one quarter square mile of one another. He cut their throats
and, with the exception of the third woman, used his knife to mutilate their dead
bodies. His identity was never conclusively established.

A journalistic sensation, the murders were widely and not necessarily accurately
reported in newspapers, broadsheets, and penny dreadfuls. Serial killings with sexual overtones were a unique phenomenon in the reporters' experience. In describing the events and their perpetrator, they drew upon the familiar conventions of
popular melodrama and Gothic horror—SLAUGHTER BY THE EAST-END FIEND and
HORRIBLE MURDER BY THE MONSTER OF THE EAST-END were among the headlines

that cast the story in lurid hues. Jack the Ripper soon became mythic, the archetype of the sex murderer, although in fact he did not rape his victims. Before long, imitators with their own dark and violent desires would perpetuate the myth and the horror. In 1889, only a year after the original crimes, a copycat killer terrorized London with another series of murders. Two years later, across the Atlantic, yet another ripper murdered and mutilated a prostitute in a Manhattan hotel. Such crimes would become all too familiar in the next century.

While Jack and his first successors laid their trail of carnage, others who dealt in sexualized violence were also active. As the Victorian period approached its end, pornographers and their trade continued to flourish. In addition to its long-established practice of reducing women and anyone vulnerable to objects and victims, of representing sexuality as the sum of body parts and mechanical acts, pornography increasingly went further. Bestiality, sodomy, and the most sadistic brutalities were among its common themes by the end of the century.

Around 1890 the monument of all Victorian pornography was published. In a purported autobiography, *My Secret Life*, the pseudonymous author, "Walter," ranged obsessively through the entire spectrum of sexual behavior. Nothing was too perverse, no physiological detail too basic for his notice. He chose his title with unintentional irony. Anything but secretive, he explicitly told all in eleven volumes and a total of 4,200 pages.

As "Walter" penned his personal sexual inventory with fixated industriousness, others were busily engaged in their own version of sexual cataloging. In the interest of scientific advancement, the sexologists literally and figuratively dissected bodies into parts for objective study. They labeled all the diverse expressions of human sexuality and sorted them into abstract categories of "normal" and "abnormal" behavior. Not unlike the pornographer, theirs was a fragmented view of the sexual body. At least one of their number, the German sexologist Krafft-Ebing, additionally validated pornography's representation of women as inherent victims. In his *Psychopathia Sexualis* he illuminated what he believed to be the "normal" activity of men and contrasting passivity of women—the basis for the "natural" male-dominant, often sadomasochistic relationship of the sexes.

But, fortunately for Victorian sexuality and the welfare of women, as late as 1900 people generally knew little or nothing of the work of sexologists. Neither did any but an obsessive minority indulge in pornography or share the dark desires it served. The majority thus lacked the facility to objectify sex and eroticize violence.

Many, of course, escaped momentarily into the lurid fantasies of fiction, but and long to be able to give my time and energy solely to those public affairs that legitimately relate to the honourable trust which you have committed to me."

(General Harrison's term in the Senate expired March 4, 1887, and the Legislature to choose his successor was to be elected in the fall of 1886. That campaign was largely General Harrison's campaign. He was almost the only prominent Republican in Indiana who felt confident of carrying the State, or who thought it worth while even to attempt to carry the Legislature. The result attested General Harrison's wisdom and his work. The Republicans carried the State, and came within a hair's-breadth of carrying the Legislature. By a goodly majority was General Harrison chosen the next President, in preference to President Cleveland. The final returns of the Presidential election show that General Harrison received 238 electoral votes, and Mr. Cleveland 168. General Harrison has the happiness to be united to a sympathetic and intelligent wife, and both emphatically declare Marriage is not a failure.

THE MURDER OF MARY KELLY IN WHITECHAPEL.

... deeply the commission of yet another murderous outrage on an unfortunate woman in Whitechapel has stirred the heart of London can hardly be imagined by those living at any distance from the Metropolis. The stillness of the Home Office, the discipline of Great Scotland-yard, and the routine life of every town household have been ruffled by this ghastly assassination, one more in the series of sanguinary outrages in Whitechapel which have shocked humanity. The morning of Lord Mayor's Day was chosen for the perpetration of this hideous crime. While London was decking itself in flags and garlands of flowers, and preparing for a day of festivity, in which thousands of the poor were charitably invited by Lord Mayor Whitehead to join, almost in the midst of the preparation a deed was being done of which one can think only with shuddering horror. The tragedy took place very near the sites of the former Whitechapel murders.

DORSET-STREET,

lying almost under the shadow of Spitalfields Church, is a short street, composed largely of common lodging-houses, in one of which Annie Chapman, a previous victim, used sometimes to lodge. About half way down this street on the right-hand side is

MILLER'S-COURT,

the entrance to which is a narrow arched passage, and within a few yards of which, by the way, there licensed genially through the murky air a partly torn-down bill announcing a reward of £100 for the discovery of the murderer on the last occasion. There are six two-roomed houses in Miller's-court, all of them owned by

MR. J. M'CARRTY,

a grocer, whose shop in Dorset-street forms one corner of the entrance to the court. The houses are let out in separate rooms "furnished"—that is to say, there are in each of them a bed and a table, and, perhaps, one or two odds and ends. For these rooms rents are supposed to be paid daily, but of course they will sometimes get a good deal in arrear. This was the case with one of the tenants, who had occupied a ground-floor room on the right-hand side of the court for about twelve months. This was the poor young woman, Mary Kelly, the victim of the murderer familiarly called "Jack the Ripper."

HOW THE MURDER WAS DISCOVERED.

It appears that by the Ninth of November, Mary Kelly, described as a comely, fair young woman, of the "unfortunate" class, was as much as fourteen shillings in arrear with her rent, and the landlord sent one of his men about eleven o'clock in the morning to see what he could get. The door was fastened, not that it had been locked from the inside, but having a catch-lock the person who had gone out last had merely slammed the door behind him, and it had thus become fastened. The man, failing to get any answer by knocking, went to the window, which had been broken and patched by rags for some time past, and on pushing the rags aside was startled by the sight of blood,

HARRY BOWYER, "INDIAN HARRY."

who is also sketched by one of our Artists, ran back in some alarm to the shop, and told Mr. M'Carthy, his employer, what he had seen, and the two returned. It soon became evident to them that another murder had been committed, and they instantly ran for the police. Officers were at once on the spot, and a communication was made to Dr. Phillips, of Spital-square, the divisional surgeon, who arrived within ten minutes or so of the discovery of the affair—at about a quarter-past eleven, that is to say. It is understood that one of the first steps taken was to dispatch a telegram to Scotland-yard giving information of the occurrence, and intimating that everything had been left absolutely untouched, in order to facilitate the employment of bloodhounds if it were thought expedient to try them. For some reason the hounds were not employed.

DR. PHILLIPS

had by this time been joined by other medical gentlemen, including Dr. Dukes and Dr. Bond, of Westminster Hospital. The spectacle that was presented on the door being thrown open was ghastly in the extreme. The body of Mary Kelly was so horribly hacked and gashed that, but for the long hair, it was scarcely possible to say with any certainty that it was the body of a woman lying entirely naked on the wretched bed, with legs outspread and drawn up to the trunk. The ears and nose had been slashed off, the flesh cut from one cheek, and the throat cut through to the bone. In addition to this, one breast had been removed, the flesh roughly torn from the thigh, and the abdomen ripped up in previous cases, the organs having been removed from the trunk and laid on the table beside the bed. In addition to the various mutilations thus described there were miscellaneous cuts and slashes about the person of the unfortunate young woman, as though her fiendish assailant, having exhausted his ingenuity in systematic destruction, had

given a few random parting strokes before pocketing his weapon and going out into the night. The police safeguarded Miller's-court. Two men were stationed at the head of the court to keep out all persons, but in the road—in Dorset-street, that is—for some days there was a shifting throng of people largely composed of the roughest of women and labouring men.

MRS. PAUMIER'S SUSPICIONS.

Mrs. Paumier, who sells roasted chestnuts, as limned, at the corner of Widegate-street; a thoroughfare about two minutes' walk from the scene of the murder, stated that about twelve o'clock that (Friday) morning a man dressed like a gentleman came to her and said—

"I suppose you have heard about the murder in Dorset-street?" She replied that she had. Whereupon the man grinned, and said, "I know more about it than you." He then stared into her face and went down Sandy's-row, another narrow thoroughfare which cuts across Widegate-street. When he had got some way off, however, he looked back, as if to see whether she was watching him, and then vanished. Mrs. Paumier said the man had a black moustache, was about 5 ft. 6 in. high, and wore a black silk hat, a black coat, and speckled trousers. He also carried a black shiny bag, about a foot in depth and a foot and a half in length. Mrs. Paumier stated further that the same man accosted three young girls whom she knows on the previous night, and they chaffed him, and asked him what he had in the bag, and he replied, "Something that the ladies don't like!"

they shared the comforting knowledge that the only liquid truly spilled in that realm was ink, not blood. Similarly, although the real-life rampage of Jack the Ripper had deeply horrified the newspaper-reading public, it was still imbued with the unreality of fiction—atrocity at a safe remove from the experience of all but the immediate neighborhood. And, like other journalistic sensations, its currency was short-lived. Throughout the Victorian period, for most people, the more absorbing preoccupation was not the suffering of others, but the everyday joys—and ills—of their own susceptible flesh.

CHAPTER 6

Flesh and Blood

POUDRE D'AMOUR

A toilet powder for the complexion, also for the nursery, roughness of the skin,
after shaving, &c. Hygienic, and prepared with pure and harmless materials.
Price 1s.

—Advertisement, *Bow Bells* magazine,

October 11, 1895

Poudre d'amour—Powder of Love. As the product's name suggests, caring for the
erotic side of life sometimes required tending to the unromantic ills and imperfec-
tions of the flesh. Rough skin was among the least of the troubles that beset Victorian bodies. The same magazine page that advertised the French talcum powder
also helped to promote Madame Frain's Famous Female Mixture—"*powerful* and
effective" but "will not injure the most delicate"—and Clarke's World-Famed
Blood Mixture for "Scrofula, Scurvy, Eczema, Bad Legs, Skin and Blood Diseases,
Pimples, and Sores of all kinds."

All over England and America, other magazines and papers advertised an array
of similar products. Many purportedly alleviated such general ills and complaints
as acne, digestive problems, constipation, and toothache. Others, like Madame
Frain's mixture (purveyed to induce abortion), were for treating or preventing
conditions directly related to sexuality—Lydia E. Pinkham's Vegetable Com-

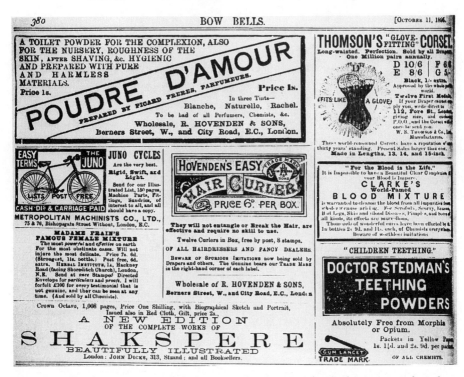

Late Victorian advertisements, including Poudre d'amour, Clarke's Blood Mixture, and Madame Frain's Famous Female Mixture for "obstinate cases" of pregnancy

pound for menstrual cramps and other "female weaknesses," pessaries for dropped wombs, diaphragms ("The Wife's Protectors"), syringes for douching, and condoms, probably used less for contraception than for guarding against venereal disease. "RUBBER GOODS," proclaimed a typical advertisement in an 1898 issue of *Photo Bits,* a slightly naughty gentlemen's magazine, *"Men, be careful! Prevention is better than Cure!"*

Other than patent medicines and related products, people had recourse to home remedies—hot baths, herbal teas, and potions—for minor ailments. For more serious ills, those who could afford it consulted doctors. As last resorts, there were also private hospitals, health spas, and sanitoriums for the well-off, and charitable institutions for the poor. No one, regardless of sex, or however circumspect and virtuous, was immune from everyday bodily troubles, or even from the threat of venereal infection. But, because of the monthly cycle, childbirth, menopause, and limited medical knowledge about the female body, women were more liable than men to suffer from the ills and discomforts of the flesh and blood.

Once a Month

Victorian girls probably entered puberty at a somewhat later age than would their descendants in the next century. Nineteenth-century statistics are scarce and not necessarily accurate, but all sources considered, it appears that the majority began menstruating during their mid-teens. While some girls were undoubtedly surprised by the event, most, it seems, had had some advance preparation. In the 1890s Dr. Helen P. Kennedy surveyed 125 American high school girls and found that over half had received at least a measure of instruction from their mothers. For girls who could not count on maternal frankness, older sisters, friends, perhaps a teacher, and, by the end of the century, a few guidance books for young women were alternative sources of information.

For most of the Victorian era, menstruating must have been something of an inconvenience for most women. In England the disposable sanitary towel did not appear on the market until the 1880s and, at a shilling or two a dozen, was not universally affordable. In America, Johnson and Johnson's "Lister's Towel" was first manufactured in 1896 but did not reach many women, and it would be twenty-five more years before Kimberley Clark brought out the Kotex sanitary napkin. Before the development of such products, women used homemade pads or diapers of flannel or other absorbent material that they washed and reused. These were bulky, awkward to wear, and often chafed the skin.

Some women additionally suffered from premenstrual symptoms or painful periods. Novelist Olive Schreiner, author of *The Story of an African Farm* (1883), found working difficult just before her period, and poet Elizabeth Barrett Browning was troubled by menstrual cramps. Reflecting the conventional beliefs of their day, doctors were apt to attribute menstrual problems such as pain and heavy flow to social or moral excesses rather than to physiological causes. Rich food, dancing, late nights, "prurient incitations" from "thoughts, books, pictures, &c.," as well as "indulgences in unlawful contacts," were all to be avoided. Masturbation among girls and women did not arouse the same concern as male "solitary vice" and the wastage of sperm, but it was nonetheless widely proscribed as yet another cause of menstrual discomforts and general female debility.

Remedies for cramps and related problems were no more advanced than medical knowledge of their causes. Opium was easily available and led to addiction in some women, Elizabeth Barrett Browning perhaps among them; and Lydia Pinkham's compound was a suspension of roots and seeds in 19 percent alcohol. Although undoubtedly there were women who suffered from troublesome periods, the majority did not perpetually have to resort to dubious patent medicines. As many women doctors insisted, menstruation was not an illness, and in most women of good health, serious cyclical disruptions of normal activity were rare. This would not have been startling news to women in general—neither to those who continued to run middle-class households and pursue their regular social life, nor to the working-class women who never missed a day at the factory, shop, or home in which they served. In other words, the image of the weak, vaporing Victorian woman languishing prone on her fainting couch several days a month is largely a myth.

It was created principally by nineteenth-century medical men and sustained by others who found it a convenient rationale for denying women access to higher education and the professions. Operating from cultural assumptions and incomplete understanding of the female body, male doctors especially were apt to exaggerate normal cyclical discomforts and inconveniences into debilitating illness. In the August 1875 issue of the *American Journal of Obstetrics and Diseases of Women and Children,* Dr. A. F. A. King, professor of obstetrics at George Washington University, summarized the medical consensus that menstruation was an essentially unhealthy "modification" of the "natural" female "procreative office." "In the strictest sense of the word, therefore, menstruation is a disease . . . a departure from nature."

From there it was no less than logical to conclude that women were victims of their periods and unfit for positions of responsibility outside the home. Equally, they were unable to bear the strain of a university education, which required a level of "equanimity" that only men could achieve. Furthermore, the experts claimed, intellectual activity would worsen ordinary cyclical infirmities and possibly result in permanent damage to the female organs and reproductive functioning. They were not so worried about the effects of physical labor on working-class women. Happily for the existing order of things, doctors and other middle-class authorities were less likely to consider factory work and domestic service to be as harmful or as difficult for the menstruating woman as mental exertion.

Misguided Gynecology

Apart from its utility in helping to maintain the status quo, the idea of menstruation as disease was part of a larger medical tendency to equate femininity and pathology. As doctors would have it, the ovaries and uterus were the culprits in female ill health of all kinds. Headaches, sore throats, indigestion, disorders of the kidneys, liver, or heart, even tuberculosis—all these and more they diagnosed as symptoms of a primary "disease of the womb." At mid-century in both England

and America, treatments were mostly ineffectual as well as horrific. They included injections of milk, water, or tea into the uterus; the application of leeches to the vulva or cervix; and cautery, either by chemical means such as silver nitrate or with a "white-hot iron" instrument—and, excepting perhaps a little opium or alcohol, no anesthetic was used for this procedure. Later in the century doctors added surgery to their gynecological repertoire. Removal of the ovaries was the most common operation. In rare cases, where a woman's symptoms included nympho-mania or incorrigible masturbation, the clitoris was excised.

Wisely, the majority of women apparently ignored the medical characterization of femininity as illness, avoided the worst "cures," and continued to go about their daily business. Some, however, accepted the role of invalid, even used it to escape the burden of constant reproduction and the monotony of domestic responsibili-ties. Others, almost exclusively women of means, found a more dramatic way to protest both the confines of their lives and medicine's effort to enfeeble femininity. This was hysteria, a syndrome that became widespread in England, the United States, and throughout Europe. It showed itself variously in fainting spells, thrash-ing limbs, inability to speak, loss of appetite, fits of coughing or sneezing, and hys-terical screaming, laughing, or crying.

Doctors responded inconsistently. On the one hand, most insisted that hysteria had a physical cause, none other, of course, than a diseased womb—the word "hysteria" in fact comes from the Greek word for uterus. Yet the profession must also have regarded it as a behavioral disorder, for treatment was not so much med-ical as punitive. Among the measures doctors advocated (and received fees for) were stern lectures, suffocation until the fits stopped, beating the patient across the face and body with wet towels, embarrassing her in front of family and friends, and threatening to give her cold showers or shave her head. Apparently, fear and humiliation were powerful weapons in gynecology's arsenal. In other words, while doctors held fast to the dogma of the defective womb, they must have had an inkling of the true nature of hysteria. Not a disease, and social rather than physical in origin, it was women's rebellion against the limitations on their lives and the medicalization of their bodies.

The final crisis in woman's supposed life of disease was menopause. Doctors generally associated "the changes" or "cessation" with illness, especially mental disorder. This they believed might take many forms—delirium, mania, melancho-lia, suicidal tendencies, perversion of moral instincts, uncontrollable peevishness, dipsomania, erotomania, and so on. The predominantly male medical establish-ment also linked menopause (as it came to be known in the 1870s) to a number of physical complaints, including rheumatism, hemorrhoids, diarrhea, constipation, and even syphilis. Treatments for menopause and its purported symptoms ranged from diets, rest cures, and patent medicines to such misguided procedures as cautery, astringent washes, and the insertion of pessaries to correct the position of the womb. According to prevailing cultural prejudice, the woman who survived menopause and the ministrations of her physicians had little to look forward to. Her sexual and reproductive life now at an end, her value accordingly diminished, menopause signaled "the death of the woman in the woman," as one medical authority proclaimed it.

Several women doctors and many of their patients knew better. While some medical women adhered to the tenets of their training and adopted the masculine view of menopause as disease, others took an alternative approach. Except in cases of hemorrhaging, they insisted, medical intervention was unnecessary, and healthy diet and moderate habits would alleviate routine symptoms like hot flashes. Further, they said, the women who remained well far outnumbered those who fell sick. And, far from being a debilitating illness, the change of life was often a time of increased physical energy and enhanced intellectual and creative endeavor.

Eliza Farnham, the social reformer and author of *Woman and Her Era* (1864), agreed. She described menopause as a "regenerative" period, "where the ultimate brightest glory of earthly Womanhood alone is seen or enjoyed." A participant in Dr. Clelia Mosher's 1892 survey of middle-class American women supported this view. The respondent reported steadily improving health, no "nervous disturbance" whatever, and impressive stores of energy—she did all her own housework and walked "15 miles without feeling it." Not only that, but she wrote and published three books in six years. She confessed, however, to something of a decline in "*passionate* feeling," but "intercourse is still agreeable to me," she hastened to add. As Farnham believed, many other women must have taken pleasure in their advancing age, new activities, and freedom from the responsibilities of motherhood. The trouble was, she explained, that "universal masculine judgment" dictated that menopause was only to be viewed as "a loss of Power."

Delicate and Dangerous Conditions

The devaluation of the menopausal woman and the medical conception of menstruation as disease grew out of the widespread conviction that reproduction was the primary female purpose. Dr. King, the American obstetrics professor, declared pregnancy to be the "only *strictly* natural course" of womanhood. But with dubious logic doctors also stressed the delicate condition of the expectant mother. She was to avoid ugly or upsetting sights, angry thoughts, erotic fantasies, her husband's breath if he had indulged in tobacco or alcohol, and too much reading or intellectual stimulation.

Maternity or "lying-in" hospitals existed in the Victorian period, but the majority of women gave birth at home. Middle-class women would have had a doctor in attendance. Those who could not afford the physician's fee were assisted by a local midwife or perhaps a friend or family member with practical experience. Albert Goodwin, son of a Stoke pottery worker and a domestic servingwoman, was born in 1890 into a comparatively prosperous working-class household. In his memoirs he told the story of his birth and preparations for it, all under the auspices of "Nurse Lewis," who was not a trained nurse but "the woman from the shop next door, . . . a motherly person . . . with a reputation for successful deliveries":

> A strong wooden box, which had usually contained "Hudson Soap" or tins of salmon had to be procured . . . so that it could be placed against the bottom bedrail and be a purchase for the woman to press her feet against at the time of delivery. . . . A bath tin holding 2 gals of water was also a most important item at these times.
>
> . . . And the preparation for the birth included the getting down of the bed from upstairs and re-erection in the "parlour". Preparation for a fire in the parlour grate must be made and plenty of candles (4d. per dozen) must be got in so that there could be all the light necessary. The fire in the kitchen must be banked up for the night so that if the accouchment took place at an awkward time there would be plenty of hot water at a few minutes notice. This fire was the only means of heating and therefore a big iron kettle . . . was placed on the hob of the grate ready to pop on the fire. . . . All these things had to be done in the hope that the delivery would be normal and straightforward because if the doctor had to be called a bill would be presented and as it was a matter of a guinea, it became a matter of economic necessity to try and avoid this. My entry was a normal one except that I was told later I cried for 17 hrs non-stop and drove everybody up the wall.

While births could often be as uncomplicated as Goodwin's, it was an ironic truth that the culmination of Victorian woman's purportedly healthiest state was the event that put her life at greatest risk. For women of both the middle and working classes, childbirth carried with it a number of potential complications. Among them were infection, slipped uterus, and irreparable pelvic tearing. Poverty, inadequate diet, overwork during pregnancy, and, in some cases, industrial diseases probably increased the potential for birth complications among working women.

At the same time, maternal childbed deaths did not clearly relate to social class. Neither the doctors who presided over middle-class births nor working-class midwives were necessarily able to deal adequately with such labor emergencies as hemorrhaging. Additionally, whether attended by doctor or midwife, all women were at risk of serious infection. The septic condition known as childbed or puerperal fever was caused by the common streptococci bacteria. These, despite increasingly hygienic practices in the medical profession—scrubbing up, for instance—could easily be carried in the nose or on the hands of the birth attendant. Some doctors refused to believe that they could be implicated in childbed infection and callously claimed that the streptococci originated in the vagina and were activated by sexual intercourse in the later stages of pregnancy.

Because of health risks associated with childbirth, economic pressures on working people, and, quite possibly, sheer physical and emotional exhaustion, many married women and their husbands, regardless of class, tried to limit the size of their families. There were also those who campaigned for birth control out of a concern for overpopulation and the poverty and social problems they believed it would engender. Other social reformers and feminists advocated family planning as a means of improving the physical and psychological welfare of women. Through tracts distributed by such groups, advertisements for patent medicines, as well as information shared among mothers, daughters, sisters, and female friends, most women had some knowledge of existing means of birth control.

The problem was that much of the information was inaccurate or incomplete, and several of the methods were widely unacceptable, inaccessible to many, or unreliable. Women and men alike generally held the condom in disfavor because of its long-standing association with prostitution and disease. The more acceptable as well as relatively dependable diaphragm, available since mid-century, was principally for middle-class wives who could afford both the device and the doctor's fee for fitting it. Douching, which was not effective anyway, was widely recommended but was not a practical option for the many working-class women who lacked privacy and a sufficient water supply. Among both the middle and the working classes, the most common form of contraception was probably coitus interruptus. Because of the uncertainty of the method, however, many experts advised against it and instead recommended that women bear the responsibility of family limitation through douching and the use of the vaginal sponge, which grew in popularity during the second half of the nineteenth century.

Although some doctors fitted diaphragms or privately dispensed birth control information, in the main they publicly opposed all mechanical means of contraception. They also denounced coitus interruptus, arguing that it was a form of masturbation that could lead to physical and mental illness. Anxious to promote their own authority and respectability, they supported three "natural" strategies: abstinence, prolonged nursing, and rhythm. The first was difficult for most people but, if adopted, at least it worked. The others did not. The fallibility of the rhythm method was augmented by the profession's general misunderstanding of the monthly cycle. According to medical consensus, the "safe period" for intercourse was ten to twelve days after the menses—precisely the time when a woman was in fact *most* likely to conceive.

Whether or not she followed misguided medical advice, no woman was safe from unwanted pregnancy. Many simply resigned themselves to the situation, but the more desperate resorted to abortion. Among the choices of means were a number of patent medicines taken orally. Many, like Madame Frain's mixture, were useless. Others, such as strong purgatives or diachylon, a lead compound in pill form, could potentially produce the desired result. There were also efficacious folk remedies such as ergot of rye and slippery elm. But reliable abortifacients were also poisonous and had to be used with care. Instrumental procedures were more dangerous still. Whether performed by an abortionist or the woman herself, the insertion into the womb of metal probes, knitting needles, or sharpened wooden implements could cause serious internal damage or fatal infection. While a few qualified doctors secretly performed abortions, most refused and publicly took to the moral high ground, opposing the practice—and leaving women to their own devices and the attendant risks.

The Veil of Modesty Torn Aside

Apart from real or medically created problems with the monthly cycle and reproduction, there were other conditions mainly or exclusively female. Anemia, vaginal infections, and cancers of the breast, cervix, uterus, and ovaries—the symptoms of any of these would have been more than enough to prompt many women to seek medical attention. Because they had the necessary time and means, middle-class women were the group who had the greatest recourse to doctors. They were also, therefore, more likely than working-class women to suffer from misguided, even harmful treatments and, perhaps in some cases, willful abuse in the guise of medical authority.

Among women who could afford to visit a doctor, there were no doubt some who resisted doing so out of an excess of modesty. In *Studies in the Psychology of Sex* Havelock Ellis relayed an anecdote, originally told by the actress Fanny Kemble, about another of her profession who was "accustomed to appear in tights, but who died a martyr to modesty rather than allow a surgeon to see her inflamed knee." If this apocryphal-sounding story is true, it was also exceptional. Most women with a health problem abandoned modesty and accepted medical examination as a necessary unpleasantness.

For problems involving the female reproductive organs, internal examination by hand and speculum, a metal instrument for dilating the vagina, was routine. At the best of times such procedures required considerable forbearance on the patient's part, and her discomfort could easily be magnified by a clumsy or insensitive doctor. Some medical men, influenced apparently by the prevailing obsession with female hysteria and associated nymphomania, mistook forbearance for pleasure and claimed that a number of respectable women were sexually aroused by medical intrusion into their bodies. A twenty-five-year-old British physician, Robert Brudenell Carter, implied that some "young unmarried women, of the middle class of society" regarded the doctor's speculum as a pleasurable alternative to "solitary vice" and asked "every medical practitioner . . . to institute an examination of the sexual organs."

Such claims by doctors may have had some basis in reality, but they also echoed a motif in the male pornographic imagination—the doctor-as-seducer theme—and actual instances were probably very rare. Certainly, tales of patients' arousal do not appear to have been widely credited and possibly contributed to the already low esteem in which certain groups held male doctors. The author of the 1856 *Hints to Husbands*, by "One of the Guild," spoke for others of his kind who were opposed to "man-midwifery"—the practice of obstetrics and gynecology by men. He inveighed against the "hateful indecency" of internal examination by hand. The physician, he warned his fellow husbands, "is mortal like other men" and, he added with emphasis, "*the very inmost secrets of your wife's person* are known to him, the veil of modesty has been rudely torn aside, and the sanctity of marriage exists but in the name." Not surprisingly, he further deplored the speculum, the use of which "is now becoming general; and its employment plunges its wretched victim, woman, down into the lowest deep of infamy and degradation."

Feminists who campaigned for enhanced political, economic, and educational rights for women also objected to the speculum examination. It was, they argued, the ultimate symbol of women's subordinate social position and definition principally in terms of sex. In 1887 one of their leaders, Josephine Butler, described the procedure as "the concrete expression of the will and determination of a certain portion of male humanity to subject womanhood to be an instrument to the convenience and lust of men." Physician Elizabeth Blackwell condemned the "common resort" to the speculum as an "evil" that was performed recklessly and often unnecessarily. In their excessive use of it, she contended, male doctors were violating women and abusing their professional power.

The concern she shared with other women about the propriety and necessity of the speculum examination was at the center of the larger issue of male domination of the medical profession. Blackwell herself was among the first of the pioneers who successfully challenged women's exclusion from the schools of medicine. More and more women followed her example, and by 1900 a number were practicing in Britain and America. But for the most part medicine remained a profession for men. The choices for most Victorian women were to submit to their not always informed or compassionate ministrations, or to rely instead upon midwives, folk remedies, and patent medicines. The only other alternative was endurance while nature took its course and either effected a cure or brought final release from suffering.

Upon the Rack of Sex

Preoccupied with the medicalization of women, doctors did not devote comparable attention to the male sexual body. As men themselves for the most part, they were not inclined to view masculinity as an illness. For the Victorians, the central problem of the male body was social rather than medical. To function effectively as leaders, economic contributors, husbands, and fathers of healthy offspring, men needed to establish and maintain a balance between unrestricted carnal gratification and self-control. To prevent the wastage of valuable energy and sperm, sexual urges had to be properly managed.

"Man is forever stretched out upon the rack of sex," wrote the autobiographer William Bowyer, keeper of ceramics at the Victoria and Albert Museum, recalling his days as a young man in Victorian London. But there were ways to lessen the torture. A determined man could limit his sexual encounters and avoid masturbation by cultivating pure thoughts, working hard, and above all by espousing the Victorians' favorite strategy, sport. Medical intervention was generally not called for.

The main exceptions were cases of intractable masturbation and chronic nocturnal emission. In the most extreme circumstances a doctor might perform surgery to restrict blood circulation to the genitals and inhibit erection. Otherwise, there were a number of patent preventives on the market. These included a belt-like apparatus that encased the genitals, a device to keep the bedcovers from coming into contact with susceptible body parts, ointments to make the genitals too tender to touch comfortably, and urethral rings. These were worn on the penis at night, and the sharp inner points with which they were equipped caused pain enough to awaken the wearer at the start of an erection.

The boys and men who underwent such abuse must inevitably have developed feelings of shame or fear concerning their sexuality. But those who escaped the indignity of the urethral ring and comparable "treatments" were not necessarily free from sexual guilt and anxieties. With the widespread Victorian concern about sperm-wasting "solitary vice," there was a proliferation of antimasturbation scare tracts distributed by religious groups and various societies. Few men would have reached adulthood without encountering one, and the typically grim warnings about the insanity and disease that would eventually plague the masturbator must have adversely affected the sexual attitudes of many sensitive readers.

Others, it seems, remained happily worry-free, for the simple reason that they were entirely mystified as to the cause of all the admonitory furor. In his autobiography John Paton, a baker's apprentice in turn-of-the-century Scotland, recollected that as a young man he had been both a dedicated athlete and reader of weekly magazines "devoted to the cult of bodily health":

> These weeklies were curious productions. Amid the deep-breathing exercises and the model dietaries were scattered, as a sort of recurring theme, cautionary paragraphs against something they euphemistically termed "secret vice". "Secret vice", it appeared was THE danger to guard against. . . .
>
> The editors, evidently, were all hot and bothered by the awful thing—whatever it was. The nameless thing excited my curiosity and greatly exercised my mind. It was obviously of great importance but I'd no idea what it could be.

He inquired among contemporaries at his athletic club and found that they too were "puzzled."

Finally, upon asking a senior member, Paton was disappointed to learn that the "secret vice" was nothing more than masturbation. "My lively imagination," he explained, "had been busy with the possibilities of unheard-of and exciting things." He had previously conducted his private experiments and was now blasé about the whole business. But others, he reported, were more enthralled and, suffering no ill effects, persisted in their indulgence:

> Masturbation was no novelty. It had been familiar to me for years as quite general among my associates. Some of the boys I knew were addicts—and made

no secret of it. Like others of my kind, I'd been at one time experimental, but it didn't attract me greatly and I formed no habit. I couldn't understand what the fuss was about. The fellows who were known to me as addicted to the practice were no different physically from the rest. Quite manifestly from their athletic feats, they were not "feeble" nor did they lack "vitality".

Apart from the dubious education on offer in the antimasturbation literature, boys and young men learned about sex from talking among themselves in the street, at school, or in the workplace. Bowyer remembered that when he was a junior bank employee "the chief topic of conversation among the Boy Clerks at the Savings Bank was sex. 'Talking smut', as it was called, was as popular as it is in any boarding-school for older boys." Paton had similar memories of the "'blue' stories and anecdotes" that were "inexhaustible" in the bakehouse where he had been apprenticed. He had also gained some rudimentary knowledge of female "private parts" from a work of pornography loaned him by a friend. Another autobiographer, Birmingham-born journalist V. W. Garratt, acquired his earliest sexual knowledge from Bible class, where the "gestures and whisperings" of his schoolmates helped to clarify "the sex lore of Leviticus." In the end, a young man learned from experience, whether it was a homoerotic schoolboy relationship (which might be anything from affectionately platonic to actively sexual), a tentative encounter with a willing female acquaintance, or a visit to a brothel, although this last was not the established rite of passage in England and America that it was in France.

Male sexual education, in other words, was generally haphazard. As a result, there was much that the average man did not know about his own body, including perhaps the ills to which it was prey. While men's bodies were never medicalized to the extent that women's were, there were a few predominantly male afflictions that required a doctor's attention. Men more than women, for example, were apt to develop bladder or kidney stones and certain types of hernias. Additionally, some older men suffered from an inflamed or enlarged prostate; the former made ejaculation and urination painful, while common side effects of the latter were a dropped anus and severe hemorrhoids. Cancers of the penis and prostate were also risks for some men—as preventives, doctors prescribed better personal hygiene and, as the nineteenth century wore on, circumcision. Finally, however deficient their sexual education might have been, most men knew that promiscuity or simple bad luck could bring them into contact with a venereal disease. And there was one in particular that they dreaded.

Contagion

Syphilis had been around for centuries, but public anxiety was perhaps never greater than it was in the mid-nineteenth century. The second major venereal disease, gonorrhea, did not generally cause the same level of concern—perhaps because it did not manifest itself as dramatically. The symptoms of syphilis could be fearful indeed. Caused by a bacterium (*Treponema pallidum*) and transmitted principally through sexual intercourse, the disease has three stages. The first is marked by the appearance of an ulcerous sore at the site of infection and enlargement of nearby lymph nodes; left untreated, the infection progresses to stage two, whose symptoms may include new lesions anywhere on the body, fever, painful joints, and hair loss; finally, without effective treatment, tertiary syphilis develops, with characteristic tumorlike masses in the soft tissues, and may be followed by damage to the vital organs, paralysis, deafness, blindness, or dementia. In the Victorian period there was no certain cure. The usual treatment was a compound of mercury, applied topically or ingested in pill form, depending on the precise symptoms. This was little better than the disease—mercury is poisonous, and in many patients produced such nightmarish side effects as ulcerated jaws, tongues, and palates, swollen purple gums, loosened teeth, fetid breath, and excess salivation.

Apart from the dread that its symptoms and treatment inspired, syphilis caused acute concern on broader social and moral grounds. The result was the passage of the Contagious Diseases Acts, enforced from 1864 to 1883. Ostensibly conceived to curb venereal disease, especially syphilis, among soldiers and sailors, the legislation was in practice directed at the prostitutes the men used. Any woman in a port or garrison town suspected of being a prostitute was compelled to submit to a speculum examination for venereal infection. Those found to be infected were detained for treatment in special hospitals.

Feminists of the day opposed the Acts, recognizing them for what they were—an attempt to make scapegoats out of one vulnerable group. Economic desperation drove most women into prostitution while, conversely, the men who demanded their services had each made a free choice. Although prostitutes did in fact constitute the greatest number of female syphilitics, directing the legislation at them, and not at their clients as well, effectively condoned men's sexual excesses and overlooked their complicity in the spread of venereal disease. The Acts, argued feminists, officially reinforced a double standard of morality—one for men, another, harsher one for women. They condemned the predominantly male medical profession for its part in executing the laws, and from that point the speculum examination became for them a symbol of the subjection of all women by all men.

Feminist critics were also angered by the fact that there was no protection for wives. Treating prostitutes did not stop infected husbands from transmitting disease to their wives. Marriage manuals echoed the feminists' concern. In his manual for young husbands, Sylvanus Stall issued stern warnings about the "moral wrong" and "great physical risk" of philandering. This was not unfounded moralizing. As Elizabeth Blackwell and other physicians recognized, so-called female complaints could often be traced to venereal infection brought home by husbands.

After 1857, when divorce became available to the middle class and prosperous members of the working class, a number of women charged their husbands with the transmission of venereal disease. Among the court records from the late 1850s and early 1860s is the petition of Jane Brocas, an upper-middle-class wife whose husband, Bernard, infected her with syphilis during her pregnancy. The doctor who treated her advised a period of abstinence from sexual intercourse. But Bernard continued to force himself on her, "in spite of her entreaties," and infected her a second time. When she begged him to have a thought for the gravity and infectiousness of his disease, he heartlessly replied that he would "'use' her as long as he chose." It was "not that he cared for her," he added, but simply that "he chose to make 'use' of her."

Although Bernard's behavior was especially cruel and irresponsible, the plight of his wife was not unique. Divorce petitions by women who charged that their husbands had infected them with a venereal disease accounted for almost one-fifth of all petitions filed by wives between 1858 and 1901. Such actions helped to upset the double standard imbedded in the Contagious Diseases Acts by holding the men answerable for their role in the spread of venereal infection. The courts for the most part ruled in favor of the wives.

Struck Powerless of Body and Mind

Venereal disease was undoubtedly the most devastating assailant of both the sexual body and the relationship of men and women. But there were other ills, often not physical in origin, which eroded romance and denied fulfillment. Sexual problems troubled some people occasionally, others constantly. In either circumstance, "mutual connections," as the anonymous author of *Men's Duties to Women* (1852) delicately phrased it, could engender "disappointment, grief, remorse and misery."

Impotence was a common source of such disappointment. Although it could be caused by a physiological condition such as diabetes, the Victorians correctly understood it as principally a psychological disorder when it occurred in young men.

Nervous bridegrooms were particularly susceptible to the problem. Charles Kingsley spoke for many when he confided to Fanny his concern that on their wedding night he might be "struck powerless of body and mind." While his fear turned out to be unfounded, others were not so fortunate. One bridegroom, caught in the vicious circle of his own anxiety, tried repeatedly throughout his wedding night, never once achieving the desired result. In the morning, desperate that his impotence should at least not be obvious to the hotel maid, he sprinkled red ink on the sheet. While this unhappy tale (recounted at a later date to Freud) confirms the importance the Victorians placed on female virginity, it also helps to dispel the stereotype of the trembling bride at the mercy of her lust-crazed groom. Sometimes this must indeed have been so, but on other occasions, clearly, it was the inexperienced husband whose terror was the greater.

In most cases, impotence was a temporary condition. In others, however, it was chronic. There is a certain irony in the fact that the sexologist Havelock Ellis was impotent throughout most, if not all, of his life. He did at least find alternative gratification in a specialized form of voyeurism: "undinism," as he called it, or sexual arousal from the sight of women urinating. This he celebrated in a sonnet with the somewhat sacrilegious title "Madonna":

> My lady once leapt sudden from the bed,
> Whereon she lay naked beside my heart,
> And stood with perfect poise, straight legs apart,
> And then from clustered hair of brownish red
> A wondrous fountain curve, all shyness fled,
> Arched like a liquid rainbow in the air,
> She cares not, she, what other women care,
> But gazed as it fell and faltered and was shed.

Taking on an exalted tone, the second stanza incongruously combines an image of "Virgin throned with saints above," and the poet's final tribute to his subject— "Life's symbol of joy's golden stream." Ellis's impotence was decidedly not of the ordinary kind.

Rarer, it seems, than male impotence was a condition in women that impeded intercourse. Vaginismus, a sudden and painful contraction of the vaginal muscles, could have a physical cause such as an inflammation of the bladder or vagina. But, like impotence, its origins were often emotional or psychological. Overcome with dread at the sex act, an unprepared or misinformed bride might have found that her body reacted accordingly. More commonly, however, such an aversion to intimacy did not manifest in so distinctively physical a manner. Women who feared or disliked sex simply found excuses to avoid it, refused it outright, or devised ways to tolerate it on occasion.

Poor general health, fear of pregnancy, or insufficiency of attraction to her spouse were all reasons why a woman might appear to be frigid—"passionless," as people in the nineteenth century were more likely to say. Sometimes it might also have been an attitude that a woman consciously cultivated as a way of exerting control in a relationship in which she felt otherwise powerless. In the first half of the Victorian period, expert opinion was divided as to whether passionlessness was indeed a dysfunction or simply the "normal" female state. Dr. Acton, the notorious author of *The Functions and Disorders of the Reproductive Organs* (1857), was the era's most dogmatic proponent of the latter view, and he had his followers— even though countless couples knew otherwise. As the century wore on, however, authorities moved toward a consensus that some measure of passion was natural and healthy in a woman. They were also increasingly inclined to blame a wife's coldness on a husband's inept or selfishly demanding lovemaking. Tenderness and moderation on the man's part were the usual recommendation.

But there were some circumstances in which this generally sound advice would not have served. Some couples' sexual difficulties arose from a want of desire on one or both sides, or from irreversible incompatibility of sexual needs and preferences. Often it must have been a combination of these factors in marriages that suffered from lack of the erotic. This seems to have been true, for instance, in the troubled relationship of the Archbishop of Canterbury Edward Benson and his wife, Mary. When they married in 1859, he was thirty, his bride eighteen. Although she was purportedly of a passionate disposition, she did not discover her true sexual nature until the age of thirty or so—and then it was not Edward, nor indeed any man, to whom she was attracted. After a series of attachments to women, she fell irrevocably in love with the daughter of her husband's predecessor as Archbishop. As for Benson, he suffered from chronic neuralgia, irritability, depressions, and constant preoccupation with work—all signs of sexual frustration.

Advances and Abuses

Frustration and its ills were by no means the common lot. There were many who enjoyed their measure of erotic fulfillment and knew little, if anything, of sexual dysfunction. The fortunate among them lived out their lives free from the worst ravages of disease, and without the trauma of harmful medical intervention. Most people had their occasional pains and discomforts, attended to them in the best ways they knew, and the rest of the time did what they could to enjoy the benefits of health and sexuality.

As the century drew to a close, medical science was making certain advances. Procedures to ensure antiseptic childbirth were rapidly becoming routine. Meanwhile, a developing knowledge of bacteriology was slowly eroding the fear of syphilis. In 1910 the arsenic derivative Salvarsan would replace the old, more dangerous mercury treatment. Antibiotics would later prove to be safer still and effective against both of the major venereal diseases.

Although growing more enlightened in some respects, most doctors publicly continued to oppose all but the rhythm method of birth control. On both sides of the Atlantic it would fall to early-twentieth-century crusaders like Margaret Sanger and Marie Stopes to provide women with the contraceptive information they needed to take control of their own bodies and lives. As many of their successors would do almost a hundred years in the future, turn-of-the-century medical men persisted in the profession's earlier policy of medicalizing menstruation, menopause, and femininity itself—some American doctors claimed to have removed from fifteen hundred to two thousand ovaries apiece. With medical advances and abuses came treatises, papers, theories, and analyses. Talk—and with that, sex became ever more part of the realm of medical abstraction, less by degrees an affair of warm flesh and blood.

At the end of their era, the greatest number of Victorian men and women remained unaware of how far doctors and related "experts" had already encroached upon their sexuality. Not yet personally affected for the most part, they carried on much as before. Whether in sickness or in health, they fell in love, looked after one another, and in all their various ways, carefully, quietly nurtured their mutual passion.

CHAPTER 7

The Remaking of Lovemaking

I am not a famous or even an infamous man, but I have had a love affair with
my only wife, in sunshine and showers, from the day when I first saw her
twenty-eight years ago.

—Reverend Edward John Hardy, dedication,
The Love Affairs of Some Famous Men, 1897

Reverend Hardy, a more obscure clergyman and author than his older contemporary Charles Kingsley, was clearly a no less devoted husband. Blessed in his own
union, he took an optimistic view of marriage in general. But he was also a realist
who knew that it was not a natural and inevitable state of felicity. He regarded it,
rather, as a crucial social institution to be maintained through ever-greater understanding of its difficulties and rewards. "The problem of the union of man and
woman," he wrote in the preface to *Love Affairs*, "must always remain the supreme
and central question of society; and this book is a small contribution to its elucidation." He then proceeded to discuss a number of individual marriages—many of
them as happy as his own, others anything but.

Almost a half-century earlier, the anonymous author of *Men's Duties to Women*
(1852) had also contributed to the "elucidation" of society's "supreme" union.
Like Hardy, this author regarded the institution positively, though with a pragma-
tism that would have dampened all but the most enthusiastic of romantics: "That

the amount of human suffering both physical and moral, is far greater in the unmarried than in the married classes of society, (in proportion with the population,) is proved by the statistical reports of health and morals." Clearly no sentimentalist, he or she also hastened to point out that emotional and sexual fulfillment were by no means universally the lot of the married.

Although this author wrote at mid-century and the reverend near its end, both acknowledged the same fundamental truths about the Victorian marriage. First, not everyone reaped its full rewards, and some knew only regret. More important, between the extremes of blissful and miserable wedlock, there were infinite variations in circumstance, behavior, and degree of mutual satisfaction. The couple's age, class, health, and level of prosperity all played their parts in distinguishing each union from the next. So too did individual temperaments and sexual proclivities. While every marriage represented the norm, each couple in its own unique way, conventionally or otherwise, for better or for worse, remade the ideal of lovemaking.

Countless in number, many of their stories are now lost to history. But others survived in memory to be told again. Overall, the impression that comes down through the years is that there were many like Reverend Hardy—great silent numbers of them, now mostly nameless—who found in reality the companionship, romance, and sexual joy that the ideal had promised.

For Better for Worse, for Richer for Poorer

In chronicling the love lives of the famous, Hardy exhibited the Victorian zeal for classification, arranging his subjects according to their professions. Much of his attention he devoted to men of letters. No one, he maintained, quoting the contemporary essayist James Payn, "derives so much benefit from the wedded state as do the brethren of the pen." Nathaniel Hawthorne, the Irish novelist Charles Lever, and the journalist George Augustus Sala were among the happy literary husbands whom Hardy found to have gained both personally and professionally from their unions.

But, staunch supporter of marriage though he was, the reverend was honest enough to admit that some writers experienced little but matrimonial woe. This was sometimes because "as husbands they did not amount to much." In other cases they were part of an "ill-assorted couple." Edward Bulwer-Lytton and his wife, Rosina, were incompatible by nature; Charles and Catherine Dickens grew apart over the years. But, as Hardy also recognized, similarity of interests and temperament did not necessarily guarantee marital tranquility.

Thomas Carlyle, the author of *Sartor Resartus* (1833–34) and *Past and Present* (1843), and his wife, Jane, a noted literary hostess and witty letter writer, were the mutual combatants in one of Victorian England's most notoriously turbulent marriages. According to Hardy, both husband and wife were high-strung, difficult personalities, and the "domestic barometer" frequently registered "stormy." But if they were the "chief tormentors of one another," they were also "sole comforters," and the marriage was not unsuccessful. It lasted forty years and enabled both to grow within it as distinct individuals. In the end, their friend Tennyson was witty but too harsh when he remarked that "it was a good thing that Carlyle and Mrs. Carlyle did marry each other, for otherwise there might have been four unhappy people instead of two."

Although Hardy principally took notice of the hapless marriages of some literary men, he would presumably have conceded that there were men in other callings whose marital troubles were more dramatic. Several British imperialists were distinguished by their spectacularly unfortunate marriages. The opposite of mild-mannered husbands, they were difficult men and often the principal architects of their marital disasters.

Charles Johnson Brooke, the second white raja of Sarawak, in present-day Malaysia, had been through a number of local mistresses before he finally married at age forty, around the time of his succession in 1868. An uncompromising misogynist, he maintained that marriage reduced an officer's efficiency by 99 percent. Perhaps to stay in peak form himself, he was cold and cruel to his own wife. By the sound of things, he also had a nasty temper. As the story goes, he sealed the fate of an already deteriorated union when he destroyed his wife's pet doves and served them in a pie for dinner. It was a consistent ending to a wretched marriage.

While neither imperial power nor literary renown could ensure marital felicity, empire builders, famous authors, and middle-class couples in general were prosperous enough that their marriages had the potential to flourish in reasonable material comfort. Not least of all, most people of means had enough physical energy for sexual expression. In contrast, working-class marriages were at a particular disadvantage from the constant hard work, diminished health, and poor living conditions that many couples had no choice but to endure. In some households deprivation expressed itself in drunkenness and violence. But this was not inevitable. Many working people recognized that marriage afforded their best chance of economic betterment, and they strove to "pull together" and maintain domestic harmony.

> At mid-century, the journalist and social investigator Henry Mayhew recorded the working day of a couple who were tailors. "I must begin work at six in the morning, and sit close at it till eleven at night," explained the husband. "My wife slaves night and day, as I do; and very often she has less rest than myself, for she has to stop up after I have gone to bed to attend to her domestic duties."

For this couple and many like them, hardship took its toll on lovemaking. Yet it did not necessarily eliminate all caring. In the tailor's sparse words and the unromantic scenario evoked, there still lingers the man's compassion for his wife and a glimmer of the pride both must have taken in their shared effort to make a home together.

Infidelities

Victorian convention dictated that those who found themselves in less than perfect marriages make the best of their troubles, whether they arose from circumstance or temperament. Not everyone, however, was able to follow the proprieties of the day. Sheer emotional misery, economic misfortune, or irrepressible sexual exuberance drove some people to seek comfort and passion outside their marriages.

> By 1858 Charles Dickens's twenty-two-year-old marriage was intolerably strained, and he and Catherine separated. Dickens had already formed an attachment to the actress Ellen Ternan and, the following year, provided for her accommodation in London's Ampthill Square. The couple endured gossip and censure that never entirely dissipated. In spite of it all, the relationship lasted until the end of Dickens's life. Ellen was with him when he died in the early evening of June 9, 1870, but received no invitation to his burial five days later at Westminster Abbey.

The working people for whom Dickens's novels show so much sympathy were sometimes compelled by economic pressures to enter into irregular relationships. For the urban poor, subsistence under any conditions was a struggle. Women and men alike did whatever was necessary to survive.

A woman whose name is now forgotten was finding it increasingly difficult to feed her children. Her husband had been out of work for a long period. Finally, in desperation, she followed the example of other women who had been in her situation. She called herself a "grass widow" and took up with another man who could look after her and the children. The community generally was tolerant.

An impoverished husband and father, his name unrecorded, had little choice of employment. Like many of his kind, he was forced to live away from his family to obtain work. He ended up cohabiting with another woman. This served two pressing needs. It assuaged the loneliness and physical longings that were for him intolerable. And—no small boon when times were hard—it was cheaper than living alone.

Well beyond the working-class neighborhoods of industrial cities, those who governed Victoria's dominions made arrangements all their own. Out in the Empire, the exigencies of everyday life could not always be answered by the conventions of home. These receded in the minds of many men who were far from England and whose needs were immediate. Although some managed to bring their wives out, there were also those who delayed marriage and maintained a native mistress instead. Others took more casual lovers, most of them young, not all of them female. And still others wanted both worlds—marriage and additional liaisons as they chose.

In his youth Sir George Goldie, the creator of Nigeria, had lived happily with a young Arab woman in the Egyptian Sudan. When he returned to England he led for a time the life of a rake before shocking his immediate circle by running off to Paris with the family governess. Having compromised both her and himself, he was forced to marry her in 1871. True to character, he was soon unfaithful. In 1877 West Africa beckoned as a refuge, both from his intrigues and from his unsuccessful marriage—yet another ill-fated match among the men who built the Empire.

Life was generally more sedate and likely often duller in prosperous middle-class America than it was in Her Majesty's imperial outposts. But at least a few solid citizens of the New World managed to find, or create, their own form of adventure.

Mabel Loomis Todd was an attractive young housewife who lived a life of erotic intrigue. She enjoyed many occasions of "sweet communion"—her exalted way of referring to sexual intercourse—and not all took place within the sanctity of marriage. But, unlike the adulteresses of fiction, Mabel was never tossed out into the street by an outraged husband, nor did she sustain any substantial loss of community standing. She proved that Victorian life did not always imitate art, nor vice versa.

In the early 1880s she and her husband, David, moved from Washington, D.C., to Amherst, Massachusetts, where he took up a position as instructor in astronomy and director of the college observatory. No ordinary faculty wife, Mabel soon began an affair with the college treasurer, Austin Dickinson, brother of the poet Emily. Austin was not only Amherst's social leader but a longtime married man. He was fifty-three. Mabel was twenty-four.

Like many Victorian couples during periods of separation, they were devoted and pining correspondents. "I love you—and I love you," he declared in a letter of 1885, "and I kiss you all over." She echoed his words in a letter of her own, written in April 1890. "I love you," she fervently avowed, "and I want you bitterly." Their impassioned affair was also a lasting one. It had not yet run its fevered course when Austin died in 1895. For Mabel, the habit of loving communication and communion did not die with her lover. "Well, my beloved," she said to him through the medium of her journal three months after his death, "you do not go away at all. I feel you here in me, enfolding me, this instant."

Mabel's husband, with whom she continued to enjoy a rich sex life and a "very happy & tender & devoted" companionship, knew all about the affair and was in fact a good-natured collaborator. When the lovers were enjoying an assignation in his house, he would signal his return by whistling a tune. It was the least he could do. He himself was not "what might be called a monogamous animal," as Mabel acknowledged. "He had most of the women guests who came to our house," his daughter would later recall. When Austin died, the deeply grieving Mabel had no qualms about confiding to her always supportive spouse, "I shall never be the same again, of course." And, indeed, some of her vital, passionate spirit had died along with her lover. David remained much as ever—a sympathetic, loving, and cheerfully unfaithful husband.

Unorthodox Unions

While some marriages departed from convention through infidelity or estrangement, others did so by more extraordinary routes. Two such unions incorporated eccentricity shading into the perverse. Three others—all part of one story—were each unique in the ways that they realized a Victorian version of chivalric devotion.

In 1873 the poet and photographer Arthur Munby, a man of middle-class background, married Hannah Cullwick, a maid-of-all-work. A marriage that cut so far across class divides was in itself unusual. Stranger still was the couple's intimate life. Hannah maintained her old role as a servant in Arthur's household and rarely assumed the part of a middle-class housewife. Their sexual relations probably did not include intercourse but centered instead upon an eroticized enactment of their social difference—a difference exaggerated by the racist and sadomasochistic overtones of their sexual play. At Arthur's request, Hannah would black her face "with oil & lead." To this he sometimes added chains. She called him "Massa"—he kissed and fondled her, his wife and "slave."

Yet love there was in this unorthodox partnership. Early in the marriage Hannah confided to her diary,

> I have the inward comfort of knowing that I am loved & honoured & admired & that I am united in heart and soul as well as married at church to the truest, best, & handsomest man in my eyes that ever was born. . . . And he is pleased with me & after all this there can be no doubt of our being made for each other.

Eventually, some doubt would enter her mind. In 1877, tired of his need to dominate, she left Arthur and returned to service in the country. The couple's bond was never severed, however. They lived together for short periods over the years and visited frequently during separations. Decades into the next century, a few people, now elderly themselves, would remember long ago seeing an old couple, arms linked, still deeply engrossed in one another and in their unconventional but, in its own way, loving union.

At the very moment, perhaps, that Hannah was blacking her face for Arthur's pleasure, an unnamed clergyman of mature years and unimpeachable reputation was also becoming aroused by the thrill of subordination—in this instance, his own. As he bent over, buttocks bared, his "young and pretty" wife administered the rod with "extraordinary passion." Not everyone had recourse to the flagellant brothels of London.

A contemporary of both the vicar and Munby appears to have been of a more conventional bent. Yet Heneage Dering's plan to contract a marriage in the customary way soon took an unusual turn. In 1859 the young officer of the Coldstream Guards fell in love with Rebecca Orpen. When he approached her aunt and guardian, Lady Chatterton, for permission to propose to Rebecca, things went drastically wrong. As it happened, Lady Chatterton misunderstood, thought the proposal was for her, and accepted. Not wanting to hurt and humiliate a lady, the overly chivalrous young man married her, even though she was old enough to have been his mother.

Some years later, in 1867, his real love, Rebecca, married his friend Marmion Ferrers. United by their shared Catholic faith, the two couples took up residence together at Baddesley Clinton, the Ferrers' family home in Warwickshire, a picturesque house complete with a moat. Here the foursome devoted themselves to philanthropy, religion, and study. Rebecca, a talented artist, painted the group harmoniously at work in Baddesley Clinton's library.

Lady Chatterton died in 1876. The widower stayed on with his two friends. Just how he managed to control his passion while living in such near-intimacy with his love has gone untold. Marmion Ferrers died eight years later. In 1885, when a year's suitable mourning had passed, Rebecca married her original suitor. Happily, more than a quarter-century after his proposal had gone awry, Heneage Dering's patience was finally rewarded. He lived to enjoy it until 1892; Rebecca died in 1923. Inseparable in death as they had been in life, the two couples were buried side by side in the churchyard near Baddesley Clinton.

Felicity

Singular stories like that of the Derings and Ferrers, accounts of eccentric or dramatically unhappy marriages, and scandals among the famous have survived from the Victorian age in large number. Mostly forgotten are the typical—all those marriages characterized by routine ups and downs, daily companionship, small amusements shared, private pleasures enjoyed. Unremarkable, such unions generally went unrecorded. As Reverend Hardy well appreciated,

> when husband and wife pull along happily together they forget themselves and each other, and do not speak about their happiness at all. . . . Matrimonial failures strive and cry in the streets, whereas the successes enjoy domestic felicity at their own fireplaces and say nothing about it.

Still, Hardy persevered in his project of identifying successful marriages and categorizing them by the husbands' professions. He found several politicians and statesmen—Gladstone, for one—who had achieved conjugal peace and contentment. Happier still, Hardy believed, were scientists. This, he explained with blithe oversimplicity, was because "the contemplation of Nature's calm and orderly working exercises a soothing influence upon her students." Diligently, he collected testimonials to sustain his conviction. In 1849 Michael Faraday, discoverer of electromagnetic induction, had described himself as still "supremely happy" after twenty-eight years of marriage. More than anything else, his marriage had contributed to his "earthly happiness and healthful state of mind." And, as the reverend collector of scientific love affairs also reported, "James Nasmyth, the inventor of the steam-hammer, speaking of his wife, said: 'Forty-two years of married life finds us the same devoted cronies that we were at the beginning.'"

Hardy was further pleased to observe many marital successes among ministers, scholars, and teachers. Delicacy no doubt prevented him from mentioning the one-time young mistress of Charles Dickens. Yet her later life lent support to the favorable view of clerical and academic unions.

> In 1876, six years after the death of her lover, Ellen Ternan made a quintessentially respectable marriage to George Wharton Robinson, the clergyman principal of the high school in Margate, a Kentish seaside resort. Although financial difficulties would subsequently trouble the pair, the early years were good ones, and George and Ellen made an admirable couple. He was an Oxford graduate, rowing enthusiast, and model of the muscular Christian gentleman. His new wife, the former professional actress, contentedly fashioned herself into an exemplary schoolmaster's wife. She taught the younger boys spelling and directed school theatrical performances. And she who had once turned her back on convention soon embraced it closer still as the devoted mother of two young children.

If Ellen Ternan can be said to have changed the course of her earlier life, there were many more who did so by rising above circumstances far less promising than hers. Many working-class people from backgrounds almost unimaginably deprived—of tenderness as much as material comfort—overcame their beginnings and achieved self-respect and contentment through marriage. Engrossed in cataloging the loves of the renowned, Reverend Hardy did not comment on the marital successes of the humble. But had he wished to do so, he would not have found it easy. Working people by and large kept their personal lives to themselves. Even those articulate enough to write their autobiographies were usually reticent when it came to matters of the heart. In silence more than utterance they expressed their feelings.

The cabinetmaker and tradesman George Acorn grew up in the slums of Victorian London and during his childhood witnessed many "violent quarrels" between his mother and father. But as an adult he managed to escape the cycle of frustration, abuse, and unhappiness that had marked his parents' marriage. He had read, he explained, both quality literature and penny romances and, from these, acquired a vision of how the relationship of men and women might ideally be. After a short-lived infatuation with a young woman he soon judged "shallow-brained," he fell in love with his future wife, Grace, whom he had met at chapel. "I will not say much about Grace, our relationship is too dear for that." True to his word, he added only that compared to her, his first love was now to him "as the moon's light waning when the sun rises." He ended his memoir in the conventional and hopeful fashion of the fiction he relished. He and Grace had married, settled peacefully into their home together, and recently become parents. "And that young life," he concluded, "is . . . a cause of thankfulness that through the failures and mistakes of the past, future lives may be brighter and happier."

Love Letters

Unlike most of the working class, middle-class people had the leisure to record their feelings, and some did in fact leave behind glimpses of their private lives. The majority, however, were as Reverend Hardy pictured—content to "enjoy domestic felicity at their own fireplaces and say nothing about it." The voices of a few must now speak for the many.

In love letters, diaries, and a few other sources are preserved the words of couples who knew overall contentment and physical joy. They and all the others like them who are now forgotten may not invariably have achieved the erotic intensity of fiction or the romanticism of love poetry and valentine verse. But they remade lovemaking in ways that were individual yet, in the end, not so far off the ideal. This comes through even in as matter-of-fact a document as the questionnaire used by Dr. Clelia Mosher in her survey of American women. One respondent, known as Mrs. C, described the "complete physical harmony" she enjoyed with her husband. Their sexual relationship, she confided, was the expression of their "true and passionate love."

Alice Baldwin, an American army wife, undoubtedly would have agreed. She cared for her husband and pined for him physically in his absence. "Oh how rejoiced I shall be," she wrote in 1869, "to see your dear face once more, to feel myself clasped in your sheltering arms. Those dear strong arms have always loved and comforted me."

The earthy humor of her other letters, written during periods of separation the following year, further reveal a woman contented with her spouse and entirely comfortable with the sexual side of life. In October 1870 she reported that as she was looking out her train window during a stop at an Illinois station, a man had exposed himself to her. "I thought he might have saved himself the trouble," was her brisk comment, "because I had seen one before."

In December she teased her husband about an old girlfriend, Nellie Smith, whom he had once considered marrying. "I thought I held *undivided* your love. Well, its too late now. Nellie Smith don't know what she escaped. She would have been killed at one nab of your old long Tom!!!" The "old long Tom" that she had so enthusiastically punctuated was nineteenth-century slang for penis.

Other correspondents coping with separation from their spouses were not generally as forthright as the irrepressible Alice. But their remembered enjoyments and longings while apart are tangible nonetheless.

"I want to put my arms around your waist—and pat your black hair and say how sweet!" yearned Lincoln Clark, a devoted husband of eleven years, writing to his wife in 1847. "It would do me just as much good as it did ten years and a half ago—and I have the vanity to believe that the pleasure would not all be on one side."

Jane Burnett also had to endure the absence of her spouse, who was away serving in the California legislature in 1857. "I am almost crazy to see you," she wrote. "This being away from you is torture. . . . How long are we to be separated, must it be much longer, I want to sleep in your arms again."

"Would that I could *kiss you all over*—and then *eat* you *up*," was the longing desire of Civil War wife Emily Lovell in 1862, as she wrote to her husband of thirteen years. He replied in kind. "Kiss me dear sweetheart, a thousand warm and loving kisses, take me to your beautiful arms and let me for a while enjoy a heaven upon earth."

It was perhaps separation that calmed the storms in the marriage of Jane and Thomas Carlyle. Although they often had difficulty being together, they missed one another when apart, and their letters reveal their true devotion to one another. On Jane's birthday in July 1844, her husband sent a gift and a letter that Hardy reproduced. In it Carlyle addresses his wife by the pet name "Goody":

> One ought to have said what the inner man sufficiently feels: that one is right glad to see the brave little Goody with the mind's and the heart's eye . . . and wishes and prays all good in this world. . . . And now, dearest, here is a small gift, one of the smallest ever sent. . . . a little jewel box, and there, you see, is the key. Blessings on thee with it! I wish I had diamonds to fill the places with for my little wifie. . . . And so, dear Goody, kiss me and take my good wishes. While I am here there will never want one to wish thee all good. Adieu on the birthday, and may the worst of our days be all done, and the best still coming. Thine evermore.

"Oh, my darling," Jane replied with feeling, "I want to give you an emphatic kiss rather than to write." She promised to keep it for him until they were together again.

Charles Kingsley also wrote to Fanny with constant "yearning love" when the couple had to be separated. Characteristically, in such letters he often mixed the erotic with the religious. He saw nothing blasphemous in calling their marriage bed an altar. Words seldom failed him, but they were not always enough. Sometimes he accompanied his passionate outpourings with ink drawings he had made of himself and Fanny, both naked. In one they are swept away on an ocean wave, intertwined with one another and lashed to a wooden cross. In another compelling image they have become winged figures who rise through a sunlit sky to heaven—still joined in intercourse. Fanny lovingly saved the drawings in her journal.

Oh! For Five Minutes More

The temporary separations that everyday life sometimes occasioned were small preparation indeed for the final parting. When the death of a spouse ended decades of loving and sharing, the survivor's sense of loss was immeasurable. When the novelist Charles Lever's wife, Kate, died, reported Hardy, "he felt as if his right hand had lost its cunning." Among the normally reserved working class it was often only in bereavement that a lifetime of common experience found expression in words. In his 1898 autobiography, *The Martyrdom of the Mine*, the miner Edward Rymer wrote movingly of his wife's last moments and his own desolation:

> She lingered and suffered . . . then sank to rest in my presence, while my very soul seemed to lose hope somehow, and sent me adrift on a dark and trackless future—lonely and desolate without her. We had braved the storm and ruthless tempest in all its fury for 40 years.

"Five minutes more of your dear company in this world. Oh that I had you yet for but five minutes," lamented Thomas Carlyle in a reminiscence of his wife written shortly after she died in 1866. They had been married forty years, and he wanted those last vanished minutes to "tell her all" of his lifelong admiration, regard, and love. His subsequent literary output dwindled. Her death, he confessed, "shattered my whole existence into immeasurable ruin."

Charles Kingsley would have understood. In early December 1874 his beloved Fanny fell ill with a form of angina. On being told by her doctor that she would not recover, he said, "My own death-warrant was signed with those words." For three weeks, all the while suffering from a cough himself, he sat by his wife's bedside in a bitterly cold room, where all the windows were open to assist her breathing. As they spent those last days together, now a middle-aged couple in their fifties, they recalled their younger years shared and reread their favorite poets—Milton, Shakespeare, Wordsworth, and Arnold. They planned the details of Fanny's funeral, and Charles sketched the tombstone she wanted—a circle representing eternity, and enclosed within it, a spray of passionflowers, the symbol of their love.

Christmas came and went, with Fanny still ill and Charles coughing continually. Three days later his cold had turned to pneumonia and he was forced to take to his bed. For nearly a month husband and wife lay in their separate beds, she in her drafty room, he in a constantly warm one. They communicated by penciled notes. After a week of such separation he could stand it no more, evaded the nurse who attended him, and went again to Fanny's bedside. "This is heaven," he said, as he held her hand. "Don't speak." It was their last encounter.

He was now completely bedridden, sedated with opiates, and only sporadically lucid. On January 20 his condition worsened, and he asked his oldest child, Rose, whether Fanny knew. "She knows all," was the reply. Charles took this to mean that Fanny had already passed away, although in fact she would live another sixteen years. Believing that his desire that they should go together had been realized, he soon sank into a coma and remained that way until he died just before noon on the twenty-third. Perhaps, as he let go of life, he saw a vision of himself and Fanny raised to heaven—forever united in their love.

The Fullness of Passion

A compelling couple by any reckoning, the Kingsleys are also striking for the vividness and detail with which their memory has survived. Their marriage stands for numberless other joyful unions between men and women who are no longer remembered. Not everyone, of course, understood or enacted sexuality in the same way, and many individual stories are now forever lost. Neither was everyone content. The Victorians' firmly held belief in the faithful productive marriage could not guarantee marital success, happiness, or sexual fulfillment. Even so, only a few couples divorced—the annual average in England was 148 divorces in the 1850s, rising to 582 in the 1890s. For the most part people sought other solutions to their marital problems, or learned to live with them.

Yet if true love was beyond the grasp of some unfortunate individuals, and if it was infinitely variable among those who knew it, the Victorians still collectively demonstrated their will toward passion in all its sensual, emotional, and spiritual aspects. Together they developed a sexual mystique that both expressed and protected passion. Although by the close of their era the transformation of sex into talk had begun, most couples continued to celebrate the joys of silence. "Thou art . . . unspeakably beloved," wrote Nathaniel Hawthorne to his wife at mid-century. Near its end Reverend Hardy was moved by the sentiment and quoted it in *Love Affairs*.

Knowing little of the graphicness of pornography and the clinic, the Victorians cultivated the nuanced words of romance and the language of gestures, blushes, and telling glances. Cherishing the sensual yet nurturing the intangible, they enjoyed the fullness of passion. "How much more delicious," Charles Kingsley wrote to Fanny shortly before they married, "when in each others' arms, the flesh & the spirit shall tend the same way, increasing each other's delight!" And many undoubtedly knew such delight. But inevitably there were also those less fortunate. In the end it is their experience against which the best of Victorian passion must be weighed.

CHAPTER 8

The Best and the Worst

It was the best of times, it was the worst of times.

—Charles Dickens, *A Tale of Two Cities*, 1859

In the famous opening line of his tale of London and Paris, Dickens was characterizing the era in which he set the novel—the late eighteenth century, the time of the French Revolution. But in the same passage he added that much the same "superlative degree of comparison" also distinguished his own age. He was speaking generally and, even though he must have composed the line while in the early, heated phase of his affair with Ellen Ternan, he presumably did not have sex specifically in mind. Yet his words evoke certain images that help to complete the picture of Victorian sexuality.

One of history's great ironies is that a tenacious myth of prudery should have clung to an age in fact so rich in strategies to accommodate and nurture the erotic. The revelations of clothing, the sexual overtones of sport, the ribaldry of the music hall, the suggestiveness of romantic fiction and valentines, the physical closeness that even decorous courtship allowed, the passionate (if irregular) liaisons of Charles Dickens and others, the intimate histories of couples like the Kingsleys—all testify to the Victorians' capacity for erotic feeling and expression. In reality and imagination, whether through personal experience or vicariously through popular entertainments, most people knew something of the best that sexuality could offer.

It was the very regard the Victorians had for sex, publicly as well as privately—it was the very intensity of their emotions and bodily responses—that created a painful contrast in some individuals' lives. Men and women caught in unhappy marriages, others who had loved and lost, and still others who had never found love at all must have felt their plight all the more keenly in a sexual world where passion was a powerful force. Poverty, bad health, ill-assorted matches, unattractive physical appearance, or a combination of these contributed to misfortune in love. Many a barren reality stood divided from the cultural ideals of romance, happy marriage, and sexual fulfillment. This sometimes unbridgeable divide, this bitter contrast, was the worst of Victorian sexuality.

In other words, while passion was the main theme of the sexual history of the Victorians, the counterpoint was the profound disappointments of some private lives. This did not go entirely unrecognized at the time. A few works of art, some fiction, and the records of real life reflected the contrast between desire gratified and denied, between intimacy and loneliness, happiness and hardship.

Imprisoned Hearts

Economic and social advantage gave some people every opportunity to realize passion. Reduced circumstances, meanwhile, placed others on its margins, observing but not partaking of its pleasures. No one captured this disparity more poignantly than the artist Rebecca Solomon.

Her painting *The Governess,* which she first exhibited at the Royal Academy in 1854, depicts a scene that would have been familiar to most middle-class Victorians. A man and woman have come together at the piano, symbol and enabler of romance. She is about to play or perhaps has just finished doing so; he is seated close by. They might be married, engaged, courting, or, at the very least, flirting. This shows in their rapt expressions, locked gaze, and the position of their bodies, turned toward one another. Warm intense colors—her coral-pink dress, his dark burgundy jacket, the shades of red and burgundy in the room's furnishings—enhance the effect of vitality and passion. In this commonplace image of Victorian domestic and social life the artist encapsulated a world where everyday objects and activities such as playing the piano kindled and expressed sexual feeling.

The scene occupies just over half the entire painting. Portrayed on the other side, giving instruction to her young pupil, is the figure from whom the picture took its name. The governess contrasts sharply with the couple enjoying their interlude at the piano. Although sharing the same picture space, she sits apart from the colorful scenario of passion unfolding. Unlike the room's decor and the other

Passion gratified and denied: Rebecca Solomon, The Governess, *1854*

figures' clothing, her attire is a drab shade of black. This perhaps indicates bereavement and mourning, or the artist may have chosen the dark hue as a more general symbol of sadness and loneliness.

As an impoverished gentlewoman the governess of the painting, like her real-life counterpart, was in an ambivalent and isolated social position. Above the rank of servant, she was also below that of guest or relative. With her marginal economic and social position went a straitened sexual existence. However passionate by nature a governess might have been, her situation demanded that she never show it or act upon it. The painted figure's sad expression and sidelong look at the couple indicate that romantic and sexual gratification was not something she voluntarily relinquished. Appropriately enough, *The Governess* was exhibited with accompanying lines from clergyman and popular nineteenth-century writer Martin Tupper's 1843 poem "Of Neglect":

> Ye too, the friendless, yet dependent, that find nor home nor lover,
> Sad imprisoned hearts, captive to the net of circumstance.

A far cry from Becky Sharp, the adventuress-governess in William Thackeray's *Vanity Fair* (1847–48), Rebecca Solomon's forlorn subject must have struck a particularly sensitive chord with the painter herself, for, as a female artist, she was subject to certain prejudices of the day. In the famous Victorian humor magazine *Punch,* for example, cartoons were apt to depict creative women not only as less competent than their male counterparts but also as unattractive old-maid stereotypes. Solomon, as it turned out, never married; she lived for a time with her brothers (one of whom was painter Abraham Solomon) but ended her days alone. She was sensitive to the plight of the governess because, perhaps, hers was yet another sad imprisoned heart.

Chaste and Unchaste Toil

It was inevitable that some women would be left to fend for themselves without the economic and emotional security of marriage. Throughout the second half of the nineteenth century the English female population exceeded the male. In an 1896 collection of essays, *The Civilisation of Our Day,* an unnamed contributor reported that the 1891 census returns for England and Wales showed that, out of a total population of some twenty-nine million, there were nearly nine hundred thousand more women than men. In literature and art governesses and teachers stood for superfluous middle-class women caught in a web of economic need, loneliness, and sexuality unfulfilled.

More desperate still was the situation of their working-class counterparts. Sympathetic artists and writers often used the figure of the oppressed needlewoman to embody all unattached and impoverished female workers at the lower end of the social scale. In the words of the painter Richard Redgrave, the aim was to "call attention to the trials and struggles of the poor and oppressed." Redgrave and others generally portrayed the needlewoman as frail, overworked, alone, and virtuous. His 1846 painting *The Sempstress* shows a woman with tired eyes and a careworn expression plying her solitary trade in a sparsely furnished garret lit by a single candle stub. George Reynolds offered a similar but more glamorous version of the same figure—the heroine of his 1850 serial *The Seamstress* is a "pale and pensive," "slightly formed," but beautiful model of "virginal artlessness."

While such visions of noble solitude and chaste toil inspired sympathy for the material and emotional deprivations of working-class women, they also softened the grim reality. Like others engaged in sweated labor, many needlewomen did not spend their days in comparatively spacious, if cheerless, garrets. Instead they had to endure overcrowded and unhygienic workplaces. Their trade could damage their health far beyond mere paleness and fragility, the long hours of close work in wretched conditions often resulting in blindness as well as general debility. And while many might have preferred sexual chastity, they did not have the luxury of such a choice. With incomes generally below subsistence level, it was a commonplace for needlewomen to resort occasionally to prostitution in order to survive. But if art and fiction glossed the real experience of sweated female labor, they at least suggested something of the human toll that poverty extracted. Beyond that, in the figure of the solitary needlewoman, they evoked the acute loneliness of every woman whose circumstances made it unlikely, if not impossible, for her to attain the ideals embodied in popular romance, valentines, and middle-class courting rituals.

Lonely Bachelors

Artists and writers apparently did not find the theme of the lonely bachelor as compelling as that of the excluded female. Popular romance often portrayed the unmarried male as the kind of carefree rake epitomized by Charles before his marriage to Bella in Charles Reade's *A Terrible Temptation*. In real life, unhappy single men perhaps went unnoticed, or people mistook them for confirmed and contented bachelors. But the correspondence pages of the most widely read magazines told a different story. Over many years men repeatedly wrote in, seeking first the companionship of suitable females and eventually the felicity of marriage.

It was not the way of the Victorian man to wear emotion on his sleeve. Yet the masculine lonely heart showed itself between the lines of all the letters whose writers described themselves as "very affectionate," "fond of home," "loving," or "of loving disposition," and who hoped to meet women as "loving and domestic" as themselves. The fact that so many men wrote at all was in itself revealing. Clearly, even though the numerical imbalance of the sexes favored men, not every bachelor was such by choice.

There were various reasons why some men who wished to marry found it difficult to do so. Economics was undoubtedly one factor. Many men in their twenties were not well enough established financially to set up a home and support a wife and family; accordingly, they delayed marriage until their circumstances had improved. The problem sometimes was that by the time a man in this situation had a secure job and a little money saved, he was no longer part of a social circle that included eligible women among whom he might find a wife. This is suggested by a number of letters from men in their thirties and forties who pursued matrimony through the correspondence pages of magazines.

At any age, a poor physical appearance might have been a contributing cause of involuntary bachelorhood. Although some men who advertised for wives professed to handsomeness, others were reticent on the subject of looks, some possibly out of modesty, but others out of a wish to avoid discouraging or misleading prospective respondents. One honest hopeful who wrote to the *London Journal* in 1874 apologetically admitted that he was "not considered good-looking." Other correspondents who may well have had marriage on their minds sought remedies for thinness, unruly hair, bad skin, and baldness. The insecurity about appearance that some men felt was not unfounded. The prevalence of Victorian valentines in which the female sender made fun of the male recipient's physical deficiencies indicates women's generally exacting standards. And both sexes read the sort of fiction in which the men who won the women were conventionally handsome or, at least, attractive in their own unique way.

With or without good appearance and sound finances, a combination of shyness, inarticulateness, and fear of rejection was often a barrier between unhappy bachelors and the wedded bliss they craved. The *London Journal* and *Reynolds's Miscellany* received letters from young women who were aggrieved or exasperated at men who did not make their feelings and intentions clear. Such men themselves also wrote in with frustrated tales of their own diffidence and shortcomings in the art of courtship. The magazines' experts sympathized and did their best to alleviate the "desperation" of some of the correspondents.

Their advice was consistent and firm. Declaration, they maintained, was the only course—in matters of the heart, frankness was the better part of manliness. But in 1853 the *London Journal* also issued the caution that honor as well as success demanded that candor be "coupled with a delicate tone and gentlemanly demeanour." A quick and decisive mustering of the necessary manly courage to speak out was also crucial. As the *Journal*'s ever-sensible adviser put it in 1854, "hesitation in love is as fatal as in war."

Subsequent correspondence pages do not indicate the outcome of such concerns and guidance. Some correspondents presumably acted upon the experts' recommendations and the results were happy. Some perhaps tried and failed. Others never reached the point of decisive frankness and continued to languish in solitary discontent. Like the lonely women who existed on the margins of passion, some men, too, lived out their lives beyond the pale of romantic and sexual gratification.

Reaching for Passion

Commonplace as they were, shyness, fear of rejection, unfavorable appearance, and economic hardship did not in the end stop most people from pursuing sexual love and marriage. From all levels of society, well off or poor, whatever their temperament and appearance, both women and men reached for passion's ideal. But the unfortunate among them held on to it only briefly—before it slipped from their grasp.

Rejection was not only the fear of some, but the reality of others. Artists reflected this in paintings such as Philip Calderon's *Broken Vows* (1856), which depicts a young woman who has just discovered that her suitor does not reciprocate her love and loyalty. Sorrow and defeat show in her anguished expression, the tear on one cheek, and her limp posture as she swoons against a garden wall. On its other side the unfaithful young man lightheartedly flirts with another woman.

Meanwhile, in both art and life, men also suffered from passionate dreams unfulfilled. Ford Madox Brown's *The Stages of Cruelty*, begun in 1856 and completed in 1890, shows a young man with a tortured countenance vainly trying to extract the least sign of affection from his beloved. Seated nearby, she glances callously at him; in her hand is a piece of embroidery with a needle lodged at its center—an image symbolic of a stabbed heart. From time to time the *London Journal*'s correspondence pages carried letters from men similarly wounded by women who treated them disdainfully. M. H., for one, was hurt because "a very handsome girl" with whom he had fallen in love had merely "used him as a foil, in order to make another young man more attentive." From the viewpoint of an eligible young woman whose future economic and social well-being depended entirely on whatever marriage she could make, such behavior was reasonable. Even so, the strategically insincere "shafts of the flirt" must certainly have injured, sometimes permanently scarred, many a sensitive man who had deserved better.

But worse still was the fate of the abandoned women who made their way to the Thomas Coram Foundling Hospital, the principal London charitable institution that cared for children born out of wedlock. The hospital's applicants were women who had babies under one year old, had been deserted by the fathers, and were without means to support their children. Some of the women had become pregnant as a result of brief forays into prostitution, usually out of economic desperation; others had been raped, often by an employer. Many others had been conventionally courted, then seduced by promises of marriage. "He courted me and promised me marriage" was the story told over and over by the Foundling Hospital's applicants. Sometimes the absconding fathers were simply callous; more often they were immature, irresponsible, and frightened of the economic and emotional pressures of marriage and fatherhood.

Through their own efforts and with the support of family, friends, and sympathetic employers, most of the women managed. And they did so without necessarily enduring universal moral censure—that the Victorians were coldly condemning of the least sexual transgression is yet another myth. Still, the situation of these deserted mothers is especially moving, for, of all the many readers of popular romance, young working-class women were among the most avid, the most willing to pin their hopes on fiction's promise of the inseparability of sex and marriage. In reality, abandoned and unwed, some had been betrayed by lovers and the ideal alike.

Once a Girl's Wed

Of the women who actually made it to the altar there were those who found disappointment and little, if any, romance on its other side. Autobiographer William Bowyer recalled that in his youth he had many times observed "the unforgettable heart-breaking degradation of radiant young brides into bedraggled slatterns broken in a year or two by poverty and child-bearing and the drunkenness of their husbands." The theme of a late Victorian music hall song became a daily reality in the lives of numberless working women:

> When first they come courting,
> how nice they behave
> For a smile and a kiss
> how humbly they crave
> But when once a girl's wed,
> she's a drudge and a slave.

Even so, the experience of unwed mothers who succumbed to promises of marriage suggests that whatever its potential drawbacks were, matrimony was still a widely desired goal of working women, and preferable to a life of lonely struggle. The closing lines of the music hall song reflected a common sentiment:

> I think we would all prefer
> marriage with strife
> Than to be on the shelf
> and be nobody's wife.

The middle-class women who sought and achieved marriage mostly escaped the daily drudgery that came with material hardship. Yet for them the tedium and demands of household management must often have weighed heavily and seemed far removed from the carefree life that many must have expected wedlock to guarantee. In *The Five Talents of Women* (1888), one of his several treatises on the relationship of the sexes, Reverend Hardy was firm in advising brides-to-be that "the wife who can make herself most useful is she whose home is likely to be the happiest":

> Men are selfish creatures at bottom—every one of them. Edwin before marriage is ready to go through fire and water, and to endure any hardship for his beloved Angelina; but after marriage, should the dinner be a quarter of an hour late, or the joint be overdone or underdone, or any of the domestic wheels drag a little, Edwin will lay all the blame on Angelina. Let Angelina, therefore, before marriage learn how to keep all the wheels properly oiled.

In other words, the wife who irritated her husband with domestic deficiencies was responsible for *his* unhappiness as well as her own. What did not occur to the knowing reverend, nor undoubtedly to many others, was the alternative proposition: exacting husbands of Edwin's sort might have done something about their own irascible temperaments.

In some working- and middle-class households alike, the accumulated pressures of poverty and drudgery or of mere tedious routine reached an intolerable level. In many cases, incompatible personalities sparked, and alcohol fueled, the unhappy situation. The result was domestic violence. More often than not, the most severe abuse was instigated and inflicted by men. But, disinclined to submit passively, many Victorian women fought back.

Court records, memoirs, and commentaries not only told the stories of battered wives but also revealed scenarios of reciprocal combat. Hitherto harmless domestic articles—crockery, umbrellas, fireplace pokers, small pieces of furniture—frequently became the missiles in such conflict. Even shoes and boots, those common and generally innocuous sexual fetish objects, figured in accounts of marital violence. The bedroom was often the battleground, and when the fight escalated there was a convenient weapon much favored by both husbands and wives. A fixture of the Victorian bedroom—but also the least romantic of the commonly deployed household weaponry—the chamber pot was ready to hand for emptying over the head of an offending spouse. While effectively making a point, such an act, it need hardly be said, found no place in the civilized misunderstandings permitted by romantic fiction and the marital ideal.

Sex, Love, and Death

Whether tranquil or violent, happy or not, passionately loving or otherwise, every relationship between men and women ran its course beneath an unavoidable shadow. Ideally, in fiction and reality, worthy couples were supposed to enjoy not only lifelong love but also longevity. In fact, although average life expectancy was rising, accident, illness, or childbirth all might suddenly end a couple's time together. In an age whose most prominent public figure, the queen herself, mourned her husband for forty years, most people could not help but be acutely aware of the imminence of death in the lives of the great and humble alike. So much did this awareness govern popular consciousness that the symbols and rituals of death found expression even in life's smallest and most mundane details. While dedicated principally to providing entertainment, the *London Journal* did not deem it out of the way to advise on the niceties of such minutiae as the trim on mourning handkerchiefs—"a wide border of black for close mourning, and narrower as the black is lightened."

Generally the Victorians accepted the idea of death and its nearness with relative stoicism. But they dreaded nonetheless the actual, final parting from a loved one. "When a few days separation is so hard to bear what would life be worth if we were separated by death," wrote American wife Elizabeth Harbert to her absent husband in 1879. It made her "tremble," she continued, "to think of the possibility of anguish in the human heart—." She was not alone in the sentiment. Charles Kingsley, for one, had desired above all else to avoid the pain of separation by dying at the same time as his beloved Fanny. "Five minutes more . . . Oh that I had you yet for but five minutes"—the sorrowful and futile plea of the bereaved Thomas Carlyle must have been the mute cry of countless mourning Victorian lovers, once separated forever in life from their mates.

The constant consciousness of the end inexorably coming, the elaborate rituals of mourning, and the profound grief that death engendered might on the surface seem entirely at odds with the passion and vitality that imbued so much of Victorian life. Yet, looking deeper, it appears that sexual love and death coexisted with a good measure of harmony in Victorian culture and sensibility. Some of fiction's characters, such as Marion and Walter in the *Bow Bells* serial *Marion's Fate*, experience death as the culmination of passion, as they die entwined in each other's arms. Kingsley portrayed a similar theme in the drawing of himself and Fanny rising as one to heaven. In reality, most people did not have either the melodramatic lives or deaths of fictional characters; nor did they possess Kingsley's imaginative ability to merge the spiritual and the erotic. But their age was one in which belief in an afterlife was general, and many bereaved lovers must have taken comfort from the certitude that a heavenly reunion eventually awaited them.

In the meantime the Victorian sense of death's nearness and inevitability was an incentive to pursue sexual love with unflagging purpose and intensity. "Love me, lady love me!" before "in the grave I lie" was the message of a valentine verse from about 1850:

> The last star is declining
> Lady be thou my light.

Already secure in love, but acutely aware of "how rapidly the years are whirling by," Elizabeth Harbert fervently resolved that she and her husband would strive to "crowd as much happiness as is possible into every day." Without doubt, she represented the feeling and determination of a great number of her contemporaries. As so many Victorians well knew, with death hovering ever near, the sweetness of passion was to be savored all the more.

Ecstasy Is Wordless

Like any age before or since, the Victorians had to reconcile life, sexuality, and the inevitability of death. More than history has generally acknowledged, they met this profoundly human challenge openly and effectively. As in any era, their sexual world was an imperfect place—it endowed many with its blessings but degraded or excluded others. Yet the Victorian sexual mystique offered what a later era's explicitness would increasingly withhold. For the unhappily married, the jilted, and the lonely, there was leeway for the romantic imagination. In an age of discreet sexual expression, there was no little gratification to be taken from an approving glance, a small act of kindness, or a few appreciative words from a member of the opposite sex.

If none of these signs of favor were forthcoming, or if they led to nothing, people could at least turn for solace to the happier realms of popular romance and love poetry. This was not escapism pure and simple, for the ideals embodied in such fiction and poetry held out hope to those who had yet to attain the fullness of passion. For some, the hope proffered was false, but this does not negate that they and others could draw real sustenance from the promise that

The innocent dreams of the coming time,
The beautiful dreams, the dreams sublime,

. . . .

Will surely be true at last.

As these lines suggest, at the quiet heart of the Victorian sexual mystique there existed possibility.

For the most part, this possibility has not been adequately recognized by historians of Victorian sexuality. With only a few exceptions, neither have they explored the lives of those who realized the ideal of passion. Because they have not looked far beyond the perspective of their own "liberated" or "authentic" sexual eras, some have seen mainly the supposed pruderies or the most sordid aspects of sex and the Victorians. Others, out of a conviction that the historical truth must be told about exclusion and brutality, have focused on prostitution, marital violence, or the like.

While it is important not to ignore or make light of the injustices and abuses of the Victorians' sexual world, it is no less truthful, and more representative of common experience, to remember the era's passionate devotion to both managing and nurturing the erotic. What ought to linger most vividly in recollection are the images of the best of Victorian sex: A woman's blush and the masculine response it inspired. The good-natured nudges and winks of the music hall. Valentines inscribed tersely but feelingly "with sweet kisses." A gentleman's delight at the accidental revelations of a lady's crinoline. "Love's joyous impulse"—the stuff of popular romance. Working people, like George Acorn, reading and seeing in fiction a vision of possibility to be pursued and attained. The love letters and love between husbands and wives, the obscure as well as the famous. A woman in a coral-pink gown, her lover attentively nearby as she touches the piano keys and turns radiantly toward him. . . .

It has not been, nor will it ever be, a straightforward undertaking to re-create the sexual joy that many Victorians knew. Of their courtships, gratifications, and marital successes few records remain; often they never existed at all. Reverend Hardy recognized this when he prepared his treatise on love affairs, remarking that "one unhappy alliance makes more noise than a hundred that are happy." The successes, as he concluded, were apt to "say nothing." The Victorians' reticence undoubtedly served eroticism well. But it was no boon to the subsequent writing of their sexual history.

A sentiment expressed in one of the many fictional romances of the day captures both the Victorian sexual mystique and the problem it poses for those who would now recollect it. In the 1874 serial *Mary Rivenhall's Prophecy* there is a passage in which a man and woman heatedly embrace, thrilling to "every long, close kiss." The anonymous author brought the scene to a close with a tacit acknowledgment that love stories can only be told in part—for "ecstacy itself is wordless." Too mindful of the erotic, too reserved to leave behind explicit comment, most passionate Victorians must silently have agreed.

Epilogue

What does all this perpetual discussion of sex mean? Wherefore this constant analysis of the passions? How comes it that the novels of today are filled with nothing but sex, sex, sex?

—*Reynolds's News,* April 21, 1895

Although the commentator may have been exaggerating for journalistic effect, his or her observation was not an isolated one. In the *Daily Chronicle*'s issue of February 6, 1894, a reviewer had also remarked that "the bulk of novels published nowadays" explored "the relations of sex." The increasing directness with which the subject was probed in late-nineteenth-century literature reflected people's need to learn more about sexuality, eradicate the unfair inequities between men and women, and reduce the physical risks associated with sex. While the Victorians well understood passion, they also recognized the flaws in their sexual world, and reformers of all kinds—writers, feminists, legislators, scientists, and doctors—worked to master the problems.

The trouble was, what ought to have been a purely humanitarian endeavor was widely exploited, especially from the beginning of the twentieth century. The scientific, medical, and legal authorities who sorted and labeled human sexual variety—the same authorities who diffused their analyses, theories, and studies—spared little thought for the potentially inhibiting effect on both the collective and individual experience of sexuality. Passion began to decline, while sex ever more thrived as a professional specialty. And, if many of the specialists had altruistic motives, most also gained in status and prosperity.

In a parallel development, others, too, found sex and people's natural interest in it to be a ready source of gain. The principle "sex sells" had been known in the nineteenth century, but early-twentieth-century advertisers were more prolific and blatant in its use. In one full-color advertisement from around 1910, the realistically lithographed model, her garments loose enough to show off the tip of one breast, lies back in apparently orgasmic ecstasy over the tiny bar of Plantol Soap she holds in her hand. A 1916 tobacco advertisement also invoked sex to sell its product. The illustration shows a soldier on leave from World War I; he and his female companion are enjoying a romantic outing in a small boat on a secluded waterway. His suggestion that they "tie up in the shade for a bit" is laden with innuendo and leads directly to the commercial climax: together, the pair are about to take mutual pleasure in *"Kenilworths . . . the most soothing and seductive cigarettes imaginable."*

Similarly, as the early-twentieth-century fashion and entertainment industries increasingly commercialized, they promoted sex more flagrantly than ever before—daring flapper fashions and steamy silent films were among the signs of a new sexual age. The more that advertising, fashion, and entertainment used sex for their commercial purposes, the more it became a commodity—an object to be owned or consumed, rather than passion to be felt. It is significant that what was once perceived more than spoken acquired a name. In the 1920s the popular slang for attractiveness to the opposite sex was "it"—not only was passion declining, but sex appeal had been neutered.

The processes of turning sex into commercial commodity and category of endless professional and quasi-professional talk have continued through the twentieth century. Publicly diminished, passion today must exist privately—hidden, as if in the shame we wrongly attributed to the Victorians. At once palpable and discreet, their passion openly flourished. Looking back, straining beyond our own weltering culture of sex, we can distinguish it still.

Notes

After first references in each chapter, I have used shortened titles in these notes.

INTRODUCTION

2 *Historians of the 1970s:* For example, Ronald Pearsall, *Public Purity, Private Shame: Victorian Sexual Hypocrisy Exposed* (1976); Milton Rugoff, *Prudery and Passion* (1971); Eric Trudgill, *Madonnas and Magdalens: The Origins and Development of Victorian Sexual Attitudes* (1976). See also Stephen Marcus, *The Other Victorians: A Study of Sexuality and Pornography in Mid-Nineteenth Century England* (1964), widely influential in the decade after publication.

2 *Michel Foucault: The History of Sexuality*, vol. 1, *An Introduction* (1976; trans. R. Hurley, 1978; reprint, 1980). My recurring theme of the transformation of sex into talk is adapted from Foucault's theory of sexual discourse.

2 *Peter Gay: The Bourgeois Experience: Victoria to Freud*, vol. 1, *Education of the Senses* (1984); vol. 2, *The Tender Passion* (1986; reprint, 1987); see 1: 468, for examples of earlier revisionist work.

2 *Subsequent research:* Among the latest, Michael Mason, *The Making of Victorian Sexuality* (1994); and Michael Mason, *The Making of Victorian Sexual*

Attitudes (1994); other studies from the 1980s and 1990s are cited below where appropriate.

2 *exception:* Stephen Kern, *The Culture of Love: Victorians to Moderns* (1992), 82–83, 338–39, passim. See also Lawrence Stone's review of Roy Porter and Lesley Hall, *The Facts of Life: The Creation of Sexual Knowledge in Britain, 1650–1950,* in the *Times Literary Supplement,* March 10, 1995, 4–5. I was unable to obtain a copy of Porter and Hall's book before this book went to press.

3 *chicken bosoms:* Lately perpetuated by Diane Ackerman, *A Natural History of Love* (1994), 88.

3 *public as well as private:* First noted by Peter Bailey, "Parasexuality and Glamour: The Victorian Barmaid as Cultural Prototype," *Gender & History* 2 (1990), 148.

4 *enormous readership:* On the cultural impact of popular fiction and magazines, see Patricia Anderson, *The Printed Image and the Transformation of Popular Culture, 1790–1860* (1991; reprint, 1994).

4 *other sexualities:* On same-sex love, see, among others, Richard Davenport-Hines, *Sex, Death and Punishment: Attitudes to Sex and Sexuality in Britain since the Renaissance* (1991), 105–55; Lillian Faderman, *Surpassing the Love of Men: Romantic Friendships and Love between Women from the Renaissance to the Present* (1981); Kenneth Plummer, ed., *The Making of the Modern Homosexual* (1981); Jeffrey Weeks, *Coming Out: Homosexual Politics in Britain from the Nineteenth Century to the Present* (1977); Jeffrey Weeks, *Sex, Politics and Society: The Regulation of Sexuality since 1800* (1981; 2d ed., 1989), 96–121; on the cult of the child, see James Kincaid, *Child-Loving: The Erotic Child and Victorian Culture* (1992).

4 *heterosexuality:* Much of the history remains to be written: see Jonathan Ned Katz, "The Invention of Heterosexuality," *Socialist Review* 20 (1990): 8–9; Ivan Illich, *Gender* (1982), 149 and 149 n. 110; Andrew H. Miller, Editor's Introduction, Special Issue: Victorian Sexualities, *Victorian Studies* 36 (1993): 269–72.

4 *"otherness":* Influentially articulated by Simone de Beauvoir, *The Second Sex,* trans. H. M. Parshley (1953; reprint, 1989), xxii–xxxv.

4 *woman not merely the oppressed "other":* "Power is everywhere" (Foucault, *History of Sexuality,* 1: 93–94) and "comes from below" as well as above; see also Illich, *Gender,* 114–16.

5 *gender:* Illich, *Gender;* Ludmilla Jordanova, *Sexual Visions: Images of Gender in Science and Medicine between the Eighteenth and Twentieth Centuries* (1989),

13–18; Elaine Showalter, "Introduction: The Rise of Gender," in *Speaking of Gender,* ed. E. Showalter (1989).

5 *gather information visually:* Interpretations here are informal versions of my approach in Anderson, *Printed Image.*

THE VICTORIAN SEXUAL MYSTIQUE

7 *Victorian sexual mystique:* Though both sexes actively created the mystique, it is a reflection of the inequities of the time that men's words outnumber those of women in this chapter.

7 *Charles Kingsley to Fanny Grenfell, October 1843:* Quoted in Susan Chitty, *The Beast and the Monk: A Life of Charles Kingsley* (1974), 82.

7 *"my blood boils":* Fanny Grenfell to Charles Kingsley, July 1843, quoted in Peter Gay, *The Tender Passion* (1986; reprint, 1987), 306.

8 *rise [of] myths and errors:* Michael Mason, *The Making of Victorian Sexuality* (1994), 8–20.

8 *the pearl:* Colin McDowell, "Learning the Ropes," review of *Pearls: Ornament and Obsession,* by Kristin Joyce and Shellei Addison, *Times Literary Supplement,* December 4, 1992, 26; on the magazine *The Pearl,* see Peter Fryer, ed., *Forbidden Books of the Victorians: Henry Spencer Ashbee's Bibliographies of Erotica* (1970), 138–42.

8 *Cora Pearl:* Polly Binder, *The Truth About Cora Pearl* (1986); Cyril Pearl, *The Girl with the Swansdown Seat* (1955), 146–47.

8 *limbs and legs:* Remarks on usage are based on a range of Victorian sources; see also Valerie Steele, *Fashion and Eroticism: Ideals of Feminine Beauty from the Victorian Era to the Jazz Age* (1985), 112–13.

9 *female leg in view:* Examples are from period illustrations and Steele, *Fashion and Eroticism,* 114, 116–17, passim.

9 *Reverend Francis Kilvert:* See, among others, Frederick Grice, *Francis Kilvert and his World* (1982); A. L. Le Quesne, *After Kilvert* (1978); David Lockwood, ed., *Kilvert, the Victorian: A New Selection from Kilvert's Diaries* (1993).

9 *"delicately beautiful limbs":* Quoted in James Walvin, *Victorian Values* (1987; reprint, 1988), 135.

10 *"no censor of legs":* "Fashion Notes, by Iris," *Bow Bells,* n.s., 32 (1895): 321.

10 *prudishly covered legs of pianos:* Among others, Russell Goldfarb, *Repression and Victorian Literature* (1970), 43; and Stephen Kern, *Anatomy and Destiny:*

A Cultural History of the Human Body (1975), 2, have repeated the popular lore about frilled piano legs as a universal sign of Victorian prudery, although reliably documented examples are rare and unrepresentative of conventional practice. Skeptics like myself include Cyril Ehrlich, *The Piano: A History* (1976; revised ed., 1990), 130; Peter Gay, *Education of the Senses,* (1984), 495; F. Barry Smith, "Sexuality in Britain, 1800–1900: Some Suggested Revisions," in *A Widening Sphere: Changing Roles of Victorian Women,* ed. Martha Vicinus (1977), 183; Steele, *Fashion and Eroticism,* 113.

10 *decorating fashion:* Jenni Calder, *The Victorian Home* (1977); Charlotte Gere, *Nineteenth-Century Decoration* (1989); F. G. Roe, *Victorian Furniture* (1952); Peter Thornton, *Authentic Decor: The Domestic Interior, 1620–1920* (1984).

10 *"externals of the female generative organs . . . sexualised":* Orford Northcote, "Dress in its Relationship to Sex," *Adult: The Journal of Sex* 1 (1897): 79.

11 *similarity to female posterior: London Journal,* n.s., 4 (1885): 257, shows another example comparable to the one used here. While not necessarily calculated or consciously perceived, resemblances between clothing and furniture indicate the breadth of Victorian sensuality; see also Casey Finch, "'Hooked and Buttoned Together': Victorian Underwear and Representations of the Female Body," *Victorian Studies* 34 (1991): 354–55, 358.

12 *six turn-of-the-century photographs:* Graham Ovenden and Peter Mendes, *Victorian Erotic Photography* (1973), 88, which also includes other examples of dress and undress in pornography.

12 *masculine attention on the stocking:* "De l'Adultère: conseils pratiques," *Gil Blas,* 1890, quoted in Steele, *Fashion and Eroticism,* 199.

12 *crinoline [as] fashion item:* Elizabeth Ewing, *Dress and Undress: A History of Women's Underwear* (1978), 72.

12 *inconvenience for women:* Victorian commentary quoted in Pearl, *Girl with the Swansdown Seat,* 206; he identifies the first commentator as Mr. J. Robertson Scott.

13 *riddle of the day:* Quoted ibid.

13 *photographic spoof:* Stereoscopic photograph, c. 1860, reproduced in William C. Darrah, *The World of Stereographs* (1977), 59.

13 *controversies over feminine underpants:* I have pieced together my discussion from C. Willett Cunnington and Phillis Cunnington, *The History of Underclothes* (1951; revised ed., 1981), 72–73; Ewing, *Dress and Undress,* 56, 61, 85; Steele, *Fashion and Eroticism,* 198–99.

15 *nude bathing on English beaches:* Pearl, *Girl with the Swansdown Seat,* 217–28; Walvin, *Victorian Values,* 134–35.

15 *Kilvert . . . observer of nude female bathers:* Quoted in Pearl, *Girl with the Swansdown Seat,* 227; Walvin, *Victorian Values,* 135.

15 *Other seaside sights . . . every English beach:* Sources in this passage quoted in Pearl, *Girl with the Swansdown Seat,* 220, 222, 224, 226.

17 *myth [of] hypocritical respectability:* Fostered by Kern, *Anatomy and Destiny;* Ronald Pearsall, *Public Purity, Private Shame: Victorian Sexual Hypocrisy Exposed* (1976); others are noted in Gay, *Education of the Senses,* 466.

17 *pleasure within limits:* For related discussion, see Peter Bailey, "Parasexuality and Glamour: The Victorian Barmaid as Cultural Prototype," *Gender & History* 2 (1990): 148–49.

17 *"natural" or "normal" sex:* Sex is not "natural" or "normal" in the sense of being purely biological but is, and was, shaped—or constructed—by the social and cultural attitudes of particular times and places; see Pat Caplan, introduction to P. Caplan, ed., *The Cultural Construction of Sexuality* (1987), 1–30; Katz, "The Invention of Heterosexuality," 7–34; Thomas Laqueur, *Making Sex: Body and Gender from the Greeks to Freud* (1990); Robert A. Padgug, "Sexual Matters: On Conceptualizing Sexuality in History," in *Passion and Power: Sexuality in History,* ed. Kathy Peiss and Christina Simmons (1989), 21–25; Peiss and Simmons, *Passion and Power,* introduction; Jeffrey Weeks, "Questions of Identity," in Caplan, *Cultural Construction of Sexuality,* 31–38; Jeffrey Weeks, *Sexuality and Its Discontents: Meanings, Myths and Modern Sexualities* (1985).

18 *eighteenth century, heterosexuality:* To avoid a lengthy digression I have not elaborated; for an introduction, see Paul-Gabriel Bouce, ed., *Sexuality in Eighteenth-Century Britain* (1982).

18 *divergent heterosexual types:* For humorous or otherwise tolerant treatment, see "The Naughty Lord and the Gay Young Lady," ballad sheet, c. 1860, in Charles Hindley, *Curiosities of Street Literature* (1871; reprint 1970), 134; see also ibid., 35 and 131.

18 *the adulteress:* On the prevailing Victorian attitude and its reflection in fiction and visual art, see Sally Mitchell, *The Fallen Angel: Chastity, Class and Women's Reading, 1835–1880* (1981); Lynda Nead, *Myths of Sexuality: Representations of Women in Victorian Britain* (1988), 48–90.

19 *The Lustful Turk:* First published, 1828; for excerpts and commentary, see Fryer, *Forbidden Books,* 126–27; Stephen Marcus, *The Other Victorians: A Study of Sexuality and Pornography in Mid-Nineteenth Century England* (1964), 197–216; Peter Webb, "Victorian Erotica," in *The Sexual Dimension in Literature,* ed. Alan Bold (1983), 97–99.

19 *gentlemen authors acknowledge women's weapons:* Novelist Charles Reade, for example, whom I discuss in chapter 4; E. C. Grenville Murray, *Sidelights on English Society: Sketches from Life, Social and Satirical* (2d ed., 1883), 12–15, on "the flirt's power."

20 *"What can be Man's . . . ":* Alfred Austin, "The Season," quoted in Pearl, *Girl with the Swansdown Seat,* 208; Austin was poet laureate in the 1890s.

20 *"For this you study coquetry . . . ":* Hints on Husband Catching* (1846), iv–v.

20 *marriage a mixed blessing:* On the limitations of marriage for women, see Mitchell, *Fallen Angel,* 175.

20 *"matrimony . . . the signal of emancipation . . . ":* Hints on Husband Catching,* iv.

21 *some left behind memoirs:* Though often marked by omissions and reticences, memoirs are reminders of the human variety that must be countered against generalizations about a period and its culture; for excerpts and commentary, see John Burnett, ed., *Destiny Obscure: Autobiographies of Childhood, Education and Family* (1982; reprint, 1984); Burnett, ed., *Useful Toil: Autobiographies of Working People from the 1820s to the 1920s* (1974; reprint, 1984); Valerie Sanders, *The Private Lives of Victorian Women: Autobiography in Nineteenth-Century England* (1989); David Vincent, *Bread, Knowledge and Freedom: A Study of Nineteenth-Century Working Class Autobiography* (1982).

22 *Victorian period began to give way:* Elaine Showalter, *Sexual Anarchy: Gender and Culture at the Fin de Siècle* (1991).

22 *New words:* Dates given for "heterosexuality" and "homosexuality" are from Lawrence Birken, *Consuming Desire: Sexual Science and the Emergence of a Culture of Abundance, 1871–1914* (1988), 93.

22 *Oscar Wilde:* On his trials and imprisonment, see Richard Ellmann, *Oscar Wilde* (1988), chaps. 18 and 19.

22 *little awareness of lesbian identity:* This had much to do with women's subordinate social position and lack of independence; for discussion, see Jeffrey Weeks, *Sex, Politics and Society: The Regulation of Sexuality since 1800* (1981; 2d ed., 1989), 115–17.

22 *Men and Women's Club:* Judith Walkowitz, *City of Dreadful Delight: Narratives of Sexual Danger in Late-Victorian London* (1992), chap. 5.

23 *rise of sexology:* Birken, *Consuming Desire,* 40–56; Vern L. Bullough, *Science in the Bedroom: A History of Sex Research* (1994); Paul Robinson, *The Modernization of Sex* (1976), 1–41; Weeks, *Sex, Politics and Society,* 141–59.

23 *Havelock Ellis: Man and Woman: Study of Human Secondary Sexual Characteristics* ([1893]; 2d ed., 1897).

23 *occasional observer might complain:* George W. E. Russell, *An Onlooker's Note-Book* (1902), 266–67; reissue, *Collections and Recollections* (1909), 326–28.

BOSOMS AND BUSTLES

25 *Revelations of Girlhood:* Subtitle: *Habits and Customs Explained* (n.d.), 7, "Sex, Population, Eugenics," box 3, John Johnson Collection, Bodleian Library, Oxford.

25 *"Note, the graceful undulations . . . ":* Ibid.

25 *George W. M. Reynolds:* E. F. Bleiler, "Introduction to the Dover Edition of *Wagner, the Wehr-Wolf*" (1975); Margaret Dalziel, *Popular Fiction One Hundred Years Ago* (1957), 35–45; *Bookseller,* July 3, 1879, 600–601; Anne Humpherys, "G. W. M. Reynolds: Popular Literature and Popular Politics," in *Innovators and Preachers,* ed. Joel Wiener (1985); Victor E. Neuburg, *Popular Literature* (1977), 156–62; Montague Summers, *A Gothic Bibliography* (1940); portrait in *Reynolds's Miscellany* 1 (1846): 1.

26 *millions of readers:* R. D. Altick, *The English Common Reader: A Social History of the Mass Reading Public, 1800–1900* (1957), 384; for at least two decades after his death in 1879, Reynolds's books were still reissued and widely read in both England and America.

26 *Wagner, the Wehr-Wolf:* By George W. M. Reynolds, serialized, *Reynolds's Miscellany* 1 (1847).

26 *abducted into white slavery:* Reynolds, *Wagner,* ibid., 1: 337; illustration reproduced in Patricia Anderson, *The Printed Image and the Transformation of Popular Culture, 1790–1860* (1991; reprint, 1994).

26 *"little wavelets . . . ":* Reynolds, *Wagner,* quoted in Dalziel, *Popular Fiction,* 38.

28 *"dreamlike voluptuousness":* George W. M. Reynolds, *The Mysteries of the Court of London,* vol. 1 (1850): 42.

28 *"glowing bosoms":* Ibid., 120; Dalziel, *Popular Fiction,* 38, 41.

28 *cleavage everywhere in popular romance:* For example, Malcolm Errym [J. M. Rymer], *Nightshade; or Claude Duval, the Dashing Highwayman* (1865), 401; *London Reader* 1 (1863): 609; 2 (1863–64): 289, 609; Thomas Prest, *Angelina; or, The Mystery of St. Mark's Abbey* (1849), 81; Eugène Sue, *Martin, the Foundling; or, Memoirs of a Valet de Chambre, London Journal* 5 (1847): 111.

28 *woman plucked from death: London Journal,* n.s., 3 (1885): 1.

28 *full-breasted woman held sway: Beautiful Women: or, the Album Book of Beauty* (1858); Reverend Edward John Hardy, *The Five Talents of Women: A Book for Girls and Women* (1888), 23; *London Journal* 8 (1849): 322–24.

28 *minor poets:* For example, Joseph Ashby-Sterry, "Miss Lizzie Leslie," *Boudoir Ballads* (3d ed., 1877), 208; see also "An Etching," *Cassell's Magazine*, n.s., 3 (1871): 25.

29 *"Who will not admit . . . ": Revelations of Girlhood,* 7.

29 *"her lovely breasts . . . ": The Disembodied Spirit* [1860s], quoted in Ronald Pearsall, *The Worm in the Bud: The World of Victorian Sexuality* (1969; reprint, 1983), 94.

29 *woman [with] torso exposed:* Graham Ovenden and Peter Mendes, *Victorian Erotic Photography* (1973), 15.

29 *the corset:* Casey Finch, "'Hooked and Buttoned Together': Victorian Underwear and Representations of the Female Body," *Victorian Studies* 34 (1991): 337–63; David Kunzle, "Dress Reform as Antifeminism: A Response to Helene E. Roberts's 'The Exquisite Slave: The Role of Clothes in the Making of the Victorian Woman,'" *Signs* 2 (1977): 570–79; David Kunzle, *Fashion and Fetishism: A Social History of the Corset, Tight-Lacing and Other Forms of Body Sculpture in the West* (1982); Pearsall, *Worm in the Bud*, 159–60; Helene E. Roberts, "The Exquisite Slave: The Role of Clothes in the Making of the Victorian Woman," *Signs* 2 (1977): 554–69; Valerie Steele, *Fashion and Eroticism: Ideals of Feminine Beauty from the Victorian Era to the Jazz Age* (1985), 161–91, 200–205; Norah Waugh, *Corsets and Crinolines* (1954).

30 *Letters and commentary: Englishwoman's Domestic Magazine* 3–16 (1867–74), correspondence pages; "Words to Women" (n.d.), anti-corset tract, "Sex, Population, Eugenics," box 3, John Johnson Collection, Bodleian Library, Oxford; W. F. Wilkinson, "Health of Body and Mind," *Good Words* 7 (1866): 121.

31 *"I . . . never feel prouder . . . ": Englishwoman's Domestic Magazine* 3 (1867): 223–24.

31 *ideal Victorian woman:* Marianne Farningham, *Girlhood* (1869), 16–24, 69–74; "Is.Is.," "Woman's Mission," *Westminster Review* 52 (1850): 352–79; *London Journal* 1 (1845): 53; 3 (1846): 35; 21 (1855): 255; 59 (1874): 63; *Revelations of Girlhood*, 4–5; *Reynolds's Miscellany* 14 (1855): 120, 174, 189, 197, 376; *Cassell's Illustrated Family Paper* 2 (1855): 163. See also Deborah Gorham, *The Victorian Girl and the Feminine Ideal* (1982); Lynda Nead, *Myths of Sexuality: Representations of Women in Victorian Britain* (1988), 12–47; Judith Row-

botham, *Good Girls Make Good Wives: Guidance for Girls in Victorian Fiction* (1989).

31 *femininity had two sides:* Hardy, *Five Talents of Women*, 23: a woman pleases "by the beauty of her body . . . and her conduct."

31 *[corset's] dual purpose:* Kunzle, "Dress Reform as Antifeminism," 578–79; Stephen Kern, *Anatomy and Destiny: A Cultural History of the Human Body* (1975), 13.

31 *Decency of dress signaled decency of behavior:* Finch, "'Hooked and Buttoned Together,'" 343; Steele, *Fashion and Eroticism*, 176.

31 *". . . extraordinarily fascinating . . . ":* "Alfred," *Englishwoman's Domestic Magazine* (1871), quoted in Steele, *Fashion and Eroticism*, 181–82.

32 *orgasmic "excitations":* Ibid., 183–84.

32 *corset removal—association with sexual encounter:* Ashby-Sterry, "Georgie's Girdle," *Boudoir Ballads*, 158 ("girdle" also meant corset in the nineteenth century); Peter Fryer, ed., *Forbidden Books of the Victorians: Henry Spencer Ashbee's Bibliographies of Erotica* (1970), 72; Steele, *Fashion and Eroticism*, 175.

32 *heroines symbolized propriety and sexuality:* For example, Paul Pimlico, *The Factory Girl*, serialized, *Reynolds's Miscellany* 3 (1849); G. W. M. Reynolds, *The Seamstress*, serialized, ibid. 4 (1850); Reynolds, *The Massacre of Glencoe*, serialized, ibid. 10 (1853): 65–66.

32 *Louisa:* Anderson, *Printed Image*, 127.

33 *books and magazine[s] identified womanly with wifely:* Hardy, *Five Talents of Women*, 23–24; *A Lady in Search of a Husband* (1847), 1; *London Journal* 1 (1845): 53; 5 (1847): 40; *Reynolds's Miscellany* 14 (1855): 174; *Cassell's Paper* 2 (1855): 163; for related theoretical discussion, see Anderson, *Printed Image*, 126–29.

34 *Attractive socialites . . . in magazines and advertising:* "Leaders of London Society," *Pearson's Magazine* 1 (1896): 266–70; "The Queen of Romania," *Girl's Own Paper* 8 (1886): 257; art reproductions of biblical figures, *Harmsworth Magazine* 1 (1898–99): passim; personification of liberty, *London Journal* 7 (1848): 129; personification of romance, *Reynolds's Miscellany* 1 (1846–47): title page.

34 *Pears' Soap advertisement:* "Baby's Delight," "Soap," box 4, John Johnson Collection, Bodleian Library, Oxford.

34 *Fanny Kemble: London Journal* 5 (1847): 209; and comparable illustrations: ibid., 225; 6 (1848): 305; 7 (1848): 353.

34 *actresses led the way in fashion:* Steele, *Fashion and Eroticism,* 131.

34 *beauty hints and advice:* For instance, *Bow Bells,* n.s., 33 (1896): 35.

34 *advertisements for Pears' Soap:* Among others, "The Temple of Beauty," depicting Lillie Langtry, Adelina Patti, and three other "professional beauties"—"Miss Fortescue," "Mad. Marie Roze," and "Miss Mary Anderson"—each holding a bar of Pears' Soap, "Soap," box 4, John Johnson Collection, Bodleian Library, Oxford.

37 *theatrical women as sexual beings:* Tracy C. Davis, *Actresses as Working Women: Their Social Identity in Victorian Culture* (1991), 105–62; see also J. S. Bratton, "Jenny Hill: Sex and Sexism in the Victorian Music Hall," in *Music Hall: Performance and Style,* ed. J. S. Bratton (1986), 107–8.

37 *the dancer Finette:* For a reproduction of her visiting card, see Davis, *Actresses as Working Women,* between 102 and 103.

39 *Cross-dressing:* For theoretical approaches, see, among a growing number of others, Marjorie Garber, *Vested Interests: Cross-Dressing and Cultural Anxiety* (1992). Although interesting, such analyses are outside the scope of this book—and, as Liam Hudson said of Garber, *Vested Interests,* it (like others of its kind) "casts over the whole business of desiring one another such a pall of gloom" (*Times Literary Supplement,* May 28, 1993, 10).

40 "*. . . girls appear in fleshing tights . . .* ": Letter to the London County Council, October 14, 1889, quoted ibid., 150.

40 "*fully exposed . . .* ": W. A. Coote, 1894 verbal submission to London County Council, Greater London Record Office, quoted ibid., 129, slightly reworked here for grammatical sense.

40 *torn tights:* Examples cited ibid., 135–36.

41 "*The warm close substance . . .* ": George Augustus Sala (with James Campbell Reddie), *The Mysteries of Verbena House* (1882), quoted in Henry Ashbee, *Catena librorum tacendorum* (1885), reprinted in Fryer, *Forbidden Books,* 133–34.

41 "*merry arses . . .* ": Examples, ibid., 24, 72, passim.

41 *the bustle:* C. W. Cunnington and P. Cunnington, *Handbook of English Costume in the Nineteenth Century* (1973), 519–20; Elizabeth Ewing, *Dress and Undress: A History of Women's Underwear* (1978), 81.

42 *model named after Lillie Langtry:* Cited ibid.

44 "*those regions as intimate . . .* ": "De l'Adultère: conseils pratiques," *Gil Blas,* 1890, quoted in Steele, *Fashion and Eroticism,* 199; see also Northcote, "Dress in its Relationship to Sex," 79; Sala, *The Mysteries of Verbena House,* quoted in Fryer, *Forbidden Books,* 133.

45 *conspicuous changes:* On women's suffrage, education, and related gender issues, see Susan Kingsley Kent, *Sex and Suffrage in Britain, 1860–1914* (1987); David Rubinstein, *Before the Suffragettes: Women's Emancipation in the 1890s* (1986); on dress reform, see Steele, *Fashion and Eroticism*, 145–58; on scientific and medical interest in sexuality and the female body, see, among others, Barbara Ehrenreich and Dierdre English, *For Her Own Good: 150 Years of the Experts' Advice to Women* (1978); Ludmilla Jordanova, *Sexual Visions: Images of Gender in Science and Medicine between the Eighteenth and Twentieth Centuries* (1989).

46 *sexual attractiveness became a commodity:* On the growth of a consumer culture and commodification of beauty and sexuality, see Rosemary Betterton, ed., *Looking On: Femininity in the Visual Arts and Media* (1987), 13; Rachel Bowlby, *Just Looking: Consumer Culture in Dreiser, Gissing, and Zola* (1985); Thomas Richards, *The Commodity Culture of Victorian England: Advertising and Spectacle, 1851–1914* (1990).

46 *lowered tolerance for plumpness: Bow Bells*, n.s., 32 (1895): 313; "Fashion Notes by Iris," ibid., 321; Virginia Harned on dieting, ibid., n.s., 33 (1896): 35; *Cassell's Magazine*, n.s., [unnumbered vol.] (1900): 458, 461, 462; "A Lovable Anomaly" (Eily), ibid., 53; *London Journal*, n.s., 24 (1895): 161, 341, 481, Nov. suppl., facing p. 1; ibid., 33 (1900): Jan. suppl., 2, 3; Feb. suppl., 2–7; *Photo Bits* 1 (1898): 23, passim.

46 *bustle had shrunk:* Cunnington, *Handbook of English Costume*, 520.

46 *anorexic young women:* Joan Jacobs Brumberg, *Fasting Girls: The Emergence of Anorexia Nervosa as a Modern Disease* (1988); Noelle Caskey, "Interpreting Anorexia Nervosa," in *The Female Body in Western Culture: Contemporary Perspectives*, ed. Susan Rubin Suleiman (1986); Finch, "'Hooked and Buttoned Together,'" 341; Helena Michie, *The Flesh Made Word: Female Figures and Women's Bodies* (1989; reprint, 1990), 17–28.

47 *corseted waist smaller:* Steele, *Fashion and Eroticism*, 163.

47 *aging wife cast into shadows: A Wild Love, London Journal*, n.s., 4 (1885): Dec. suppl., 1–4; see also *Pearson's Magazine* 1 (1896): 69–77, 168; Arthur Marwick, *Beauty in History: Society, Politics and Personal Appearance, c. 1500 to the Present* (1988), 225.

48 *Slimness . . . youth and attractiveness not as intimate as later:* For example, *Strand Magazine* 12 (1896): 10, 154; *Pearson's Magazine* 1 (1896): 564. On the wide-ranging aftermath of the increasingly restrictive feminine ideal that emerged at the end of the nineteenth century, see Naomi Wolf, *The Beauty Myth* (1991).

MUSCLES AND MANHOOD

49 *Rosa Fielding, 1867:* Quoted in Stephen Marcus, *The Other Victorians: A Study of Sexuality and Pornography in Mid-Nineteenth Century England* (1964), 227. The original referred to the officer's "beautiful cousin," to whom he was betrothed; to give the modern reader the correct context, I have changed "cousin" to "fiancée."

50 *weapons . . . [as] phallic symbols:* John S. Farmer and W. E. Henley, *Slang and Its Analogues,* vol. 5 (1902; reprint, 1965), s.v. "pistol," "prick," and "weapon"; see also this chapter's discussion of *Captain Pink, of the Plungers*; Peter Gay, *Education of the Senses* (1984), 148; Ronald Pearsall, *The Worm in the Bud: The World of Victorian Sexuality* (1969; reprint, 1983), 482.

50 *feats of nerve and strength: Amy; or, Love and Madness* (1847), 25, 49, 105.

50 *biceps brandish manly arsenal:* Ibid., 137, 217, 265, 273, 313, 361, passim.

50 *weapon-wielding escapades: The Black Pirate; or, the Phantom Ship* (1839; reprint, 1848), 105, 129, 193, 217, 241, 273; *The Boy Brigand; or, the Dark King of the Mountains* (1865), 105, 233, 241; *The Boy Pirate; or, Life on the Ocean* (1865), 97, 225, 289, 345, 361, 417, 441; Pierce Egan, *Paul Jones; the Pirate* (c. 1850), 177, 185, 329, 385; Malcolm Errym, *Nightshade* (1865), passim (Claude Duval, "the dashing highwayman," also appears in W. H. Ainsworth, *Talbot Harland,* serialized, *Bow Bells,* n.s., 12 [1870]); *Pedlar's Acre; or, the Wife of Seven Husbands* (1848; reprint, 1854), 177; Thomas Prest, *The Death Ship; or, the Pirate's Bride and the Maniac of the Deep* (1846), 97–99; Prest, *The Harvest Home: A Domestic Romance* (1852), 129, 145. See also J. Medcraft, *Bibliography of the Penny Bloods of Edward Lloyd* (1945); Montague Summers, *A Gothic Bibliography* (1940).

51 *magazine fiction [for] adolescent males:* For example, *Beeton's Boy's Annual* (1870): 88, 200; *Boy's Leisure Hour* 1 (1884): 81; ibid., 2 (1885): 369.

52 *1884 illustration [of] a warrior:* Ibid., 1 (1884): 241.

53 *"roaring like a bull" . . . "weary hands":* The Silver Digger, London Reader 1 (1863): 433–34; for conciseness and clarity, I have telescoped two concurrent encounters.

53 *Susannah Reynolds:* E. F. Bleiler, "Introduction to the Dover Edition of *Wagner, the Wehr-Wolf*" (1975), ix; Summers, *Gothic Bibliography,* 147; *Gretna Green; or, All for Love* (1848), 18, 73, 81, 297, 305, 377, 385, for examples of weapon-brandishing male characters.

54 *ideal of Victorian manhood:* Mark Carnes and Clyde Griffen, *Meanings for*

Manhood: Construction of Masculinity in Victorian America (1990); Mark Girouard, *The Return to Camelot: Chivalry and the English Gentleman* (1981); J. A. Mangan and James Walvin, eds., *Manliness and Morality: Middle-Class Masculinity in Britain and America, 1800–1940* (1987); Norman Vance, "The Ideal of Manliness," in *The Victorian Public School: Studies in the Development of an Educational Institution,* ed. Brian Simon and Ian Bradley (1975); Vance, *The Sinews of the Spirit: The Ideal of Christian Manliness in Victorian Literature and Religious Thought* (1985).

54 *boy's papers [and] athletic life:* See logo, illustration, p. 53, above; *Boy's Own Annual* 1 (1879): logo with balls, cricket bat, and other sporting equipment; ibid., 6 (1883) and 16 (1893–94), both covering topics such as football, lacrosse, gymnastics, and the overall value of athletic ability; *Boy's Own Magazine* 5 (1859): passim; see also John Springhall, "Building Character in the British Boy: The Attempt to Extend Christian Manliness to Working-Class Adolescents, 1880–1914," in Mangan and Walvin, *Manliness and Morality,* 64–69.

54 *cricket and football heroes glowing examples of manhood:* C. B. Fry "Some Famous Footballers," *Windsor Magazine* 7 (1898): 20–27; see also illustration of cricket heroes, ibid., between 90 and 91; Owen Conway, "Lord Hawke at Home: A Chat with the Captain of the Yorkshire Cricket Team," ibid., 705–9.

54 *"muscular Christianity":* Girouard, *Return to Camelot,* 142; see also Vance, *Sinews of the Spirit,* 8–28.

54 *games ethic [and] British Empire:* Ronald Hyam, *Empire and Sexuality: The British Experience* (1990), 71–73; James Walvin, "Symbols of Moral Superiority: Slavery, Sport, and the Changing World Order, 1800–1940," in Mangan and Walvin, *Manliness and Morality.*

55 *"in the history of the Empire . . . ":* J. E. C. Welldon, quoted in Hyam, *Empire and Sexuality,* 73.

55 *"self-pollution":* Sylvanus Stall, *What a Young Man Ought to Know* [1897], 30–36, 69.

55 *"a set of light-weight dumb bells . . . ":* Ibid., 84.

55 *cautionary tracts:* For example, Church of England Purity Society, *Your Duty: An Address to Sailors and Soldiers* and *A Letter of Warning to Lads,* Papers for Men, nos. 2 and 7 (n.d), "Sex, Population, Eugenics," box 2, John Johnson Collection, Bodleian Library, Oxford.

55 *manly not monastic Christianity:* Girouard, *Return to Camelot,* 142–43.

55 *"provisions":* Stereoscopic photograph, 1858, William C. Darrah, *The World of Stereographs* (1977), 59.

56 *"Tis the hard grey weather . . . ":* Quoted ibid., 136; the emphasis on *hard* English men is mine.

56 *"the Hunt" imbued with erotic symbolism:* John M. MacKenzie, "The Imperial Pioneer and Hunter and the British Masculine Stereotype in Late Victorian and Edwardian Times," in Mangan and Walvin, *Manliness and Morality,* 180–81.

56 *article on fencing: Boy's Own Magazine* 5 (1859): 347.

56 *1890s magazine image of Lord Hawke: Windsor Magazine* 7 (1898): 709; originally published in *Vanity Fair* (no date given in picture credit).

58 *"solitary sin" . . . "splendid energy":* Comments quoted in Lesley A. Hall, "Forbidden by God, Despised by Men: Masturbation, Medical Warnings, Moral Panic, and Manhood in Great Britain, 1850–1950," *Journal of the History of Sexuality* 2 (1992): 367, 370, 372.

58 *"proper subjugation of the sexual impulses . . . ":* James Foster Scott, *The Sexual Instinct,* quoted in Claudia Nelson, "Sex and the Single Boy: Ideals of Manliness and Sexuality in Victorian Literature for Boys," *Victorian Studies* 32 (1988–89), 529.

59 *"round shoulders . . . bad . . . ":* Quoted in Girouard, *Return to Camelot,* 136.

59 *"My limbs are all knots . . . ":* Quoted ibid.

59 *Confessions of a Footman:* Subtitle: *The Secrets of High Life Exposed* (n.d.), "Sex, Population, Eugenics," box 3, John Johnson Collection, Bodleian Library, Oxford.

59 *Matrimonial advertisements: London Journal* 59 (1874): 64.

60 *"Oh what a funny stick . . . ":* "Valentines," folder 1, John Johnson Collection, Bodleian Library, Oxford.

60 *tailoring:* C. W. Cunnington and P. Cunnington, *Handbook of English Costume in the Nineteenth Century* (1973), illustrations on 156–59, 162–63, 315; Claudia Brush Kidwell, "Gender Symbols or Fashionable Details," in *Men and Women: Dressing the Part,* ed. Kidwell and Valerie Steele (1989), 128.

60 *corsets [for men]:* Valerie Steele, "Clothing and Sexuality," ibid., 55; John Gloag, *Victorian Comfort* (1961), 98; David Kunzle, *Fashion and Fetishism: A Social History of the Corset, Tight-Lacing and Other Forms of Body Sculpture in the West* (1982), 232 and pl. 40, facing 105; Valerie Steele, *Fashion and Eroticism: Ideals of Feminine Beauty from the Victorian Era to the Jazz Age* (1985), 184 and 278 n. 63.

61 *"ten or twelve hours of married life . . . ": Hints on Husband Catching* (1846), 41–42.

61 *music hall:* Peter Bailey, "Champagne Charlie: Performance and Ideology in the Music Hall Swell Song," in *Music Hall: Performance and Style,* ed. J. S. Bratton (1986); Peter Bailey, *Leisure and Class in Victorian England: Rational Recreation and the Contest for Control, 1830–1885* (1978; reprint, 1987), 154–75; Susan Pennybacker, "'It was not what she said but the way in which she said it': The London County Council and the Music Halls," in *Music Hall: The Business of Pleasure,* ed. Peter Bailey (1986).

62 *Slap Bang, Here We Are Again:* Cited in Bailey, "Champagne Charlie," 57.

63 *Oxford Joe:* "Actors and Actresses," box 3: "Entertainers and Music Hall Singers, M-R," John Johnson Collection, Bodleian Library, Oxford.

63 *"to pink":* Definition, in use since 1598, from the *Shorter Oxford English Dictionary,* 3d ed.

63 *emotional devastation of manhood:* Carol Lee, *The Blind Side of Eden* (1989); Victor J. Seidler, "Reason, Desire, and Male Sexuality," in *The Cultural Construction of Sexuality,* ed. Pat Caplan (1987); Peter N. Stearns, *Be a Man! Males in Modern Society* (1979).

65 *"brutality and bestiality in the dormitories . . . ":* C. R. Nevinson, *Paint and Prejudice,* quoted in J. A. Mangan, "Social Darwinism and Upper-Class Education in Late Victorian and Edwardian England," in Mangan and Walvin, *Manliness and Morality,* 143.

65 *"There is not a war in the world . . . ":* John Ruskin, *Sesame and Lilies,* quoted in Carol Christ, "Victorian Masculinity and the Angel in the House," in *A Widening Sphere: Changing Roles of Victorian Women,* ed. Martha Vicinus (1977), 159.

66 *her feelings, the focus:* For example, *Amy,* 25.

66 *cold baths heighten testosterone:* Richard O'Mara, "The Masters Were All Wet," *Vancouver Sun Saturday Review,* May 22, 1993, C5.

67 *manhood meant muscle:* Hyam, *Empire and Sexuality,* 72–73; Nelson, "Sex and the Single Boy"; Valerie Steele, "Appearance and Identity," in Kidwell and Steele, *Men and Women,* 20. See also *Boys Will Be Girls: The Feminine Ethic and British Children's Fiction, 1857–1917* (1991), which identifies a feminine ethic imbedded in the earlier Victorian ideal of manliness. The narrowing of masculinity may in part have been a reaction (not necessarily conscious) to the blurring of gender boundaries that accompanied the rise of feminism, individualism, and consumerism; see Lawrence Birken, *Consuming Desire: Sex-*

ual Science and the Emergence of a Culture of Abundance, 1871–1914 (1988), 14; Ivan Illich, *Gender* (1982), 5, 48–58; Elaine Showalter, *Sexual Anarchy: Gender and Culture at the Fin de Siècle* (1991), 8–9.

67 *men's [clothes] became drab:* Steele, *Fashion and Eroticism,* 57–59. This was a continuing trend that had begun in the mid-eighteenth century: Steele, "Appearance and Identity," 16.

67 *turn-of-the-century fiction writers:* Martin Green, *Deeds of Adventure, Dreams of Empire* (1979).

68 *notable athletes of the day:* Apart from the example shown here are, among others, "Our Champion of the Week," *Boys of Our Empire* (1903): 881; "Leading Boy Cricketers," ibid., 886.

68 *football "precludes sentiment . . . ":* Fry, "Some Famous Footballers," 20.

The Making of Lovemaking

71 *"Lover's Lullaby":* Joseph Ashby-Sterry, *Boudoir Ballads* (3d ed., 1877), 53–54.

71 *making of lovemaking:* On the cultural construction of sexuality, see my notes to chapter 1, "The Victorian Sexual Mystique," under the key phrase *"natural" or "normal" sex.*

72 *"ravish a kiss" . . . "every fibre of her being":* Taken by Storm, *London Journal,* n.s., 3 (1885): 123.

72 *Charles Reade:* Wayne Burns, *Charles Reade: A Study in Victorian Authorship* (1961); Malcolm Elwin, *Charles Reade* (1931); Elton E. Smith, *Charles Reade* (1976).

72 *"Every day he sat for hours . . . ":* Charles Reade, *A Terrible Temptation, Cassell's Magazine,* n.s., 3 (1871): 21.

72 *"prattle her maiden love" . . . "'my own—own—own!'":* Ibid.

72 *million or more readers:* Calculated from circulation figures for *Cassell's Magazine* (200,000 or more) and the ratio 1:5, which specialists widely accept as a conservative estimate of the relationship between circulation and actual readership in the mid-nineteenth century.

74 *paintings of attractive couples:* For example, John Calcott Horsley, *Blossom Time,* n.d., and Frederick Smallfield, *Early Lovers,* 1858, reproduced in Christopher Wood, *Victorian Panorama* (1976), 162, 164.

74 *courting at the seaside:* For a photograph of working-class couples at

Yarmouth Beach, 1892, see John R. Gillis, *For Better, For Worse: British Marriages, 1600 to the Present* (1985), 277.

75 *the stereograph:* William C. Darrah, *The World of Stereographs* (1977).

75 *the piano:* Cyril Ehrlich, *The Piano: A History* (1976; revised ed., 1990); Craig H. Roell, *The Piano in America, 1890–1914* (1989), 22–27; Jane Traies, "Jones and the Working Girl: Class Marginality in Music-Hall Song, 1860–1900," in *Music Hall: Performance and Style*, ed. J. S. Bratton (1986), 25–27.

75 *Christmas and New Year's cards:* "Christmas Cards/Humorous/Novelty," ex. case 5, John Johnson Collection, Bodleian Library, Oxford.

76 *the valentine:* Frank Staff, *The Valentine and Its Origins* (1969); David Vincent, *Literacy and Popular Culture* (1989), 44–45.

77 *engraved messages:* Quoted from examples in "Valentines," boxes 8, 9, 10, John Johnson Collection, Bodleian Library, Oxford.

78 *handwritten feelings:* Quoted from examples ibid., box 8.

78 *"flinging herself passionately . . . ":* Reade, *Terrible Temptation*, 21.

78 *"two full and rosy lips . . . ":* Ibid., 1.

78 *"sip the nectar":* Taken by Storm, 123.

79 *"eyes dwelt on . . . ":* The Disembodied Spirit [1860s], quoted in Ronald Pearsall, *The Worm in the Bud: The World of Victorian Sexuality* (1969; reprint, 1983), 94.

79 *[fiction] made much of blushing:* For example, *Taken by Storm*, 121, 123; Reade, *Terrible Temptation*, 21.

79 *Havelock Ellis [on] the blush:* Studies in the Psychology of Sex ([1900]; 3d ed., 1924), 1: 74–75.

79 *"That face which has lost the power . . . ":* Cassell's Maga\?ine, n.s., 1 (1858): 144.

80 *"perfectly irresistible" . . . "earthly treasure":* Taken by Storm, 123.

80 *Charles overcome . . . bereft of "all power of resistance":* Reade, *Terrible Temptation*, 21.

80 *"Old March" wind "romps with skirts . . . ":* Ashby-Sterry, "A Breezy Ballad," *Boudoir Ballads*, 170–71.

81 *final, intense encounter:* Marion's Fate, *Bow Bells*, n.s., 11 (1870): 603–4.

81 *gloves erotic:* Valerie Steele, *Fashion and Eroticism: Ideals of Feminine Beauty from the Victorian Era to the Ja\?\? Age* (1985), 201.

81 *"Good night dear":* Valentine with miniature nightcap, "Valentines," box 9, John Johnson Collection, Bodleian Library, Oxford.

82 *William Holman Hunt, The Awakening Conscience, 1853:* Wood, *Victorian Panorama*, 137.

82 *"And to keep her piano in tune . . . "*: "Tuner's Oppor-tuner-ty," quoted in Traies, "Jones and the Working Girl," 25–26.

83 *"Lather! lather! . . . "*: "Starve Her, Joe," Collection of 12 Music Hall Songs (1893?–c. 1910), 28, British Library, London.

84 *"Man proposes . . . "*: *London Journal*, n.s., 3 (1885): 64.

84 *"Mirror your fate . . . "*: Ashby-Sterry, "Lover's Lullaby," *Boudoir Ballads*, 54.

84 *exceptions according to class:* Among some of London's urban working class, there was a comparatively relaxed attitude to premarital sexual intercourse: Françoise Barret-Ducrocq, *Love in the Time of Victoria: Sexuality, Class and Gender in Nineteenth-Century London*, trans. John Howe (1991).

85 *"blaze of your naked beauty . . . "*: Kingsley, letter to Fanny, 1843, quoted in Peter Gay, *The Tender Passion* (1986; reprint, 1987), 307.

85 *card from the 1880s:* Reproduced and quoted in Avril Lansdell, *Wedding Fashions, 1860–1980* (1983), 27.

85 *"The First Wedding Night"*: "Catalogue of the Latest Photographic Novelties," Collection of . . . Catalogues of Erotic and Obscene Books . . . (1889–1929), no. 15, British Library, London.

86 *"most ruinous" . . . "paralysis"*: Sylvanus Stall, *What a Young Husband Ought to Know* [1900], 91, 95–96.

86 *Mosher survey:* Peter Gay, *Education of the Senses* (1984), 135–44.

86 *"the indication of . . . most sacred powers . . . "*: Mary Wood-Allen, *What a Young Woman Ought to Know* ([1899]), 151.

87 *"throbbing and pulsing . . . "*: Ibid., 152.

87 *"realize the greatest pleasure . . . "*: Stall, *What a Young Husband Ought to Know*, 91.

87 *"love embrace" . . . "worth doing well"*: R. T. Trall, *Sexual Physiology* (1870), quoted in Karen Lystra, *Searching the Heart: Women, Men, and Romantic Love in Nineteenth-Century America* (1989), 113–14.

87 *Dr. William Acton: The Functions and Disorders of the Reproductive Organs* (1857), quoted in Stephen Marcus, *The Other Victorians: A Study of Sexuality and Pornography in Mid-Nineteenth Century England* (1964), 31–32, which overstates Acton's influence: see Gay, *Education of the Senses*, 467–68; see also Michael Mason, *The Making of Victorian Sexuality* (1994), 195–96.

87 *"largest number" . . . "pronounced sexual inclination"*: Stall, *What a Young Husband Ought to Know*, 127.

87 *sexual coldness a correctable condition:* Ibid., 124–26.

88 *informed and considerate approach . . . "sweet and lasting":* Ibid., 135.

88 *American wives:* Quoted in Lystra, *Searching the Heart,* 64, 72.

89 *"natural" and "normal" way:* Auguste Debay, *Hygiène et physiologie du mariage* (1848), cited in Gay, *Education of the Senses,* 151.

89 *"Then lie down . . . ":* Kingsley, letter to Fanny, October 1843, quoted in Gay, *Tender Passion,* 308.

90 *"Oh, dearest, dearest . . . ":* Nathaniel Hawthorne, letter to his wife, quoted in Lystra, *Searching the Heart,* 201.

90 *"Shall we the first night . . . ":* Kingsley, letter to Fanny, 1844, quoted in Gay, *Tender Passion,* 307.

90 *"These soft, hot damp days . . . ":* Kingsley, letter to Fanny, May 1850, quoted ibid., 310–11.

90 *number of marriages grew:* Gillis, *For Better, For Worse,* 231–32.

90 *"A Maiden's Wishes . . . ":* Pears' Soap advertisement, "Soap," box 4, John Johnson Collection, Bodleian Library, Oxford.

91 *colorful weddings:* Lansdell, *Wedding Fashions,* 25, 39–40.

91 *voices of dissent:* Carol Dyhouse, *Feminism and the Family in England, 1880–1939* (1989), 145–50, passim; Susan Kingsley Kent, *Sex and Suffrage in Britain, 1860–1914* (1987), 86–90; David Rubinstein, *Before the Suffragettes: Women's Emancipation in the 1890s* (1986), 38–50.

92 *"sweetness and light":* Matthew Arnold, *Culture and Anarchy* (1869), in *Matthew Arnold: Selected Prose,* ed. P. J. Keating (1970; reprint, 1982), 257.

Dark Desires

93 *"Epitaph on a Young Lady":* Quoted in Ronald Pearsall, *The Worm in the Bud: The World of Victorian Sexuality* (1969; reprint, 1983), 420.

93 *pornography:* Peter Fryer, ed., *Forbidden Books of the Victorians: Henry Spencer Ashbee's Bibliographies of Erotica* (1970); Stephen Marcus, *The Other Victorians: A Study of Sexuality and Pornography in Mid-Nineteenth Century England* (1964); Pearsall, *Worm in the Bud;* Peter Webb, "Victorian Erotica," in *The Sexual Dimension in Literature,* ed. Alan Bold (1983).

94 *flagellation:* Ian Gibson, *The English Vice: Beating, Sex and Shame in Victorian England* (1978).

94 *"He went on whipping me . . . ":* *The Memoirs of Dolly Morton* (1899), quoted in Webb, "Victorian Erotica," 100–101.

95   *"'Put down your slate' . . . ":* The Romance of Lust (1873–76), quoted in Gibson, *English Vice*, 273–74.

95   *"I was forced upon my knees . . . ":* The Romance of Chastisement (1866), quoted in Fryer, *Forbidden Books*, 177–78.

96   *"gradually the pain ceased . . . ":* Romance of Lust, quoted in Gibson, *English Vice*, 274.

96   *"propensity which the English most cherish . . . ":* Henry Ashbee, *Index librorum prohibitorum* (1877), quoted in Fryer, *Forbidden Books*, 22.

97   *"O If my love offended me . . . ":* Joseph Ashby-Sterry, "Pet's Punishment," *Boudoir Ballads* (3d ed., 1877), 22–23.

97   *periodical advertisements:* Society, November 18, 1899 and March 31, 1900, reproduced in Gibson, *English Vice*, facing 277 and 308.

97   *flagellant prostitutes:* Fryer, *Forbidden Books*, 23–25; Gibson, *English Vice*, 246–49, 252–59, illustration facing 309; for the social and cultural history of Victorian prostitution, see Lynda Nead, *Myths of Sexuality: Representations of Women in Victorian Britain* (1988), 91–164; Judith Walkowitz, *Prostitution and Victorian Society: Women, Class, and the State* (1980).

98   *"One of the great charms of birching . . . ":* Algernon Charles Swinburne, "Hints on Flogging" (c. 1888), quoted in Webb, "Victorian Erotica," 91.

98   *"men of the highest positions":* Ashbee, *Index,* quoted in Fryer, *Forbidden Books*, 22.

98   *"queen of her profession" . . . "belly full":* Quoted ibid., 23–24.

98   *"a print in Mrs. Berkley's memoirs . . . ":* Quoted ibid., 24; for an illustration of the "horse," see Gibson, *English Vice,* facing 308.

99   *incest:* James B. Twitchell, *Forbidden Partners: The Incest Taboo in Modern Culture* (1987).

99   *"To get a strong bodied wench . . . ":* Raped on the Railway (1894), quoted in Webb, "Victorian Erotica," 94.

99   *"As she arched up . . . ":* Quoted ibid.

99   *the doctor-rapist:* Roy Porter, "Rape—Does It Have a Historical Meaning?" in *Rape: An Historical and Cultural Enquiry,* ed. Sylvana Tomaselli and R. Porter (1986), 233–34.

99   *"I carefully raised up her clothes . . . ":* The Amatory Experiences of a Surgeon (1881), quoted in Marcus, *Other Victorians*, 239.

100   *"They seize her . . . ":* The Secret Life of Linda Brent (1882), quoted in Pearsall, *Worm in the Bud*, 425.

100   *energetic orgy:* Romance of Lust, quoted in Marcus, *Other Victorians*, 274–76.

101 *sadistic hangman:* George W. M. Reynolds, *The Mysteries of London,* 6 vols. (1845–50), cited in Ronald Pearsall, *Night's Black Angels: The Forms and Faces of Victorian Cruelty* (1975), 261.

101 *flagellant nuns:* George W. M. Reynolds, *Wagner, the Wehr-Wolf* (1857 ed.), 57.

101 *lout forces heroine into dungeon:* Illustration in Bracebridge Hemyng, *Women of London* (c. 1856), 97.

101 *"strange and extraordinary torture . . . ":* Ibid., 151; see also "Chamber of Torture," *London Journal* 1 (1845): 345.

102 *voyeuristic clergyman:* Reynolds, *Mysteries of London,* quoted in Thomas Clark, *A Letter Addressed to G. W. M. Reynolds . . .* (1850).

102 *antagonist seizes hero's fiancée:* Illustration in *Boy Pirate; or, Life on the Ocean* (1865), 25.

102 *"If you say nay . . . ":* Pierce Egan, *Paul Jones; the Pirate* (c. 1850), 16.

103 *seducers:* "The Politics of Seduction in English Popular Culture," in *The Progress of Romance: The Politics of Popular Fiction,* ed. Jean Radford (1986).

103 *Octavia "gives herself completely up ":* George W. M. Reynolds, *The Mysteries of the Court of London,* vol. 1 (1850): 42–43.

103 *the fiendish "vampyre" Varney:* Malcolm Errym, *Varney, the Vampyre* (1847); Christopher Frayling, ed., *The Vampyre: Lord Ruthven to Count Dracula* (1978), has passages from *Varney.* See also Carol Senf, *The Vampire in Nineteenth Century English Literature* (1988).

104 *he "seizes her neck" . . . "sucking noises":* Errym, *Varney,* 4.

104 *And oh, my God, my God, pity me!. . . :* Bram Stoker, *Dracula* (1897; reprint 1992), 293–94. See also Christopher Bentley, "The Monster in the Bedroom: Sexual Symbolism in Bram Stoker's *Dracula,*" in *Dracula: The Vampire and the Critics,* ed. Margaret Carter (1988), which makes the point, 33, that the eroticized content of Stoker's *Dracula* caused little or no offense to readers; Christopher Craft, "Kiss Me with Those Red Lips: Gender and Inversion in Bram Stoker's Dracula," in *Speaking of Gender,* ed. Elaine Showalter (1989); Carol L. Fry, "Fictional Conventions and Sexuality in *Dracula,*" Gail B. Griffin, "'Your Girls That You All Love Are Mine': *Dracula* and the Victorian Male Sexual Imagination," Phyllis A. Roth, "Suddenly Sexual Women in Bram Stoker's *Dracula,*" all in Carter, *Dracula*; Robert Tracy, "Loving You All Ways: Vamps, Vampires, Necrophiles and Necrofilles in Nineteenth-Century Fiction," in *Sex and Death in Victorian Literature,* ed. Regina Barreca (1990).

105 *Victorian crusade[s] against vice:* H. Montgomery Hyde, *A History of Pornography* (1964), 163–74; Iain McCalman, *Radical Underworld: Prophets, Revolutionaries, and Pornographers in London, 1795–1840* (1988), chap. 10; Judith Walkowitz, *City of Dreadful Delight: Narratives of Sexual Danger in Late-Victorian London* (1992), chaps. 3 and 4, on Stead's campaign; Jeffrey Weeks, *Sex, Politics and Society: The Regulation of Sexuality since 1800* (1981; 2d ed., 1989), 84–89.

105 *Count [Dracula] basically heterosexual:* Not everyone agrees: see, for example, Craft, "Kiss Me with Those Red Lips," on the homoerotic elements in Stoker's *Dracula*; Judith Halberstam, "Technologies of Monstrosity: Bram Stoker's *Dracula*," *Victorian Studies* 36 (1993). But whatever his sexual orientation(s), Dracula upheld the heterosexual norm indirectly—as a symbolic warning against the horror of perversion.

107 *disturbing ambiguity:* Patricia Anderson, *The Printed Image and the Transformation of Popular Culture, 1790–1860* (1991; reprint, 1994), 195.

107 *fiction's women turned the tables:* On powerful, as opposed to passive or helpless, female images in Victorian literature and art: see, for example, Nina Auerbach, *Woman and the Demon: The Life of a Victorian Myth* (1982); Camille Paglia, *Sexual Personae: Art and Decadence from Nefertiti to Emily Dickinson* (1990; reprint, 1991) also revives many strong, even threatening, representations of women as part of a larger agenda of illustrating the "amorality, aggression, sadism, voyeurism, and pornography in great art" (xiii).

107 *heroine uses stays: Fortunes and Misfortunes of a Ballet Girl* (c. 1870), 31, "Sex, Population, Eugenics," box 3, John Johnson Collection, Bodleian Library, Oxford.

107 *"'Cowards!'" she exclaims:* George Emmett, *Black-Eyed Susan; or, Pirates Ashore* (1868), 65.

107 *three rapacious female vampires:* Stoker, *Dracula*, 45–48.

107 *women "delight . . . ":* Henry Ashbee, *Centuria librorum absconditorum* (1879), quoted in Gibson, *English Vice*, 278.

108 *women beginning to erode male power:* On Victorian feminism, see, among others, Carol Dyhouse, *Feminism and the Family in England, 1880–1939* (1989); Susan Kingsley Kent, *Sex and Suffrage in Britain, 1860–1914* (1987); David Rubinstein, *Before the Suffragettes: Women's Emancipation in the 1890s* (1986).

108 *Jack the Ripper:* Jane Caputi, *The Age of Sex Crime* (1987); Christopher Frayling, "The House that Jack Built: Some Stereotypes of the Rapist in the

History of Popular Culture," in Tomaselli and Porter, *Rape;* Donald Rumbe-
low, *The Complete Jack the Ripper* (1988).

108 *journalistic sensation:* Frayling, "House that Jack Built," 187–89; Walkowitz,
City of Dreadful Delight, chap. 7.

109 *[Ripper] imitators:* Caputi, *Sex Crime,* 32, 33.

109 *pornography increasingly went further:* Pearsall, *Worm in the Bud,* 453;
Walkowitz, *City of Dreadful Delight,* 274 n. 62.

109 *My Secret Life:* By "Walter," 11 vols. (c. 1890), quoted in Marcus, *Other Victorians,* chaps. 3 and 4, which overestimates the "honesty" and realism of this
work.

109 *[sexology's] fragmented view of the sexual body:* Distinct from pornographers,
sexologists had redeeming, if often misguided, humanitarian motives. Yet,
because both pornography and sexology fragmented the body, each in its
own way thereby dehumanized sex.

109 *Psychopathia Sexualis:* By Richard von Krafft-Ebing (English trans., 1892),
cited in Lawrence Birken, *Consuming Desire: Sexual Science and the Emergence of a Culture of Abundance, 1871–1914* (1988), 102.

Flesh and Blood

114 *"RUBBER GOODS":* Photo Bits 1 (1898): 31.

114 *medical knowledge [and] the female body:* Much has been written on this subject, and the literature continues to grow. Making no attempt to be all-inclusive, I have limited myself to a few works that have provided the basic
information for this chapter.

115 *menstruating:* Janice Delaney, Mary Jane Lupton, and Emily Toth, *The Curse:
A Cultural History of Menstruation* (1988); Deidre English and Elaine
Showalter, "Victorian Women and Menstruation," in *Suffer and Be Still:
Women in the Victorian Age,* ed. Martha Vicinus (1972); Louise Lander, *Im-
ages of Bleeding: Menstruation as Ideology* (1988).

115 *most had some advance preparation:* Although Victorian young people did not
have the sexual knowledge of today's adolescents, some scholars have made
too much of girls' supposed ignorance and fear of puberty and menstruating:
see, for example, Fraser Harrison, *The Dark Angel: Aspects of Victorian Sexuality* (1977), 58–59. Ignorance, fear, and shame may well have loomed larger

for boys, most of whom had few resources other than anti-masturbation literature or ill-informed peers.

115 *Helen P. Kennedy surveyed high school girls:* Peter Gay, *Education of the Senses* (1984), 287.

115 *Rich food . . . to be avoided:* Dr. W. W. Bliss, *Woman, and Her Thirty Years' Pilgrimage* (1870), cited in Lander, *Images of Bleeding,* 20–21.

116 *menstruation an unhealthy "modification" of "procreative office . . . ":* Dr. A. F. A. King, *American Journal of Obstetrics* (August 1875), quoted in Lander, *Images of Bleeding,* 49.

116 *medical tendency to equate femininity and pathology: British Medical Journal* (1890.1): 24, 584, 905, passim; (1890.2): 27, 140, 154, passim, for a sampling; see also, among others, Barbara Ehrenreich and Dierdre English, *For Her Own Good: 150 Years of the Experts' Advice to Women* (1978), 99–120; Michel Foucault, *The History of Sexuality,* vol. 1, *An Introduction* (1976; trans. R. Hurley, 1978; reprint, 1980), 104, 146–47; Ornella Moscucci, *The Science of Woman: Gynaecology and Gender in England, 1800–1929* (1990).

117 *hysteria:* Ehrenreich and English, *For Her Own Good,* 120–26; see also Elaine Showalter, *The Female Malady: Women, Madness and English Culture, 1830–1980* (1985), chaps. 5 and 6.

117 *menopause:* Ruth Formanek, "Continuity and Change and 'The Change of Life': Premodern Views of the Menopause," in *The Meanings of Menopause: Historical, Medical, and Clinical Perspectives,* ed. R. Formanek (1990).

118 *"death of the woman in the woman":* Quoted in Ehrenreich and English, *For Her Own Good,* 100.

118 *menopause as "regenerative . . . ":* Eliza Farnham, *Woman and Her Era* (1864), quoted in Formanek, "Continuity and Change," 29.

118 *participant in Mosher's survey:* Quoted ibid., 33.

118 *"masculine judgment" . . . "loss of Power":* Farnham, *Woman,* quoted ibid., 29.

118 *pregnancy the "only strictly natural course":* King, *American Journal of Obstetrics,* quoted in Lander, *Images of Bleeding,* 49.

119 *delicate condition:* Ehrenreich and English, *For Her Own Good,* 100, 114.

119 *"A strong wooden box . . . ":* Albert Goodwin, "Autobiography," quoted in John Burnett, ed., *Destiny Obscure: Autobiographies of Childhood, Education and Family* (1982; reprint, 1984), 287.

119 *childbirth complications:* Ehrenreich and English, *For Her Own Good,* 101–2; Irvine Loudon, *Death in Childbirth: An International Study of Maternal Care and Maternal Mortality, 1800–1950* (1992), reviewed by M. A. Crowther,

Times Literary Supplement, January 22, 1993, 6; Edward Shorter, *A History of Women's Bodies* (1983).

120 *birth control:* John D'Emilio and Estelle Freedman, *Intimate Matters: A History of Sexuality in America* (1988), 57–66; Angus McLaren, *Birth Control in Nineteenth-Century England* (1978); Angus McLaren, *A History of Contraception: From Antiquity to the Present Day* (1990), chap. 6.

121 *abortion:* D'Emilio and Freedman, *Intimate Matters,* 63–66; McLaren, *Birth Control in Nineteenth-Century England,* chap. 13.

122 *"died a martyr to modesty . . . ":* Fanny Kemble, quoted in Havelock Ellis, *Studies in the Psychology of Sex* ([1900]; 3d ed., 1924), 1: 81.

122 *women regarded speculum as pleasurable:* Robert Brudenell Carter, quoted in Ehrenreich and English, *For Her Own Good,* 110.

122 *"the very inmost secrets . . . ":* Hints to Husbands (1856), 26.

123 *Josephine Butler [and] Elizabeth Blackwell condemned the speculum:* Susan Kingsley Kent, *Sex and Suffrage in Britain, 1860–1914* (1987), 120, 127.

123 *the male sexual body:* Compared to studies of the medicalization of women, parallel research on men is not extensive; my discussion is based on chapter 3, above, and additional works noted below.

123 *"Man is forever stretched out . . . ":* William Bowyer, *Brought Out in Evidence: An Autobiographical Summing-Up* (1941), 334.

123 *Medical intervention [in] cases of masturbation and nocturnal emission:* Vern L. Bullough, *Sexual Variance in Society and History* (1976), 549; Formanek, "Continuity and Change," 13; Lesley A. Hall, "Forbidden by God, Despised by Men: Masturbation, Medical Warnings, Moral Panic, and Manhood in Great Britain, 1850–1950," *Journal of the History of Sexuality* 2 (1992): 368–69.

124 *belt-like apparatus [and] urethral rings:* For illustrations, see Gay, *Education of the Senses,* facing 183; Reay Tannahill, *Sex in History* (1980), 343.

124 *"These weeklies were curious . . . ":* John Paton, *Proletarian Pilgrimage: An Autobiography* (1935), 82.

124 *"My lively imagination . . . ":* Ibid.

124 *"Masturbation was no novelty . . . ":* Ibid., 82–83.

125 *"the chief topic of conversation . . . ":* Bowyer, *Brought Out in Evidence,* 102.

125 *"'blue' stories and anecdotes":* Paton, *Proletarian Pilgrimage,* 80.

125 *"gestures and whisperings":* V. W. Garratt, *A Man in the Street* (1939), 20.

125 *rite of passage in France:* Ronald Hyam, *Empire and Sexuality: The British Experience* (1990), 60.

125 *male afflictions:* Ibid., 76–77; Shorter, *History of Women's Bodies,* also briefly discusses men's diseases, 281–84.

125 *venereal disease:* Bullough, *Sexual Variance,* 552–53; Richard Davenport-Hines, *Sex, Death and Punishment: Attitudes to Sex and Sexuality in Britain since the Renaissance* (1991), chap. 5; Shorter, *History of Women's Bodies,* 263–67; Elaine Showalter, *Sexual Anarchy: Gender and Culture at the Fin de Siècle* (1991), 188–200; for more specialized histories, see Stanislav Andreski, *Syphilis, Puritanism and Witch Hunts: Historical Explanations in the Light of Medicine and Psychoanalysis* (1989); Claude Quetel, *History of Syphilis,* trans. J. Braddock and B. Pike (1990).

126 *Contagious Diseases Acts:* Davenport-Hines, *Sex, Death and Punishment,* 167–78; Kent, *Sex and Suffrage,* 63–78, 119–22; Judith Walkowitz, *Prostitution and Victorian Society: Women, Class, and the State* (1980).

127 *stern warnings:* Sylvanus Stall, *What a Young Husband Ought to Know* ([1900]), 114–18.

127 *divorce became available:* The 1857 Matrimonial Causes Act set up civil divorce courts and procedures. Until 1857, divorce could only be obtained by Act of Parliament, a privilege withheld from all but the wealthy upper classes.

127 *women charged husbands with transmission of venereal disease:* Gail Savage, "The Wilful Communication of a Loathsome Disease: Marital Conflict and Venereal Disease in Victorian England," *Victorian Studies* 34 (1990): 35–54.

127 *Jane Brocas:* Case cited in James Hammerton, *Cruelty and Companionship: Conflict in Nineteenth-Century Married Life* (1992), 109–10.

127 *"mutual connections":* Men's Duties to Women (1852), 19.

128 *Nervous bridegrooms:* Kingsley, letter to Fanny, 1843, quoted in Susan Chitty, *The Beast and the Monk: A Life of Charles Kingsley* (1974), 86; Gay, *Education of the Senses,* 291; anecdote of the red ink, recounted ibid., 290.

128 *Ellis was impotent:* Ruth Brandon, *The New Women and the Old Men: Love, Sex and the Woman Question* (1990), 107, 242.

128 *"My lady once leapt sudden . . . ":* Havelock Ellis, "Madonna," quoted in Eric Trudgill, *Madonnas and Magdalens: The Origins and Development of Victorian Sexual Attitudes* (1976), 276; for other references by Ellis to his eccentric sexual preference, see Brandon, *New Women,* 120–21, 223.

129 *"passionless" attitude consciously cultivated:* N. F. Cott, "Passionlessness: An Interpretation of Victorian Sexual Ideology, 1790–1850," *Signs* 4 (1978): 219–36; Kent, *Sex and Suffrage,* 37.

129 *Edward Benson and his wife, Mary:* John Tosh, "Domesticity and Manliness in the Victorian Middle Class: The Family of Edward White Benson," in *Manful Assertions: Masculinities in Britain since 1800,* ed. Michael Roper and J. Tosh (1991), 51–59.

130 *fifteen hundred to two thousand ovaries:* Ehrenreich and English, *For Her Own Good,* 111.

THE REMAKING OF LOVEMAKING

131 *"problem of the union of man and woman . . . ":* Edward John Hardy, *The Love Affairs of Some Famous Men* (1897; reprint, 1972), 5.

132 *"That the amount of human suffering . . . ": Men's Duties to Women* (1852), 30.

132 *stories survived to be told again:* To evoke the diversity with which real people remade the ideals of lovemaking and marriage, I have taken an eclectic anecdotal approach; these are stories that appeal to me because each in its own way enlarges the picture of the Victorian sexual mystique.

132 *No one "derives so much benefit . . . ":* James Payn, quoted in Hardy, *Love Affairs,* 19.

132 *happy literary husbands:* Examples of Hawthorne, Lever, Sala, ibid., 19, 56–57, 63.

132 *"as husbands they did not amount to much":* Ibid., 5.

132 *Bulwer-Lytton and Dickens:* Ibid., 57–58.

133 *Thomas Carlyle and his wife, Jane:* Ibid., 75–85. See also Phyllis Rose, *Parallel Lives: Five Victorian Marriages* (1983), 243–59.

133 *"it was a good thing . . . ":* Tennyson paraphrased in Hardy, *Love Affairs,* 85.

133 *Charles Johnson Brooke:* Ronald Hyam, *Empire and Sexuality: The British Experience* (1990), 45.

133 *violence:* James Hammerton, "The Targets of 'Rough Music': Respectability and Domestic Violence in Victorian England," *Gender & History* 3 (1991): 23–44.

134 *couple who were tailors:* Henry Mayhew, *London Labour and the London Poor* (1861), quoted in Fraser Harrison, *The Dark Angel: Aspects of Victorian Sexuality* (1977), 178.

134 *Charles Dickens [and] Ellen Ternan:* Claire Tomalin, *The Invisible Woman: The Story of Nelly Ternan and Charles Dickens* (1990). See also Cyril Pearl, *The Girl with the Swansdown Seat* (1955), 81–85, for brief entertaining ac-

counts of the irregular relationships of Dickens and other famous literary and artistic lights.

135 *"grass widow"/impoverished husband and father:* Vignettes based on John R. Gillis, *For Better, For Worse: British Marriages, 1600 to the Present* (1985), 251–52.

135 *Sir George Goldie:* Hyam, *Empire and Sexuality,* 43.

136 *Mabel Loomis Todd:* Peter Gay, *Education of the Senses* (1984), 81–108.

137 *Arthur Munby and Hannah Cullwick:* Derek Hudson, *Munby: Man of Two Worlds: The Life and Diaries of Arthur J. Munby, 1828–1910* (1972); Liz Stanley, ed., *The Diaries of Hannah Cullwick, Victorian Maidservant* (1984).

137 *"I have the inward comfort of knowing . . . ":* Cullwick, quoted ibid., 273.

138 *unnamed clergyman aroused by subordination:* Henry Ashbee, *Index librorum prohibitorum* (1877), quoted in Peter Fryer, ed., *Forbidden Books of the Victorians: Henry Spencer Ashbee's Bibliographies of Erotica* (1970), 25.

138 *Heneage Dering, Rebecca Orpen, Lady Chatterton, Marmion Ferrers:* Mark Girouard, *The Return to Camelot: Chivalry and the English Gentleman* (1981), 202–4.

139 *"when husband and wife pull along happily . . . ":* Hardy, *Love Affairs,* 9.

139 *politicians and statesmen:* Ibid., chaps. 23 and 24.

139 *"contemplation of Nature's calm . . . ":* Ibid., 1897 ed., 259.

139 *Michael Faraday [on] marriage:* Ibid., 261.

139 *"'Forty-two years of married life . . . ":* James Nasmyth, quoted ibid., 265.

139 *marital successes among ministers, scholars, and teachers:* Ibid., 1972 reprint, chaps. 13, 14, and pp. 139–42.

139 *Ellen Ternan married George Wharton Robinson:* Tomalin, *Invisible Woman,* part 3.

140 *George Acorn: One of the Multitude* (1911), an autobiographical account of life among the nineteenth-century urban poor.

140 *"I will not say much" . . . "brighter and happier":* Ibid., 275, 300.

141 *Mrs. C:* John D'Emilio and Estelle Freedman, *Intimate Matters: A History of Sexuality in America* (1988), 56.

141 *Alice Baldwin:* Quoted in Karen Lystra, *Searching the Heart: Women, Men, and Romantic Love in Nineteenth-Century America* (1989), 61.

141 *Lincoln Clark:* Quoted ibid.

142 *Jane Burnett:* Quoted ibid., 62.

142 *Emily Lovell:* Quoted ibid., 63.

142 *"One ought to have said . . . ":* Thomas Carlyle to Jane Carlyle, quoted in

Hardy, *Love Affairs*, 84–85; Hardy's transcription differs slightly in spelling and punctuation from the one in Thomas and Jane Carlyle, *Collected Letters*, ed. Clyde de L. Ryals et al. (1990), 18: 132–33.

142 *"Oh, my darling . . . ":* Jane Carlyle to Thomas Carlyle, quoted in Hardy, *Love Affairs*, 85.

143 *Charles Kingsley letters [and] drawings:* Susan Chitty, *The Beast and the Monk: A Life of Charles Kingsley* (1974), illustration between 64 and 65, 126; Peter Gay, *The Tender Passion* (1986; reprint, 1987), illustration between 172 and 173, 309–10.

143 *"he felt as if his right hand . . . ":* Hardy, *Love Affairs*, 56.

143 *"She lingered and suffered . . . ":* Edward Rymer, *Martyrdom of the Mine*, quoted in David Vincent, *Bread, Knowledge and Freedom: A Study of Nineteenth-Century Working Class Autobiography* (1982), 54.

143 *"Five minutes more . . . ":* Carlyle, quoted in Rose, *Parallel Lives*, 256.

143 *"shattered my whole existence . . . ":* Carlyle, quoted in Margaret Drabble, *Oxford Companion to English Literature*, s.v. "Carlyle, Thomas," 171.

144 *Charles Kingsley['s] last days:* Chitty, *Beast and Monk*, 294–96.

145 *"Thou art . . . unspeakably beloved":* Nathaniel Hawthorne to his wife, quoted in Hardy, *Love Affairs*, 63.

145 *"How much more delicious . . . ":* Kingsley, letter to Fanny, 1843, quoted in Gay, *Tender Passion*, 308.

THE BEST AND THE WORST

147 *Dickens, Tale of Two Cities:* Ed. Andrew Sanders (1988; reprint, 1991), 1.

148 *Rebecca Solomon, The Governess, 1854:* Susan P. Casteras, *Images of Victorian Womanhood in English Art* (1987), 114–15, color plate between 128 and 129; Deborah Cherry, *Painting Women: Victorian Women Artists* (1993), 29–30.

149 *"Ye too, the friendless . . . ":* Martin Tupper, "Of Neglect," in *Proverbial Philosophy—A Book of Thoughts and Arguments* (1843), quoted in Casteras, *Images of Victorian Womanhood*, 114.

150 *creative women [depicted] as unattractive:* Ibid., 103.

150 *more women than men:* "Woman and Civilisation," in *The Civilisation of Our Day*, ed. James Samuelson (1896), 183.

150 *governesses and teachers:* Examples other than Solomon's *Governess* include Emily Osborn, *Home Thoughts*, 1856; and Richard Redgrave, *The Poor*

Teacher, 1843, and later versions; for reproductions, see Casteras, *Images of Victorian Womanhood*, 115–16.

150 *the oppressed needlewoman:* Thomas Hood, "The Song of the Shirt," 1843; John Everett Millais, *Virtue and Vice*, 1853; G. W. M. Reynolds, *The Seamstress*, serialized, *Reynolds's Miscellany* 4 (1850); and see Casteras, *Images of Victorian Womanhood*, 110–14; T. J. Edelstein, "They Sang 'The Song of the Shirt': The Visual Iconology of the Seamstress," *Victorian Studies* 23 (Winter 1980): 183–210; Sally Mitchell, "The Forgotten Woman of the Period: Penny Weekly Family Magazines of the 1840's and 1850's," in *A Widening Sphere: Changing Roles of Victorian Women*, ed. Martha Vicinus (1977), 47–48.

150 *"call attention to the trials . . . ":* Redgrave, *Art-Journal*, 1850, on his 1844 painting *The Sempstress*, quoted in Casteras, *Images of Victorian Womanhood*, 110; the painting is now lost.

150 *Redgrave, The Sempstress, 1846:* Reproduced ibid., 111, and color plate between 128 and 129.

150 *"pale and pensive" . . . "artlessness":* Quoted in Edelstein, "They sang 'The Song of the Shirt,'" 198.

151 *Reade's Terrible Temptation:* See chapter 4, above.

151 *correspondence pages of magazines:* Sampling used here: *London Journal* 2 (1845): 208; 17 (1853): 64; 19 (1854): 192; 28 (1858): 192; 32 (1860): 736; 60 (1874): 64, 416; and n.s., 3 (1885): 64, 384; *Reynolds's Miscellany* 3 (1849): 48, 415; 4 (1850): 143; 10 (1853): 64, 79.

153 *Philip Calderon, Broken Vows, 1856:* Royal Academy entry, 1857; reproduced in Casteras, *Images of Victorian Womanhood*, 89.

153 *Ford Madox Brown, The Stages of Cruelty, 1856–90:* Reproduced ibid., 93.

153 *M. H., was hurt: London Journal* 17 (1853): 64; see also ibid., 28 (1858): 192; 32 (1860): 736.

153 *Thomas Coram Foundling Hospital:* Françoise Barret-Ducrocq, *Love in the Time of Victoria: Sexuality, Class and Gender in Nineteenth-Century London*, trans. John Howe (1991).

153 *"He courted me . . . ":* Ibid., 87–94.

154 *women managed without universal censure:* Ibid., 180; Sally Mitchell, *The Fallen Angel: Chastity, Class and Women's Reading, 1835–1880* (1981), 11, 53.

154 *many readers of popular romance [were] young working-class women:* Patricia Anderson, *The Printed Image and the Transformation of Popular Culture, 1790–1860* (1991; reprint, 1994), 149–50; see also Barret-Ducrocq, *Love in the Time of Victoria*, 58–59.

154 *"the unforgettable heart-breaking degradation . . . "*: William Bowyer, *Brought Out in Evidence: An Autobiographical Summing-Up* (1941), 109.

154 *"When first they come courting . . . "*: Quoted in John R. Gillis, *For Better, For Worse: British Marriages, 1600 to the Present* (1985), 233–34.

154 *"I think we would all prefer . . . "*: Quoted ibid., 234.

155 *"the wife who can make herself most useful . . . "*: Edward John Hardy, *The Five Talents of Women: A Book for Girls and Women* (1888), 111.

155 *domestic violence:* George Acorn, *One of the Multitude* (1911), 2–3, 64–65; James Hammerton, *Cruelty and Companionship: Conflict in Nineteenth-Century Married Life* (1992); Fraser Harrison, *The Dark Angel: Aspects of Victorian Sexuality* (1977), 200–203, passim; Peter Quennell, ed., *Mayhew's London* (1984; reprint, 1987), 57.

156 *queen mourned for forty years:* Albert died in 1861 after twenty-one years of marriage. Victoria remained in virtual seclusion for the next ten years; in the subsequent thirty years, until her own death in 1901, she never appeared in public without wearing mourning.

156 *niceties of mourning handkerchiefs: London Journal,* n.s., 3 (1885): 64.

156 *"When a few days separation" . . . "anguish in the human heart":* Quoted in Karen Lystra, *Searching the Heart: Women, Men, and Romantic Love in Nineteenth-Century America* (1989), 202.

156 *Marion's Fate:* See chapter 4, above.

157 *"Love me, lady . . . be thou my light":* Valentine showing a couple with eyes romantically locked and hands clasped, "Valentines," box 1, John Johnson Collection, Bodleian Library, Oxford.

157 *"how rapidly" . . . "every day":* Quoted in Lystra, *Searching the Heart,* 202.

158 *"The innocent dreams . . . ":* "The Summer by the Sea," *Cassell's Illustrated Family Paper* 3 (1859): 230 (poet not named).

158 *a few exceptions:* Notably, Peter Gay, *Education of the Senses* (1984) and *The Tender Passion* (1986; reprint, 1987).

158 *some have seen mainly pruderies or sordid aspects:* Stephen Kern, *Anatomy and Destiny: A Cultural History of the Human Body* (1975), 1–9; Stephen Kern, *The Culture of Love: Victorians to Moderns* (1992); Stephen Marcus, *The Other Victorians: A Study of Sexuality and Pornography in Mid-Nineteenth Century England* (1964); Ronald Pearsall, *The Worm in the Bud: The World of Victorian Sexuality* (1969; reprint, 1983).

158 *Others have focused on prostitution, marital violence:* Hammerton, *Cruelty and Companionship*; Judith Walkowitz, *Prostitution and Victorian Society: Women, Class, and the State* (1980).

158 *"one unhappy alliance . . . ":* Edward John Hardy, *The Love Affairs of Some Famous Men* (1897; reprint, 1972), 9.

159 *"ecstacy itself is wordless":* Mary Rivenhall's Prophecy, *London Journal* 60 (1874): 410.

EPILOGUE

161 *". . . sex, sex, sex":* Reynolds's News, April 21, 1895, front page; also quoted in Eric Trudgill, *Madonnas and Magdalens: The Origins and Development of Victorian Sexual Attitudes* (1976), 242. The passage continues: "Influenza is not the only new disease which has come to reside among us. Another more terrible and potent plague has seized hold of the nation—sex-mania."

161 *"bulk of novels" . . . "relations of sex":* Daily Chronicle, February 6, 1894, quoted in David Rubinstein, *Before the Suffragettes: Women's Emancipation in the 1890s* (1986), 25.

162 *advertisement [for] Plantol Soap:* "Soap," box 6, John Johnson Collection, Bodleian Library, Oxford.

162 *1916 tobacco advertisement:* "Tobacco," box 3, ibid.

162 *"it":* In use by 1927 to mean sex appeal: *Shorter OED,* 3d ed.

Bibliography

COLLECTIONS

Collection of . . . Catalogues of Erotic and Obscene Books . . . [1889–1929].
   British Library, London.
Collection of 12 Music Hall Songs [1893?–c. 1910]. British Library, London.
John Johnson Collection of Printed Ephemera. Bodleian Library, Oxford.
Ono, Barry. Collection of Nineteenth Century Bloods and Penny Dreadfuls.
   British Library, London.

ESSAYS AND TRACTS

In this and the following two sections, authors are named if known.

Church of England Purity Society. *Your Duty: An Address to Sailors and Soldiers.*
   Papers for Men, no. 2. N.d. "Sex, Population, Eugenics," box 2, John Johnson
   Collection, Bodleian Library, Oxford.
————. *A Letter of Warning to Lads.* Papers for Men, no. 7. N.d. [1880s?]. "Sex, Pop-
   ulation, Eugenics," box 2, John Johnson Collection, Bodleian Library, Oxford.
Clark, Thomas. *A Letter Addressed to G. W. M. Reynolds* . . . 1850.

"Is.Is." "Woman's Mission." *Westminster Review* 52 (1850): 352–79.

Northcote, Orford. "Dress in Its Relationship to Sex," *Adult: The Journal of Sex* 1 (1897): 75–80.

"A Physician." *Revelations of Girlhood: Habits and Customs Explained.* N.d. "Sex, Population, Eugenics," box 3, John Johnson Collection, Bodleian Library, Oxford.

Wilkinson, W. F. "Health of Body and Mind." *Good Words* 7 (1866): 121.

"Woman and Civilisation." In *The Civilisation of Our Day*, edited by James Samuelson. 1896.

Words to Women. N.d. Anti-corset tract, "Sex, Population, Eugenics," box 3, John Johnson Collection, Bodleian Library, Oxford.

Fiction and Poetry

Amy; or, Love and Madness. 1847.

Ashby-Sterry, Joseph. *Boudoir Ballads*, 3d ed., 1877.

The Black Pirate; or, the Phantom Ship. 1839. Reprint, 1848.

The Boy Brigand; or, the Dark King of the Mountains. 1865.

The Boy Pirate; or, Life on the Ocean. 1865.

The Confessions of a Footman; or, the Secrets of High Life Exposed. N.d. "Sex, Population, Eugenics," box 3, John Johnson Collection, Bodleian Library, Oxford.

Egan, Pierce. *Paul Jones; the Pirate.* C. 1850.

Emmett, George. *Black-Eyed Susan; or, Pirates Ashore.* 1868.

Errym, Malcolm [Rymer, J. Malcolm]. *Nightshade; or Claude Duval, the Dashing Highwayman.* 1865.

———. *Varney, the Vampyre; or, the Feast of Blood.* 1847.

Hemyng, Bracebridge. *Women of London.* C. 1856.

Jones, Hanna Maria. *The Curate's Daughters; or, the Twin Roses of Arundale.* 1853.

A Lady in Search of a Husband. 1847.

"A Lovable Anomaly." *Cassell's Magazine*, n.s., [unnumbered vol.] (1900).

Marion's Fate: A Love Story. Serialized, *Bow Bells*, n. s., 11 (1870).

Mary Rivenhall's Prophecy. Serialized, *London Journal* 60 (1874).

Pedlar's Acre; or, the Wife of Seven Husbands. 1848. Reprint, 1854.

Pimlico, Paul. *The Factory Girl.* Serialized, *Reynolds's Miscellany* 3 (1849).

The Pirate Queen. C. 1849.

Prest, Thomas. *Angelina; or, The Mystery of St. Mark's Abbey.* 1849.

————. *The Death Ship; or, the Pirate's Bride and the Maniac of the Deep.* 1846.

————. *The Harvest Home: A Domestic Romance.* 1852.

————. *Susan Hoply; or, the Trials and Vicissitudes of a Servant Girl.* 1842.

Reade, Charles. *A Terrible Temptation.* Serialized, *Cassell's Magazine,* n.s. 3 (1871).

Reynolds, G. W. M. *The Massacre of Glencoe.* Serialized, *Reynolds's Miscellany* 10 (1853).

————. *The Mysteries of the Court of London.* Vol. 1. 1850.

————. *The Seamstress.* Serialized, *Reynolds's Miscellany* 4 (1850).

————. *Wagner: the Wehr-Wolf.* Serialized, *Reynolds's Miscellany* 1 (1847). Reprint, with introduction by E. F. Bleiler. 1975.

Reynolds, Susannah F. *Gretna Green; or, All for Love.* 1848.

The Silver Digger. Serialized, *London Reader* 1 (1863).

Stoker, Bram. *Dracula.* 1897. Reprint, 1992.

Sue, Eugène. *Martin, the Foundling; or, Memoirs of a Valet de Chambre.* Serialized, *London Journal* 5 (1847).

Taken by Storm. Serialized, *London Journal,* n.s., 3 (1885).

A Wild Love. Serialized, *London Journal,* n.s., 4 (1885).

GUIDES, MANUALS, TREATISES, AND MISCELLANEOUS

Beautiful Women; or, the Album Book of Beauty. London, 1858.

Ellis, Havelock. *Man and Woman: Study of Human Secondary Sexual Characteristics.* [1893]. 2d ed., 1897.

————. *Studies in the Psychology of Sex.* Vol. 1. [1900]. 3d ed., 1924.

Farningham, Marianne [Hearn, Marianne]. *Girlhood.* 1869.

Hardy, Reverend Edward John. *The Five Talents of Women: A Book for Girls and Women.* 1888.

————. *The Love Affairs of Some Famous Men.* 1897. Reprint, 1972.

Hints on Husband Catching: Manual for Marriageable Misses. 1846.

Hints to Husbands. 1856.

Men's Duties to Women. 1852.

Murray, E. C. Grenville. *Sidelights on English Society: Sketches from Life, Social and Satirical,* 2d ed., 1883.

Russell, George W. E. *An Onlooker's Note-Book.* 1902.

Stall, Sylvanus. *What a Young Husband Ought to Know.* [1900].

————. *What a Young Man Ought to Know.* [1897].

Wood-Allen, Mary, MD. *What a Young Girl Ought to Know.* [1897].
————. *What a Young Woman Ought to Know.* [1899].

MEMOIRS

Acorn, George. *One of the Multitude.* 1911.
Bowyer, William. *Brought Out in Evidence: An Autobiographical Summing-Up.* 1941.
Cullwick, Hannah. *The Diaries of Hannah Cullwick, Victorian Maidservant.* Edited and introduced by Liz Stanley. 1984.
Garratt, V. W. *A Man in the Street.* 1939.
Paton, John. *Proletarian Pilgrimage: An Autobiography.* 1935.

PERIODICALS

Adult: The Journal of Sex. 1897–99.
Beeton's Boy's Annual. 1870.
Bow Bells. 1870, 1874–75, 1885, 1895–96.
Boy's Leisure Hour. 1884–85.
Boys of Our Empire. 1903.
Boy's Own Annual. 1879, 1883, 1893.
Boy's Own Magazine [later *Beeton's Boy's Annual*]. 1859.
British Medical Journal. 1890.1, 1890.2.
Cassell's Magazine. 1855, 1871, 1885, 1895, 1900.
Days' Doings. An Illustrated Journal of Romantic Events, Reports, Sporting and Theatrical News. 1870.
Englishwoman's Domestic Magazine. 1867, 1874.
Girl's Own Paper. 1886–87.
Good Words. 1866.
Harmsworth Magazine. 1898–99.
London Journal. 1845, 1847–48, 1853–54, 1858, 1860, 1874–75, 1885, 1895, 1900.
London Reader. 1863–64.
Pearson's Magazine. 1896.
Penny Illustrated Paper. 1888.
Photo Bits. 1898.

Reynolds's Miscellany. 1846–60, 1869.

Strand Magazine. 1896.

Sunday at Home. 1867, 1878.

Westminster Review 1850.

Windsor Magazine. 1897–98.

SUGGESTED READING

The history of human sexuality is a comparatively new but already vast field of study. While indicating some important directions that recent research has taken, the following list is by no means comprehensive. Neither does it include every reference given in my notes. Its purpose is to draw attention to the works on sexuality and related subjects that have most substantially enriched this book.

Bailey, Peter. "Parasexuality and Glamour: The Victorian Barmaid as Cultural Prototype." *Gender and History* 2 (1990): 148–72.

Barret-Ducrocq, Françoise. *Love in the Time of Victoria: Sexuality, Class and Gender in Nineteenth-Century London.* Translated by John Howe. 1991.

Birken, Lawrence. *Sexual Science and the Emergence of a Culture of Abundance, 1871–1914.* 1988.

Caplan, Pat, ed. *The Cultural Construction of Sexuality.* 1987.

Casteras, Susan. *Images of Victorian Womanhood in English Art.* 1987.

Chitty, Susan. *The Beast and the Monk: A Life of Charles Kingsley.* 1974.

Davenport-Hines, Richard. *Sex, Death and Punishment: Attitudes to Sex and Sexuality in Britain since the Renaissance.* 1991.

Davis, Tracy C. *Actresses as Working Women: Their Social Identity in Victorian Culture.* 1991.

D'Emilio, John, and Estelle Freedman. *Intimate Matters: A History of Sexuality in America.* 1988.

Ehrenreich, Barbara, and Dierdre English. *For Her Own Good: 150 Years of the Experts' Advice to Women.* 1978.

Finch, Casey. "'Hooked and Buttoned Together': Victorian Underwear and Representations of the Female Body." *Victorian Studies* 34 (1991): 337–63.

Formanek, Ruth. "Continuity and Change and 'The Change of Life': Premodern Views of the Menopause." In *The Meanings of Menopause: Historical, Medical, and Clinical Perspectives,* edited by R. Formanek. 1990.

Foucault, Michel. *The History of Sexuality.* Volume 1, *An Introduction.* Translated by R. Hurley. 1978. Reprint, 1980.

Fryer, Peter, ed. *Forbidden Books of the Victorians: Henry Spencer Ashbee's Bibliographies of Erotica.* 1970.

Gay, Peter. *The Bourgeois Experience: Victoria to Freud.* Volume 1, *Education of the Senses.* 1984. Volume 2, *The Tender Passion.* 1986. Reprint, 1987.

Gibson, Ian. *The English Vice: Beating, Sex and Shame in Victorian England.* 1978.

Gillis, John R. *For Better, For Worse: British Marriages, 1600 to the Present.* 1988.

Girouard, Mark. *The Return to Camelot: Chivalry and the English Gentleman.* 1981.

Hall, Lesley A. "Forbidden by God, Despised by Men: Masturbation, Medical Warnings, Moral Panic, and Manhood in Great Britain, 1850–1950." *Journal of the History of Sexuality* 2 (1992): 365–87.

Hyam, Ronald. *Empire and Sexuality: The British Experience.* 1990.

Illich, Ivan. *Gender.* 1982.

Jordanova, Ludmilla. *Sexual Visions: Images of Gender in Science and Medicine between the Eighteenth and Twentieth Centuries.* 1989.

Kent, Susan Kingsley. *Sex and Suffrage in Britain, 1860–1914.* 1987.

Kunzle, David. "Dress Reform as Antifeminism: A Response to Helene E. Roberts's 'The Exquisite Slave: The Role of Clothes in the Making of the Victorian Woman.'" *Signs* 2 (1977): 570–79.

Lander, Louise. *Images of Bleeding: Menstruation as Ideology.* 1988.

Lystra, Karen. *Searching the Heart: Women, Men, and Romantic Love in Nineteenth-Century America.* 1989.

McLaren, Angus. *Birth Control in Nineteenth Century England.* 1978.

———. *A History of Contraception: From Antiquity to the Present Day.* 1990.

Mangan, J. A., and James Walvin. *Manliness and Morality: Middle-Class Masculinity in Britain and America, 1800–1940.* 1987.

Marcus, Stephen. *The Other Victorians: A Study of Sexuality and Pornography in Mid-Nineteenth Century England.* 1964.

Nead, Linda. *Myths of Sexuality: Representations of Women in Victorian Britain.* 1988.

Nelson, Claudia. "Sex and the Single Boy: Ideals of Manliness and Sexuality in Victorian Literature for Boys." *Victorian Studies* 32 (1988–89): 525–50.

Pearl, Cyril. *The Girl with the Swansdown Seat.* 1955.

Pearsall, Ronald. *The Worm in the Bud: The World of Victorian Sexuality.* 1969. Reprint, 1983.

Peiss, Kathy, and Christina Simmons, eds., with Robert A. Padgug. *Passion and Power: Sexuality in History.* 1989.

Roberts, Helene E. "The Exquisite Slave: The Role of Clothes in the Making of the Victorian Woman." *Signs* 2 (1977): 554–69.

Rubinstein, David. *Before the Suffragettes: Women's Emancipation in the 1890s.* 1986.

Showalter, Elaine. *Sexual Anarchy: Gender and Anarchy at the Fin de Siècle.* 1991.

Steele, Valerie. *Fashion and Eroticism: Ideals of Feminine Beauty from the Victorian Era to the Jazz Age.* 1985.

Tomalin, Claire. *The Invisible Woman: The Story of Nelly Ternan and Charles Dickens.* 1990.

Vicinus, Martha, ed. *A Widening Sphere: Changing Roles of Victorian Women.* 1977.

Walkowitz, Judith. *City of Dreadful Delight: Narratives of Sexual Danger in Late-Victorian London.* 1992.

Webb, Peter. "Victorian Erotica." In *The Sexual Dimension in Literature,* edited by Alan Bold. 1983.

Weeks, Jeffrey. *Sex, Politics and Society: The Regulation of Sexuality since 1800.* 1981. 2d ed., 1989.

Illustration Credits

11 *London Journal* 60 (1874): 409 (PP.6004.cc); by permission of The British Library.

27 *Reynolds's Miscellany* 1 (1847): 273 (PP.6004.baa); by permission of The British Library.

30 Author's collage and photograph.

33 Advertisement for G. W. M. Reynolds, *Mysteries of the Court of London* (1850), *Reynolds's Miscellany* 5 (1850): 300 (PP.6004.b); by permission of The British Library.

35 Bodleian, John Johnson Collection, "Actors and Actresses," box 3: "Entertainers and Music Hall Singers, M-R." Courtesy of the Bodleian Library, University of Oxford.

36 Bodleian, John Johnson Collection, "Soap," box 5*. Courtesy of the Bodleian Library, University of Oxford.

37 Bodleian, John Johnson Collection, "Soap," box 5*. Courtesy of the Bodleian Library, University of Oxford.

38 *Days' Doings*, December 24, 1870, 13; British Newspaper Library, by permission of The British Library.

43 Bodleian, John Johnson Collection, "Women's Clothes," box 1. Courtesy of the Bodleian Library, University of Oxford.

44 *Bow Bells*, n.s., 22 (1875): 44 (PP.6004.ci); by permission of The British Library.

45 *London Journal*, n.s., 4 (1885): October Ladies' Supplement, 8; by permission of The British Library.

47 *Cassell's Magazine,* n.s., [unnumbered volume] (1900): 53 (PP.6004.da); by permission of The British Library.

51 *Amy; or, Love and Madness* (1847), 1 (1206.k.21); by permission of The British Library.

52 *The Boy Pirate* (1865), 49 and 57 (1501/21); by permission of The British Library.

53 *Caractacus: Champion of the Arena, Boy's Leisure Hour* 2 (1885): 305; author's photograph.

57 *Windsor Magazine* 7 (1898): 709; author's photograph.

62 Bodleian, John Johnson Collection, "Men's Clothes," box 2. Courtesy of the Bodleian Library, University of Oxford.

64 Bodleian, John Johnson Collection, "Actors and Actresses," box 3: "Entertainers and Music Hall Singers, M-R." Courtesy of the Bodleian Library, University of Oxford.

68 *Boys of Our Empire* 3 (1903): between 460 and 461; author's photograph.

69 Bodleian, John Johnson Collection, "Soap," box 4. Courtesy of the Bodleian Library, University of Oxford.

69 Bodleian, John Johnson Collection, "Soap," box 6. Courtesy of the Bodleian Library, University of Oxford.

73 *Taken by Storm, London Journal,* n.s., 3 (1885): 121; by permission of The British Library.

74 *Windsor Magazine* 7 (1898): 157; author's photograph.

76 *Society,* n.s. 6 (1885): 451; author's photograph.

77 Bodleian, John Johnson Collection, "Valentines," boxes 2 and 8. Courtesy of the Bodleian Library, University of Oxford.

80 *Marion's Fate: A Love Story, Bow Bells,* n.s., 11 (1870): 601; by permission of The British Library.

83 Bodleian, John Johnson Collection, "Valentines," box 2. Courtesy of the Bodleian Library, University of Oxford.

102 *Boy Pirate,* 457; by permission of The British Library.

103 Malcolm Errym, *Varney, the Vampyre* (1847), 1 (12621.g.55); by permission of The British Library.

110 *Penny Illustrated Paper,* November 17, 1888, 310; British Newspaper Library, by permission of The British Library.

114 *Bow Bells,* n.s., 32 (1895): 380; by permission of The British Library.

149 Courtesy of the McCormick Collection.

Index